Alice in Genderland

Alice in Genderland
A Crossdresser Comes of Age

Richard J. Novic, M.D.

iUniverse LLC
New York   Bloomington

Contents

Introduction

I was surprised when I discovered back in the early 2000s that no one had ever told the life story of a crossdresser who had set foot out his front door.[1] Although there had been many transsexual memoirs and drag queen diaries, no one had ever dared to publish the story of a "heterosexual crossdresser" who had gone out into the world and made a little life for himself as a woman to enjoy alongside the life he led as a man.

Although I had begun an advice column for *GIRL TALK* magazine, I still thought of myself as much more of a psychiatrist than a writer—hardly the person to fill that kind of gap in the transgender record. Yet the letters that came in from my readers kept reminding me of that critical time in my life when I had first learned I was not alone. Desperate and confused then, every encouraging word and whispered confidence from a more experienced crossdresser had meant the world to me, and every printed page on the subject had been worth its weight in gold.

Now inspired—even if not naturally able—I was thrilled when some time opened up in my schedule and I had the opportunity to take on such a large writing project. Once underway, I began to believe even more in my mission as a crossdresser speaking to other crossdressers. As one of our own who had worked out a very satisfying and balanced life, I aimed to give others hope. As a psychiatrist who had found positive new ways to look at the challenges we all face, I hoped to give others pride.

As I toiled to get the details of my life down on paper in some sort of organized, engaging form, I enlisted the help of a woman friend who edits books for a living. Instead of simply providing technical feedback, she surprised me. "Anyone," she said, "who has struggled to figure out who they are and how they want to live will feel your pain and share your joy." With that, I dug deeper and aimed wider in the hope of reaching other like-minded souls.

Some of you may wonder, *What exactly is a crossdresser?* Mainstreamers often define *crossdresser* as anyone who dresses in the clothes of the opposite sex for any purpose and *fetishistic crossdresser* as any man who is aroused by wearing women's clothes. But we "fetishistic crossdressers" barely recognize that term and refer to ourselves simply as "crossdressers." How many of us are there? According to survey, 3% of male college students are aroused by wearing women's clothes,[2] and I'd assume the same to be true of the educated male population, because such an urge rarely if ever goes away and rarely if ever begins in adulthood.[3]

Crossdressers, together with male-to-female (MTF) transsexuals and drag queens, make up the MTF transgender community. There is also a small but vital female-to-male (FTM) community, which consists almost entirely of transsexuals. Yet because mine is an MTF story, I will use the term transgender to refer to the MTF side of the greater community, unless otherwise specified. Contrary to popular belief, we transgendered people are not all automatically gay. Some of us are attracted to men, and others to women or both or even each other. As it happens, most crossdressers prefer women. Who'd have thunk?

Please note that I refer to people in this book as he or she according to common courtesy and the conventions of the transgender community. Most trans people, when dressed as women, prefer *she* and, when dressed as men, prefer *he*. So if you're introduced to an elegant crossdresser at your next cocktail party, you'll score more points if you follow her cues and address her as *ma'am* rather than think yourself clever and opt for *sir*.

But alas, we crossdressers are usually married men with secret lives, so we rarely have the chance to mix with people and tell our stories, let alone publish them. So you're not likely to meet many of us on the social circuit, and the only depictions you're liable to see are those written by outsiders. All too often, these are riddled with misunderstandings and show us in a light that's either negative or silly. We are neither. Fortunately I am able to tell my tale, because of the love and support of my closest friends and family.

Although I wasn't fully aware of my womanly desires until my twenties, in retrospect I can trace them back as far as I can remember. Although no one knows for sure what causes crossdressing, many experts suspect that hormonal surges alter the development of the fetal brain and cause behavioral changes that show up later on in childhood.[4] Additionally, recent research suggests that all mental processes from depression to love are coded somewhere in the central nervous system. So I have to imagine that, as a crossdresser, I have a brain that's part female in a way that's not yet discovered, and I suspect that the same is true, only more so, for transsexuals.

In fact, there has already been some evidence in this direction. Studies by the Netherlands Institute for Brain Research show the hypothalamus of MTF transsexuals to be much more woman-like than man-like in an area known as the bed striate nucleus.[5] Perhaps this will turn out to be a biological marker of transgenderism. Perhaps not.[6] But if and when such a marker is found, transgenderism will be reclassified from the psychological into the neurological and thereby take its place among the intersex conditions. (For more, see Appendix A.)

But regardless of the cause or classification of transgenderism, the more pressing question for each person or family affected is what to do about it. As I see it, I was allotted a number of cards in life: dark hair, *fine, whatever;* white skin, *sure can't hurt;* nimble mind, *great,* the hopes and dreams of a girl, *what the hell?* Imagine being dealt something like that. Such was my predicament. How was I to play my hand with any chance of happiness or success? How was I to live with this *thing* I didn't choose, this trait I couldn't get rid of without amputating a part of who I was and what I might enjoy?

As a parent, how would you know if your son might turn out to be a crossdresser or transsexual? There's really no easy way to tell. Studies reviewed by historian Vern Bullough show that, if your young son likes to put on girls' clothes and prefers girlish activities, then there's a 6% chance he'll turn out to be a transsexual and a 2.5% chance he'll be a crossdresser, but a surprising 55% chance he'll be a noncrossdressing gay man and a 21% chance he'll be a noncrossdressing straight man.[7] (15.5% were classified as uncertain.) Please note, however, that these studies were conducted in the English-speaking world and that the path taken by effeminate boys in traditional Latin and other cultures may be markedly different.

Then again, if your son shows no interest in girlish things, you still may not be out of the woods. A small percentage of ostensibly regular boys turn out to be transgendered. That's because most crossdressers and many transsexuals are able to suppress their femininity until much later in life. I was one of those boys. So, too, might be your son—or brother, husband or father.

With that in mind, I would like to introduce you to a kind of person you might never meet but may already know. I was perhaps as stunned as any of you might be to have to deal with something like this. How could a traditional man, like me, face the fact he wanted nothing more than to indulge in the pleasures of womanhood? All the pleasures of womanhood. What a humiliating fate. It tore me up like nothing before and nothing since. I've had to grow in astonishing ways to turn this indelible curse into an invaluable blessing to go from my worst nightmare to my wildest dreams. Although my lifestyle is no doubt controversial, I feel good about who I am and how I live.

Whether you're a crossdresser or someone who has battled his/her own inner demons, I hope you find kinship and comfort in these pages. And by all means, enjoy the journey.

Richard J. Novic, M.D.
March 24, 2009

The story you are about to read is true.
Names and identifying details, however, have been changed.

I

Now and Then

There are more things in heaven and earth, Horatio,
Than are dreamt of in your philosophy.

-William Shakespeare,
Hamlet, I. v.1 66-167

Last Friday was a Friday like many others, and I was oh so ready for it. My psychiatry practice had been particularly busy that week. On the bright side, I had helped a sweet but inhibited fifty-year-old find more passion in her marriage, but on the more difficult side, I'd had to break the news to a happy-go-lucky twenty-four-year-old that he had bipolar disorder and would need medication for it. All the same, though, I'm pleased to find after fifteen years that I'm still fascinated by my patients and the challenges they face.

Thank goodness I'm not on call, I thought, as I high-tailed it out of West Hollywood in my SUV and jockeyed my way south to get on the 10 West. A few miles of freeway later, my exit sign in Santa Monica filled me with fondness for the quirky bungalow my honey had found for us there. And when I saw the purple-blue morning glories lining the back alley next to our garage, I knew I was home.

"Daddy, Daddy!" chirped my two sweet kids, from where they sat at the kitchen counter finishing their dinner with our nanny. I gave them both a kiss on the cheek and sat down to slurp some applesauce alongside them. After an impromptu game of Hide and Go Seek and a round of tickles and hugs, I grabbed a light beer from the refrigerator and headed upstairs to the master bathroom.

There I shed my shirt and tie and shaved my chest and then with a fresh blade shaved my face. While still in boxer shorts, I studied my face in the mirror and started to apply makeup. Soon I heard my wife get home from work, greet the kids, and pad upstairs. "Hi, Rick-a-dee," she sang, as she popped in and touched me affectionately on the back. She is a natural beauty, with wavy hair, high cheekbones, and a sunny disposition.

1

"Hey, you," I grinned. "I'd give you a kiss, but you might get a mouth full of lipstick."

"I'll pass," she replied with a giggle. I had to admit the bright red lips looked pretty silly with my soldier-short salt-and-pepper hair. "You can kiss me twice tomorrow," she offered.

"It's a deal."

"How did things go with that kid you had to put on Lithium?"

"Much better than I expected. How was your day?"

"Fine," she said. "We're getting closer to signing that cool new band from Orange County. But I'll tell you more about it on the way to Hanna's recital in the morning. You look like you're rushing."

"I've got an eight o'clock dinner reservation," I explained simply, considering what my wife had said she would want to know and not want to know about the softer side of my social life.

"Okay," she replied, knowing to steer clear of *Where?* and *With whom?* "Have fun. I'll see you later." She gave me a little kiss on the back of my head and noticed the different shoes I had laid out under my red velvet dress. "I'd go with the suede pumps. They're a better match." On her way out the door, she looked over her shoulder and teased, "Don't do anything I wouldn't do."

That's always been good enough for me, I thought, as I held back a chuckle and smiled, ever thankful that the love of my life allowed me the space I needed to fully express myself. Minutes later, my face all made-up, I was ready to get dressed. There was a time when putting on a bra and panties would send chills down my spine, but now all I could think of was getting out the door on time without putting a run in my pantyhose.

Once dressed and coiffed, I threw my wallet and keys into my purse and scampered down the back stairway to the garage, pleased as always that I didn't have to parade by my neighbors to get to my Ford Explorer. Its gray color and complete lack of bumper stickers were deliberate choices to reduce the chance of someone thinking, *Hey, that's Dr. Novic's car. But who's the big brunette behind the wheel?*

With the push of a button, the garage door rolled up, and it was smooth sailing out the back alley and onto the freeway. By now, driving in a wig and high heels was old hat, though there had been a time when I'd feared harassment from every car that stopped beside me at a red light.

Braving traffic on the 405 North, I made my way to the Oxwood Inn, a left-for-dead lesbian bar that's welcomed the transgender crowd since the closing of the Lodge (three-year successor to our legendary Queen Mary Show Lounge). Though I still miss my old stomping grounds, I've come to appreciate the Oxwood's soft blue light and retro-chic Nagel prints.

After almost an hour on the road, I scurried past the other early birds at the faux black-marble bar to relieve myself in the ladies' room, a place that used to feel dangerously off-limits.

"You look amazing!" a pear-shaped and obviously real girl told me, as I emerged from the tiny room.

"So do *you*," I replied, smoothing out my dress. "I mean, look at you. Who would *ever* know?"

"But I really am a girl. I am. I am—"

"Oh, sweetie, that's what we all say," I winked, enjoying the overreaction I always get from women when I play this little game with them.

Scanning the club, I spotted my friend April chatting with the bartender. She's a cute 5'7" Korean-American crossdresser with funny barbed wire tattoos around her arms, left over from her days in the army, that give her a cool biker-chick look.

"Hi, Alice!" she boomed, as I approached.

"Hey, girl," I replied, giving her a little hug and kiss. "What's new with you?"

"I met this girl here last weekend."

"Trans or genetic?"

"No, no, no, she's a real girl, and she's actually more straight than gay. We talked during the week and really seemed to hit it off. I'm hoping to see her tomorrow night."

"I'll keep my fingers crossed for you."

"How's your wife and kids?" April asked.

"We're all getting over a case of the sniffles, but I guess that's par for the course."

"Is your boyfriend coming tonight?"

"He sure is," I beamed.

"Look at you. You've got a smile going from ear to ear."

We shared a round of drinks and caught up some more, before my pal tapped me on the wrist and chimed, "Look who's here."

I turned around as the man in my life strode over. He stood a full 6'4", with broad shoulders. Although 6' myself, I'm relatively svelte and always feel like a woman next to him. Needless to say, I love it.

After some small talk, we let April know we had to rush off to make a dinner reservation. I took my guy's arm on our way out to his car and stole a little glance up at the balmy night sky. *Is this heaven?* I mused, as the womanly energy that had built up during the week exuded from my every pore.

You may wonder how this could be real. Ah, but it is.
You may think I have the best of both worlds.

I feel like I do—and am very grateful for it. But there were times when I felt like I had the worst of all worlds. Although I now lead a richly expressive life, I suffered since adolescence with a secret, a desire I was in no way equipped to handle, but one that eventually burst through my denial. In my most electrifying fantasies, I had always imagined myself to be a *woman*.

Like Alice in Wonderland, my curiosity led me to fall headlong down a rabbit hole, through desperate straits, mind-opening surprises, heart-rending changes, and boundless love. I had to rethink some of society's and my own most basic assumptions in order to be true to who I was. By the time I was back on my feet, I was a different person, living a lifestyle I hadn't known existed. I was no longer a regular guy. I was a crossdresser—and a bold one.

Around every corner, I encountered puzzles and prejudices, which I'll try to shed light on as they come up, based on my psychiatric training and understanding of transgendered and gay people, but also based on the kind of person I am. I've always been one to ask a lot of questions, observe closely, and strive for the best possible answer, whether I like it or not.

◆   ◆   ◆

I was born in 1963 into a conventional reformed Jewish family in Buffalo, New York. My father was a tall, handsome man who in his day was compared to a young Gregory Peck. He was a physician who loved internal medicine and was widely respected throughout town. As a father, he was levelheaded and consistent but not particularly playful, nor did he put much time aside for his kids. My mother was an outgoing, buxom woman who stayed home to take care of the four kids she had in the span of three years. Though at times scattered and overwhelmed, she was dedicated to bringing us up the best way she knew how, while he worked hard to send us to private schools, camps, colleges, and graduate schools. On top of it all, Mom and Dad were devoted to each other and had a marriage that was lifelong and strong.

Most of the time around the house, I was a lone boy surrounded by my mother and three sisters: Kathy, a year and a half older, and the twins, Miriam and Laura, a year and a half younger. Because the three girls were more temperamental and verbal than I, our day-to-day conversations and activities usually revolved around them. Sometimes I felt bored and left out, but more often I was happy to entertain myself or to run out and play with the other boys in the neighborhood.

Naturally, from day one, my parents expected me to act like a boy and encouraged me to act like a boy. And I, being much more inclined toward blocks and records than dolls and tea parties, did not disappoint them. Yet much to my chagrin, a trickle of girlish thoughts began to cross my mind when I was four years old and developed my own version of that charming game Step on a Crack, Break Your Mother's Back. For me, though, stepping on a crack wouldn't break my mother's back; *it would turn me into a girl.* Although one part of me had clearly chosen my own special consequence for a misstep, another recoiled in horror at the mere thought of suffering such a fate. Still, I couldn't keep from playing this game each time I glanced down at the sidewalk.

Did growing up among four females lead me to wonder about being a girl? To eventually become a crossdresser? I suppose it's possible, but I don't know of any studies to back that up. Nevertheless, the mixed feelings I had about my childhood would leave me feeling distant from my parents and vulnerable to blaming them later on.

Ironically, my mother wasn't especially interested in the trappings of femininity, but she had a keen interest in the women's movement. She brought us up with a solid serving of feminism and made sure we knew that a woman could do anything she wanted to in the world. To make her point, she insisted that women and men were equal in every respect. When I pointed out the simple fact that most boys run faster than most girls, she got annoyed, then caught her breath and said, "I mean the same in every way that matters."

"Okay, Mom," I said, somehow comforted by the sound of it.

Despite her good intentions, she enforced her sense of gender equality rather unequally. In our house, the traditional girls' chores were to be shared, but not the customary boys' duties. For instance, the indoor work, like washing the dishes, was evenly distributed among my three sisters and me, whereas the outdoor work, like mowing the lawn or shoveling the snow, wasn't even up for discussion, because it so clearly belonged to me.

I remember raking leaves with my father on a crisp, clear Saturday morning, when I was eight. "You know, this really isn't a fair way to divide up the chores," I complained, after explaining the situation.

"What do you want us to do about it?" he quipped back. "Dress you up in a sweater and skirt and march you off to school like your sisters?"

Suddenly shamed like that, I had no choice but to snort, "Of course not!" though deep inside I wondered, *What would that be like?* and found the idea uncomfortably exciting. Did it appeal to me because it would relieve me of extra chores? Perhaps that was part of it, but more likely my step-on-a-crack-get-turned-into-a-girl brain was already primed and readily triggered by the notion of any such transformation.

Although my parents didn't want to hear anything from me that might be less than hale and hearty, the people who really stamped out any sissyness I might have had were the other boys in third grade with me. We all knew we weren't supposed to act in any way like girls and could be teased mercilessly if we did. Fortunately, I was a little guy who loved dodge ball and math, who never really had a girlish personality or mannerisms, but more of a hazy curiosity about what it would be like to be a girl.

Although I was able to ignore most of my unseemly impulses, every once in a while, I would indulge them. Once, when I was nine, I wanted to see what my body would look like if I were a girl. I pushed my penis between my thighs and studied the precious little triangle of skin between my legs in the full-length mirror on the back of my bedroom door. Just then, our babysitter pushed the door open to check up on me, and her jaw dropped. I turned away instantly and tried to cover up, but it was too late. I was never more embarrassed in my life. Struck speechless, I could offer no explanation, and thankfully she simply backed away without asking for one. The only thing I could tell myself was *Wouldn't every boy wonder about something like that?*

Later that year, I remember drifting off to sleep and picturing myself in a Cinderella ball gown, then going on to picture many of the other boys in my class in ball gowns. *Weird, huh?* I thought and shrugged it off.

Even though these images and urges would ultimately lead me to crossdress, I turned down my first opportunity, one morning when I had run out of clean socks and my mother suggested I borrow my sister's. Although they were simple white cotton socks, I insisted on wearing my own dirty ones rather than compromising my fledgling male image. If my curiosity about girls' clothes was to turn into action, it would have to be in private.

Various studies have shown that crossdressers usually start dressing between the ages of nine and eleven.[8] So that makes me more or less on schedule when I first took the plunge at the tender age of eleven. Kathy and I were traveling with our grandmother to a bar mitzvah in Youngstown, Ohio. While the two of them were visiting with our cousins downstairs, I snuck a pair of my big sister's "bikini underwear" out of her suitcase. I knew it was wrong, dangerously wrong, and my heart pounded at the mere thought of getting caught. As I slid the silky briefs on under the sheets of my bed, they felt slippery, almost wet, against my bare skin. Although I still hadn't passed through puberty, adrenaline shot through me and I developed an intense erection.

I couldn't bear the excitement, fear, and shame, however, for more than a minute, before returning Kathy's underpants to her suitcase. Then I jumped back in bed and lay there like a bundle of nerves, while a debate raged between two parts of me.

"If a tree falls in the wilderness," said the side that valued peace, "with no one to hear it, does it still make a sound? Maybe not. So maybe sneaking into my sister's panties doesn't matter, because no one knows."

"But God can see me," said the side that valued truth, "and he knows what I've done."

"But I don't really believe in God, anyway," countered the peaceful side.

"Nonetheless, putting on Kathy's underwear is a very real event," the scientific side insisted. "It will always exist out there in its place, a horrible blemish on the trajectory of my life through space-time."

Back home, I fought the urge to do it again but caved in two or three more times, when I would borrow some little scrunched-up triangle from one of my sisters' drawers and then steal off to the most remote place in our house, a small walk-in closet under the eaves in the attic. There I would be quite literally *in the closet*, among the mothballs and dusty clothes, as if on some kind of insane dare pulling my pants down and panties up. Once they were on, though, I didn't know what else to do except quickly take them off and get them back to my sister's room before anyone might wonder what I was up to.

From fifth to twelfth grade, my parents sent the four of us to the Nichols School, an old private school just a few slate-shingled blocks from our home. Despite adhering to many traditions, like jacket and tie for boys, Nichols had recently opened its doors to girls, who wore plaid skirts, and tried to keep up with the times, the mid '70s, by adding a number of more progressive classes.

In seventh grade, we had sex ed with Mrs. Hobbs. One day, while learning about female anatomy, I was astonished to learn that women had openings for the urethra, vagina, and anus, all in the same little area between their legs. So I raised my hand and asked, "When a couple gets together, how can the man be sure he finds the right hole?"

"It's usually not a problem," my teacher replied, "because the urethra is very small and it's easy to tell the difference between the vagina and the anus. However, a man's penis *can* fit in the anus just like it fits in the vagina. That's what gay people do."

Nervous laughter echoed through the classroom. I was mortified my question had led in this direction. But at the same time, I was fascinated by the revelation that a man could receive intercourse like a woman, unnerved by the notion that, when gay people get together, one is the man and the other is the woman. Though I soon willed my mind on to other things, Mrs. Hobbs had made an all-too-lasting impression.

At around that time, I happened to see a preview for the movie *Rocky Horror Picture Show*. All those women and men—some of them quite grotesque—running around in ladies' lingerie, it was chilling. Although I didn't see the movie for years to come, the preview alone got into my head and haunted me for weeks. I didn't want to know why. I see now the world offers little shelter to someone trying to run from himself.

To guide my sisters and me through puberty, my mother bought us two books, *Boys and Sex* and *Girls and Sex*. Although the boys' book was meant for me, I couldn't resist checking out the girls' book. I'd skulk up to the attic to read it. There, hands trembling, I could hardly wait to turn page after page. My curiosity about womanhood, nevertheless, remained restricted to what I could ponder in private and balanced by more traditional interests.

In my early teens, I played a lot of four square and tackle football around the neighborhood. Though never the most popular kid on the block, I always had two or three good friends, and in my mid-teens we turned more to Dungeons and Dragons and other elaborate board games. Meanwhile, I got involved with sailing and club soccer. These things, plus school, made up the bulk of my life. So everything seemed normal, if not better.

I devoted myself to soccer and became one of two sophomores to make Nichols varsity. I loved the game and became friendly with some of the upperclassmen on the team. Unlike me, they were old enough to drive at night, and they started to include me in parties and bar hopping. (The drinking age was eighteen, and we all had fake ID.) For the first time, girls were beginning to notice me, and I couldn't have been more thrilled. But being more scholarly than social, I didn't really know how to comport myself around older guys or girls and ended up being cast off as a good midfielder, but a hopeless geek.

To make matters worse, junior year I discovered that, although I stood six feet tall, I was really quite thin. I hadn't developed the powerful-looking upper body the other guys had, and I knew looking wimpy wouldn't help me win their respect nor draw rave reviews from the girls. Investigating things more closely, I had to accept the fact that my torso was narrow and my wrists were small-boned. Thankfully I discovered weightlifting and poured my teenage angst into building up my body. I attacked it with real self-discipline. *No pain, no gain* was my motto. Ironically, I was to put that same skinny frame and self-discipline to far different use later on.

Amazing as it may sound, I never suspected I was different from any other sexually frustrated teenage boy until I was seventeen and first tried to masturbate. I had never dared to try it before, because my parents didn't believe in locks on bedroom or bathroom doors—nor did they believe in knocking. But spring break junior year, they and my sisters drove to Florida, while I stayed home to enjoy having the house and other car to myself. Suddenly I had a whole lot more privacy.

Eager to give masturbation a try, I sat on my bed with a *Playboy* magazine, a jar of Vaseline, and a few paper towels. I imagined I was about to have sex with the lovely lingerie-clad centerfold. I tried and tried but couldn't climax. After my right hand reached the point of exhaustion, I started in with my left. When that burned out, I went back to my right. Finally, my whole body seemed to tighten up, then explode. I felt triumphant, but my victory had been costly. My forearms felt like lead, and my penis was swollen and sore for days.

The next time I tried to get off, I stared at the pretty playmate and my mind made a subtle shift. Instead of imagining I was with her, I imagined I *was* her. And before I knew it, I was experiencing that about-to-sneeze sensation of approaching orgasm and then wow! What a feeling, but what on earth had I done to achieve it

I ran again and again into the same disturbing fact: I could either struggle for satisfaction, or I could relax, imagine I was a woman, and whammo. This fantasy had a power that was almost magical, but it was a black magic that I didn't care to use. Resorting to it felt like cracking the lid on some kind of Pandora's box, filled with horrible homosexual mysteries. Nonetheless, I drifted inexorably toward it, slowly but surely spreading my legs nearly every time I masturbated.

Why does one's sense of self so often start with the sexual? Why do so many crossdressers and transsexuals start out with centerfold fantasies and lingerie, rather than a sense of female identity? Why do so many gay and bi men begin with locker-room fantasies and furtive encounters, rather than love for another man? Maybe it's because a scared teenager can keep himself blind to the deeper truth but can't avoid the simple things he requires to reach orgasm.

As a psychiatrist, I've learned that it's very difficult for most young people to adjust to the reality of being gay, lesbian, bisexual, or transgendered. Many remain oblivious but feel empty and lack any passion inside. No doubt, some even live their whole lives in this mode of quiet desperation. Yet many like me seem to bump into things that turn us on and make us wonder if we're different. With experience, most of us discover that our differences are significant and not just sexual, but involve a large part of who we are.

Whether egged on by the erotic or not, GLBT youth typically embark on an adjustment process that begins with emptiness or confusion, then passes through shame and hopefully on to comfort and pride.[9] Although there are many obstacles along the way, the idea is to go from feeling empty and stifling yourself to feeling proud and expressing yourself. That's what it means for someone queer to be well-adjusted.

Back when I was a teenager, I hadn't a clue about any of this. I barely even knew the word transvestite. My secret proclivity for pretending I was a girl was confusing and utterly unacceptable. I suppose I judged it based on how people in my life would have judged it, for that's how I learned what was right or wrong, wholesome or sinister. My parents would have been shocked if they had caught me in panties, and instead of their usual pride in me, they would have been profoundly disappointed. My mother would have been terrified, and my father would have been furious.

But things would have been far worse if my tendencies had somehow become public knowledge at Nichols. Whether in the locker room or lunchroom, we guys spent far too much energy trying to compete with each other and put each other down by saying things like "Don't be such a pussy" or "What are ya, a faggot?" It was as if our passage into manhood depended on constant reminders of the humiliating alternatives. If word got out about me, I would've become the prime target for all this animosity and just showing up for school each day would have been a living hell.

For a while, I had simply ignored my unmanly feelings and left them to languish in the dark. But now, how could I ignore the plain fact that I couldn't come without imagining for a moment I was a woman? I scrambled for new ways to keep the lid on Pandora's box.

I came up with Universalize It, and it became my next strategy of choice. It seemed like common knowledge that everybody who didn't have a girlfriend masturbated and that their fantasies could be quite bizarre. So, I figured, how was I different from anyone else? It would be years before I realized that, though many—if not most—men have weird fantasies, very few have recurring fantasies of being a woman.

Another interesting approach was the Forbidden Fruit Defense, and it went like this: *I like putting on panties because of the thrill of the forbidden. If it weren't forbidden, I wouldn't be so thrilled.* I supposed that I'd be equally excited by anything else *verboten*. But it's funny how no other no-no's came to mind terribly often. And if I ever thought it might be exciting to break another taboo, like wearing a diaper, I might try it once but have no interest in doing it again. Eventually, when I thought it through, I realized I was awfully into *permitted* as well as forbidden fruit, as long as it was feminine. I loved the fact I was allowed to come out of the shower and wrap a towel around my waist just like a skirt.

As I struggled to find a girlfriend through the remainder of junior and on into senior year, my tension would build and my world would shake every couple of months when I would find myself alone in the house for who-knew-how-much time. It was pure torture. All at once, everything was available to me with no one to intrude, and my curiosity, reinforced by sexual excitement, would swell into an irresistible force, a compulsion that felt as horrid as an urge to kill a small animal or steal from a friend.

I would be seized by a notion like *I wonder what it's like to wear a bra* and rapidly jump to *Better do it now while I still have the chance.* Then I would head up to one of my sisters' rooms, as my heart rose in my throat. I'd put my arms through the straps of a lacy white bra—or indulge in whatever else had tweaked my interest—and chills would shoot down my spine. Only orgasm could relieve my agitation. Returning to a more sober state of mind, I'd feel ashamed of what I had done and fearful of what it might mean.

Then I might engage in wishful thinking—*Okay, got that out of my system*—or fall back on one of my other strategies to reassure myself that I was still just a regular guy. Yet the next time I had the opportunity, I'd be helpless to resist something else, like a discarded pair of tights or a high-school prom garter. On one occasion, I needed to know how it felt to insert a tampon. I nearly had a heart attack when I realized the little white contraption—that I had thought was the tampon—had actually left something behind in my body and I didn't know how to get it out!

Technically, the first time I dressed fully in women's clothes was during my senior year in high school. I had decided that this curiosity crap had to go. The next time I had the house to myself, I would try on everything and hopefully put an end to all this painful wondering. When the opportunity arose, I started with panties, then added a bra. I stuffed it with socks and pulled some tights on. Aroused as could be, I stepped into a plaid skirt, buttoned a blouse over my perky chest, and crammed my feet into my sister's clogs.

By then, I was so revved up that I thought of doing something I'd never before dared. I needed to know how it felt to be a girl having sex with a guy. Brainstorming, I scurried downstairs and opened the refrigerator. Poring over the possibilities, I grabbed a carrot and dashed back upstairs. I penetrated myself in every kitten-like position I could imagine and then had the orgasm of my life.

That was the culmination of a desperate new strategy: Try It and Hope You Don't Like It. I had worn everything a girl would wear and done everything a girl would do. Unfortunately, I'd liked it, but at least I'd be able to fend off future temptations with a sense of *Been there. Done that.*

As a child, I had stumbled into things that had shaken me up and made me wonder what it was like to be a girl, but by now, as a teenager, I was actively trying to learn more. Let's take a step back and think about the process of being exposed to something new, becoming curious, fantasizing, experimenting, and making it part of your life. Sounds to me like the basics of growing up and pursuing happiness, especially if we think of something nonsexual—like golf.

Let's say I'm an inner-city kid who has a taste for outdoor sports. From television or friends, I might hear about golf. Naturally I'd be curious to learn more and eager to give it a try, because I've a hunch I'd like it. But alas, I come from a poor family and have no access to a course. So I'll have to make do with playing putt-putt and pretending I'm a real golfer, like Tiger Woods. After years of envy, a friend, at last, offers to take me golfing and lends me a set of clubs. And guess what? I *do* like it. Well, the next thing to figure out is *Do I like it enough to make it a regular part of my life?* And ultimately, I work out a satisfying routine of work during the week, golf with my buddies on Saturday, and family time on Sunday.

If you find something *sexually* enjoyable, is it really so different from finding it enjoyable for other reasons? I was a boy with no chance to hit the links, except, of course, I didn't want to play golf, I wanted to play girl. For most of my youth, I had no opportunity to dress up and be a girl for a while. So I had to be content with my putt-putt course of borrowed bras and appropriated panties.

Why did these things pack such a sexual punch for me? Perhaps it was the unconscious resourcefulness of a testosterone-driven mind. Faced with a major roadblock to my pursuit of happiness, maybe I was just doing my utmost to savor the shreds of femininity within my reach. At the time, though, I thought I was just a boy being bad in a really twisted way. Burdened by that secret, I now had to face all the other trials and tribulations that boys face in high school and beyond.

2

Choosing a Path

Although I feared I could be gay, it just didn't make sense. I loved girls. I loved looking at them. Who needed art? I loved listening to them. Now *that* was music. I loved touching them. *So* warm and cuddly. When a pretty girl walked by, I could hardly maintain my train of thought. Women drove me mad. Men, on the other hand, never set off my radar. I experienced them as rivals, plain and simple.

I figured that, with a nice girl and a healthy sex life, my freaky fantasies would fade. *It's all just a weird reaction to being alone*, I told myself, while praying year after year for a girlfriend and an end to my virginity. *Besides, it doesn't mean anything, because I know I like women*, I would remind myself, because by popular wisdom you were either gay or straight. So therefore, I was okay: straight, normal, and natural. Nonetheless, I couldn't be sure until I had proved it by going all the way with a girl.

Though by senior year I had fooled around with a few and had gone to parties and bars regularly, I'd long since learned it wasn't going to be easy. I remember at fifteen thinking it was going to be paradise as we boys got our driver's licenses and had more chances to get together with girls without our parents around. Surely they wanted to get physical with us as much as we did with them. After all, Mom had always insisted, "Men and women are the same in every way that matters."

I'll never forget my innocence sophomore year, as I asked a cute blonde from the class ahead of me to dance at the Charity Ball, I in my navy jacket and gray flannels, she in her Laura Ashley dress. As she said yes, the fast music turned slow. Though surprised, I thought, *Maybe that's all for the better*, and assumed she felt the same. As we clumsily slow danced, I felt her stiffen. I started to sweat. She seemed to make faces at her girl friends. I did my best to ignore them.

Finally, when the song finished, she broke away and gave me a silly double clap, as if to say, *Thank god this is over*. To show I understood, I clapped too, before realizing that she had made a complete fool of me. I then shrank into the shadows for the rest of the event, until my mother arrived to pick my sisters and me up. The gap between her well-intended feminism and reality on the ground hit me that night as an unintelligible shock and would continue to vex me for years.

We boys used to say sex was like baseball. You try to get around the bases and score with a girl. First base was kissing. Second would be feeling her up. Third would be getting up her skirt. And, of course, having sex would be a home run. Surely the girls were looking to pair up and race around the bases with us, weren't they?

My turn at bat came junior year, when I finally had the chance to make out with a few girls. At first, I could hardly believe my eyes, when I saw how they would drag their feet. Nothing would happen, not a single kiss or caress, unless I made it happen, and even then, my affection might be accepted but not actively reciprocated. Later, I would loathe having to coax a girl along, nudging a hand here or a head there, and was flabbergasted at how that might be characterized as using her or worse. Who needed it?

I did . . . urgently, and not only were the girls at Nichols reluctant, but they were relatively scarce, because a lot would jump ship and date older guys. Day after day, I faced the depressing fact that teenage girls were fresh-faced flowers in bloom, while teenage boys were awkward young contenders, trying to stake out some small piece of the action. I despised all the effort and competition among us for a limited number of them. The forces of supply and demand were solidly in their favor. Eventually, I learned to play the game: to attend to a woman's whims, to relax her with a drink. Still, I wasn't savvy enough to flatter a girl if it didn't come naturally and was never willing to pretend I was a potential boyfriend if I wasn't truly interested.

I resented always having to take the initiative and hated the fact I never got hit on. The closest I ever came was once, when a girl at school inquired about me through an intermediary. I suppose most guys don't care if they don't get hit on. But there was a part of me that just wanted to take care of my body, put on a snug-fitting pair of jeans, show up at a party, and graciously enjoy whatever attention came my way. Maybe even attract an older, more experienced woman. When I stop and think about it, maybe I had so many complaints about being a teenage boy because I would've really preferred to be a teenage girl.

Still desperate to prove my manhood, late junior year I sought out less attractive, looser women and finally had sex with a wild public-school girl—but couldn't come, which only made matters worse. At least that summer I found some solace in a handjob from a girl I met in Spain. Finally, in the snowy winter of senior year, I succeeded with a free-spirited friend of a friend and sighed long with relief. Still, my pleasure was short-lived, because my consort turned out to be as free-spirited about drinking and lying as she was about sex.

As fervently as we boys wanted sex, the girls seemed to want *boyfriends* and mystifying romantic things, like a moonlight walk, a timely phone call, and frequent use of the word *we*. Thankfully I was a guy who liked the idea of being in a relationship. Simply put, if I had fun fooling around with a girl and she seemed like a nice person, I would want to see her again and again. So when the time came, it was easy to make the classic—though seldom admitted to—trade of commitment for sex.

That spring, I fell in love with a girl named Fiona. I was originally drawn to her golden-haired good looks, but she turned out to be kind, intelligent, and athletic to boot. I was lucky and about to get a lot luckier. Once her rather progressive parents could see that I was a devoted boyfriend, they allowed me to sleep over "across the hall" from her as often as we could arrange it.

As I had hoped, my freaky fantasies no longer seemed necessary now that I had a regular sex life. I jumped in bed with Fiona whenever I got the chance and had little difficulty reaching orgasm. I came every time, unless I was using a condom, and even then, I came most of the time. Tremendously relieved, I figured that that proved all this imagine-I'm-a-girl stuff was just Something Strange Connected With Masturbation—and that became my new strategy of choice.

But looking back, was I somehow still using my transgender fantasies? Often, before Fiona and I would make love, she would go off to put her diaphragm in. Meanwhile, I would take my clothes off, lie on my stomach, and pretend to fall asleep. I hoped she would see me there, be overcome with lust, and start touching me all over. And she may have actually done that once or twice. But of course, most of the time she just snuggled next to me and waited for me to make the first move. I was frustrated that I was always the one with the "Russian hands and Roman fingers" and she was the one with the body they were "Hungary" for. Back then, I felt that I just wanted sex to be more equal, but now, in retrospect, I wonder if I was really longing to dance the woman's part in our little *pas de deux*?

By the time high school graduation came around, I was riding high. I had distinguished myself academically and even won my way into Harvard. I was the handsome captain of varsity soccer complete with his lovely figure-skating girlfriend, yet part of me felt like so much less than what met the eye. After a sizzling summer, I bade Fiona an awkward farewell and headed off to college.

I blush to admit that, even as my parents and I drove onto the hallowed ground of Harvard Yard, with its centuries-old red brick, white trimmed edifices of higher learning, I had nothing loftier in mind than how I might establish some street cred through sports. I tried out for the soccer team but was cut because I lacked the quickness to compete at the division-one level. With my tail between my legs, I hastily joined the rugby team. Anyone could sign up, but the team had a swaggering image, nonetheless.

I was a good B-side player, and the fact I got anywhere at all in collegiate rugby can be explained by one thing . . . heart: wanting it more, needing it more, never mind the pain. I needed to prove my manhood over and over again. At least I wasn't a jerk about it, and in the process, I made a lot of friends and became an integral part of the preppy-athletic crowd. For the first time in my life, I was popular and felt like I belonged.

Keenly interested in computers, I decided to major in applied mathematics. I strove for a work-hard-play-hard lifestyle, but it didn't turn out to be enough. "We're not sending you to Harvard to get Cs," my father informed me over the phone, as my mother clucked in agreement. To please them, I would have to opt for a work-hard-work-hard approach. I felt torn between who I wanted to be and who my parents wanted me to be. I never would have suspected that, in the end, neither they nor I would get to choose.

From freshman week on, I was exposed to people and things that upset me far more than I was ready to admit. Whether it was the jailhouse banter of the rugby blokes or the dirty magazines at the local newsstand, it all got under my skin and stayed there. Once, a bunch of the guys at a dorm party were tossing around a porno mag featuring beautiful women—with penises. I had never before heard of such a thing. "What the hell is *this*," we all sneered.

I wasn't aware of having any gay classmates back at Nichols. And even at liberal Harvard in the People's Republic of Cambridge (as it was known by Bostonians, across the river), most people who would later turn out to be gay weren't out yet. The few that were, though, made quite an impression on me. Prissy and precious, they hung out in artsy circles, where everyone smoked. They seemed unhealthy and unnatural. *But as long as they keep their hands to themselves*, I reckoned, *then who cares what they do to each other*.

Looking back now, it seems paranoid to think my queer classmates might've gone out of their way to make passes at me. And under the influence of pot back then, I sometimes worried that even my straight friends might try it. But at least my homophobic sentiments were moderate compared to my compatriots. A few of the football players beat up two gay students as they left a dance at the Science Center. Although the gridiron goons got in trouble with school officials, most people in my social circles were nonplussed, as if the football fellas had just been overzealous in keeping perverts off campus.

For spending money, I worked part time as a night watchman. I sat at the front desk of Currier House, carried a walkie-talkie, and every few hours patrolled the newly coed dorms of the Radcliffe Quadrangle. My job was to make sure various doors were locked and to function as "the eyes and ears of the Harvard University Police Force," as Sergeant Sutherland would remind me in his r-dropping Boston accent.

On patrol in the wee hours of a Monday night, I ambled past a ladies' room in a secluded section of North House and my heart stopped. *Oh, my god, I could actually*—I didn't even want to finish the thought, as I trembled with temptation. Although there weren't any dorm rooms around, I knew it was risky. I knew it would be a humiliating have-to-leave-Harvard disgrace if I got caught. But my old familiar enemy, Compelling Curiosity, had returned. After two hard knocks on the door yielded no response, I turned the knob and pushed it open with my heart pounding.

Empty, phew! I thought. *And a one-toilet bathroom to boot. Step in.* Thump. Thump. *Lock the door. Pray that no one knocks. Now what? Well, sit down and pee like a girl, for god's sake.*

And so I did. Otherwise, I just looked around to see if a ladies' room was any different from a men's room and discovered a funny little trashcan next to the toilet that was apparently—yuck—for used tampons. My hands shook as I pulled my pants back up, and my heart didn't stop pounding until I had made it safely back into the hallway without being seen. Despite how nervous it had made me, I felt inexorably drawn to this ladies' room, shift after shift. Just as my body roamed through the night, so did my mind. Although the year was 1982, I kept drifting to *1984*, George Orwell's *1984*. Although I had read the book in high school, it now came back to haunt me. In it, the police are somehow able to read the minds of their prisoners. They then threaten each with the type of torture he fears the most. For example, lead character Winston Smith's worst nightmare is to be strapped to a chair while two cages of hungry rats are opened up next to his face. As dreadful as that sounds, what I feared from the very pit of my stomach was to be put in a dress and raped. Hmm, what was that about?

The idea of being forced into something must have asked me deep down, *Is there anything you'd like to do and not have to take responsibility for?* Being forced to wear a dress and submit sexually to a man would have given me the opportunity to enjoy being a woman, while not having to claim it as my own idea. So for me, this imagined torture was really more fantasy than fear. Years later, I learned that this kind of fantasy is well known among crossdressers. It's called forced feminization, and there is a whole genre of trans erotica devoted to it.

Another grim place I drifted to was a picture from a porn magazine that I just couldn't shake. In it, a beautiful brunette in a black negligee and stockings was on her hands and knees being taken from behind by one man, while giving oral sex to another. Casting myself as that woman, I'd feel a burst of adrenaline followed by a wave of panic. In a flash, I'd be myself again but feel like I had been brought before a court and charged with a sex crime. *It's just a strange, dark thought*, I would plead, *like when I'm angry with someone and pretend to shoot him. It's something very bad, but very far from anything I'd ever do.*

Fortunately, by day I was rarely alone and therefore less prone to such disturbing flights of fancy. But even a simple trip to The Coop (our campus department store) could potentially throw me for a loop. For some reason, ladies' lingerie was located just across from mechanical pencils and calculators. All I had to do was glance over at the sassily displayed Radcliffe panties, and I'd get hot and uncomfortable.

Once, they seemed to wink back at me and mock me. After scanning the crowd and finding no familiar faces, my pulse quickened and I considered making a purchase. Still, I realized with a shudder as I stared down at the linoleum floor, the risk of a surprise tap on the shoulder from someone I knew—anyone I knew—was just too great. Men who snuck around with women's underwear were laughingstocks, I reminded myself, thinking of a recent Steve Martin routine.

Or worse yet, they were pathetic, like the old man caught stealing frilly undies from one of the freshman laundry rooms. Rumor had it that, while being led away, he'd wailed, "How come only women get to wear pretty things?" But more horrid, still, was the notion that men who liked ladies' things were like the serial-killer transvestite psychiatrist in the movie *Dressed To Kill*. I was not that kind of man. I would not let myself become one of those disgusting transvestites. I had other plans for my life. Thus, I raised the stakes and forged a new strategy for the containment of my female side: Make It a Matter of Character.

With an iron will, I smothered that part of me during what could have been the prime of my trans girlhood. I could have been a smooth-skinned, slender beauty, but sadly I squandered my first blush of youth. At the time, though, I didn't know how jealous I would turn out to be of my classmates in their cocktail dresses, and I never would have considered dressing in drag and heading out into downtown Boston. That may have been a blessing in disguise, for had I pursued my fantasies, I might have died. HIV was spreading like wildfire, but nobody knew, so no one knew to be careful.

The reality of life from sophomore year on was that I had to work so hard in my math and science classes that I barely had time to express my male side and sexuality, let alone my female side and whatever came with it. To turn my grades around, I ended up sacrificing everything from Friday-nights-out to all but my most stalwart friends, like my junior- and senior-year roommate, Colin, a ruddy-faced former football player who worked as doggedly as I did. My only solace was my unusual love of learning, regardless of the subject. My education nourished my curiosity, while fortifying it with healthy skepticism.

I sacrificed everything except the hope of a girlfriend. Wistfully I yearned for a special someone whose slightest smile would make every hardship worthwhile. But in college, as in high school, the forces of supply and demand were still stacked against us boys, especially overworked and unhappy ones like me. And for god-knows-what reason, I wasn't willing to lower my rather superficial standards and date someone just okay looking. Sure, I'd settle for the purpose of sex here and there, but with the girls so often expecting more, I wondered whether it was worth it.

So most of the time, I had to take care of my own sexual needs, which I did about twice a week. Maybe having to tap my fantasies like that was what finally drove me to buy my first pair of panties, from a street vendor on my way to catch a train with the rest of the ruggers on tour in England. Once on board, though, just knowing I had "knickers" in my backpack made me feel too anxious and edgy to sit and talk for even a minute. So I rushed off to the tiny bathroom, tried them on, and got myself off.

Afterward, I couldn't throw the lacy little things out fast enough. Of course, I didn't want to risk getting caught with them in my luggage, but more importantly I just couldn't deal with such ongoing temptation. Keeping lingerie felt like playing with a fire that could easily burn out of control and turn me into something I didn't want to be. In this way, Make It a Matter of Character segued into Don't Play with Fire—or don't do anything you might like *too* much.

Somehow, saving some men's clothes that could mimic the look and feel of women's clothes wasn't quite as menacing. I bought a Speedo bathing suit that felt like panties, and I was especially fond of one ragged old cotton sweatshirt. Alone in bed, I used to lie back and stretch it down to my knees like a dress and imagine I was Jennifer Beals from *Flashdance*. What a feeling! All the while, I remained confident I wouldn't need this mind game as soon as I found a girlfriend and a healthy supply of real sex.

Although none of my few college flings amounted to much, one is fascinating in retrospect. It happened junior year with a girl named Deborah Collins. She was smart and interesting, and found me very attractive— though I found her a bit plain, with a biggish body and short brown hair. She was bisexual and far more freethinking than anyone I'd ever been with. One particular night, at her humble off-campus apartment, she suggested we finger each other's anuses. I couldn't help but like it. When she asked if I'd like to penetrate her that way, I agreed to give it a try. Her rear entrance felt pretty much like her front, except a little tighter. And before I had too much time to think about it, I came.

Relaxing afterward on her futon, she commented, "I noticed how much you liked that stuff. You should really try having sex with a man sometime."

Then as if she hadn't rocked my world enough, she continued, "You're really so beautiful. Let me make you up as a woman tonight. It'll be so much fun!"

I felt embarrassed and scared she was on to me. I knew it would be wildly exciting, but what if I liked it too much? My secret would be out; there'd be no turning back. "No," I said with a scowl, trying to convince myself I was more disgusted than conflicted.

"Aw, come on. You'd make such a pretty girl."

"Haven't we done enough for one night?" I replied, refusing to play with fire. Besides, I was relaxed and post-orgasmic and therefore much less tempted than if still tense and aroused. Although there was no way I could have known it at the time, Deborah was a most unusual woman, who had just made an offer I might never hear again.

Toward the end of college, I discovered my next major sport, backpacking. I loved the beauty of the wilderness and the challenge of getting around effectively and living comfortably within it, regardless of terrain or conditions. Was I compensating for that part of me that was much more Jane than Tarzan? No doubt. Still, the main thing was that backpacking, like soccer and rugby, expressed a genuine part of me. The fact that it helped smooth over others was icing on the cake.

In fact, I didn't take the compensation thing nearly as far as other crossdressers and transsexuals. Many friends and acquaintances of mine have volunteered for the armed forces and even served in elite units, like the Army Rangers and Navy Seals. I'm proud to be part of a group that includes such people. Whatever manly feats I have achieved pale in comparison.

As I approached senior year, I burned out on applied mathematics and my plan to follow it up with a Ph.D. in computer science. I had grown lonely puzzling over differential equations every day with people as nerdy as I was. I never found the kind of woman I dreamed of and didn't think graduate school in computer science would help my chances. *If the world wants me to use my brain for science*, I told myself, *it has to provide me with a girlfriend— and it hasn't*.

After surveying my options, I chose a career in medicine, because I liked the way it combined science with people-work and, my father being a doctor, I felt familiar with it. I ended up applying for medical school a year behind schedule, though, because I didn't make my final decision until mid-senior year. That gave me an extra year to spend one way or another.

I returned home after graduation and continued to feel rather glum. My parents saw how obsessed I was over whether I was making the right decision, and my father pointed out that I had lost sight of everything else in life. "Why not go off and ride a motorcycle through the back roads of Scotland," he suggested in classic Novic style. Myself a true Novic, I liked the idea and appreciated his concern.

With Mom and Dad covering my expenses, I set off for a year of low-budget travel through the British Isles, the Middle East, and Alaska. In the Mideast, I loved learning where so many of the basics of our lives come from—like the alphabet we write with and the seven-day-a-week rhythm we live by. And in Alaska, I found the most amazing summer job, as a deck hand on a tugboat pushing barges full of fuel and freight up and down the Yukon River to off-road Indian villages.

Travel pulled me out of my depression, not because it was leisurely, but just the opposite. Most of the time I was so engrossed by what I was seeing and doing that I didn't have time to dwell on my career quandary and sexual baggage. All too soon, though, it was time to go back east to medical school. But now, with batteries recharged, I was ready to buckle down again. I'd had my chance to see the world. Little did I know, but there was a whole 'nother one lurking in the shadows inside me.

Although it was 1986 and Boston bustled with young urban professionals, I swaggered into medical school with a plaid shirt and full beard and felt all the more a mountain man when I met my classmates. They were bookish and intense and never interested in taking a weekend off to go climbing or fishing, like I would. I ran the Boston Marathon that year in the very respectable time of three hours and seventeen minutes and felt buoyant and physical. Despite marching to the beat of a different drummer, I was kind to my classmates and well liked, even if I wasn't the most sensitive man in the class.

After a month, I ran into Debbie Collins at a party. Although she was there with her new boyfriend, we were both happy to see each other and exchanged phone numbers as friends. Then one morning, as Halloween approached, I started thinking about how she had wanted to dress me up as a woman. For the first time as an adult I allowed myself to imagine dolling up from head to toe and was intrigued by all the exotic things involved: not just a bra and panties, but a skirt and heels, and a purse and perfume. What would it all feel like? I'd give my trademark black beard to find out, and I felt so wound up that I couldn't begin my day until I had "relieved my tension."

"Deb," I asked in a tremulous voice, "could I take you up on your offer to dress me up as a woman this Halloween?" It was awkward enough to call an old girlfriend up for a favor, let alone something like this. I could barely hold the phone still, as I hovered back and forth between hoping she would say yes and willing her to say no.

"I'm sorry, Rick," she replied, chuckling, "but Steve and I have some friends coming in from out of town that weekend. I guess that idea really tickled your fancy."

"No, no, not really, I just thought it would be something fun and different to do," I said backing away from my scandalous request and praying that our paths would never cross again.

Now, more relieved than anything else, I took the easy way out for our class costume party. I dug up a hardhat, tool belt, winter boots, and parka and strode in as an Alaskan Pipeline worker. My thick beard was perfect for the part, though I shaved it off soon thereafter.

When it came to dating, the tide began turning when I got to medical school. Now any woman who I thought should be in my league *was* in my league. I was very pleasantly surprised, but I guess I'd gone from being a college student with no money to a medical student with decent prospects as a provider. I remember pumping my fist in the air after a chilly run along the Charles. *Your ship has arrived. Your ship has arrived!* I would finally have a regular, healthy sex life and be free of all this weird masturbation stuff.

Because the first year of medical school wasn't too difficult, I was at last able to work hard and play hard. For a while, I was dating and having sex with two different women, both freckled and fair. I spent many a night with Rachel, a smart, sensible strawberry-blonde working on her Ph.D. in the neuroscience building across from school. And I enjoyed passionate weekends with Melissa, an auburn-haired little-bit-older woman whom I had met at my sister Kathy's birthday party in New York, where she lived and wrote for an upscale women's magazine.

I was having far too much fun to masturbate much or fret about my fantasies, yet after a few months, my dandy days came to an end. "I don't know where this is going," Rachel announced squarely over a candle-lit dinner. "Do you love me? And are we serious? Or else, I'll have to stop seeing you." Thus, she lay down the Up or Out Rule by forcing me to either accept a promotion to exclusive boyfriend—and potential husband—or tender my resignation. I wasn't in love with her, so I had to resign.

Meanwhile, I had begun to fixate on Melissa's too-curly hair and curvy hips. So, as one of our weekends in New York was winding down, I decided I wouldn't make any plans to see her again. I'd stop calling and simply fade away rather than risk hurting her feelings.

As we stood on the platform in Penn Station awaiting my train, she practically read my mind. "So what's going on here?" she asked gently, but assertively. "Am I going to hear from you again?"

I couldn't believe my ears. Since when did people talk about something like that? They just kind of did it. Not knowing what to say, I stammered, "Um, ah, well, probably—"

"Okay, okay, I understand. I get the sense you're seeing someone up in Boston. I've already done that," she explained, referring to a recent triangle she'd been caught in. "I'm not going to do it again. So do what you want to do."

"It's really nothing against you." I started to squirm and fib. "I've just kind of lost interest. Maybe it's because of the long-distance thing."

"Listen. It's okay. It really wasn't working that well for me either. I just feel much better having it out in the open."

Weird, I thought as I boarded the train, *I've never seen someone handle a breakup so directly, yet so peaceably. But she's one of those New York girls with a therapist and all. Maybe they do things like that?*

As my first year of med school came to a close, I found a group of well-rounded classmates to hang out with. Among them, I clicked best with Judy, a petite Jewish girl from New Jersey who was liberal in her outlook but conservative in her clothes and demeanor. "Would you consider a roommate of the male persuasion?" I asked, upon learning she was also looking for someone to live with second year. That September, we moved into an unrenovated third-floor walk-up apartment and grew very close.

When it came to women, my interest had typically been more sexual than social. But along the way, as I had dated them, I'd begun to like them a lot as friends. Their company seemed easier and less fraught with one-upmanship. Now, with Judy, I was able to enjoy pure friendship. There was a sweetness to her that made many see her as a goody-two-shoes. But compared to the boisterous women in my family, I experienced her as an angel.

Finally living in a place with locks on the bedroom doors, I could take care of my own needs without worrying about anything more than a possible knock on the door. Gradually I got more comfortable with masturbation as a way to relax before going to sleep each night. Though I hesitated to use it, I maintained my collection of men's clothes that could mimic women's clothes. A handful of times now, I got especially imaginative and took a pair of white men's briefs, cut a hole for my head out of the crotch, and constructed a believable bra, ready to be stuffed with gym socks. Compared to that, cutting the crotch out of an old pair of shorts to make them into a miniskirt was a cinch. I never got to enjoy my creations more than once or twice, however, because I didn't dare keep such things in my drawers. So I would throw them out—very carefully—and start again from scratch the next time.

Judy and I appreciated each other's company and valued each other's opinions. Together we could be real candid about how we saw our classmates as well as various political and social issues. One particular opinion of mine at the time seems almost laughable in retrospect. I saw her standing by the sink in our tiny kitchen one day and thought aloud, "I just don't see the purpose of a skirt as opposed to pants."

"What do you mean?" she replied, in a surprised but friendly tone.

"A skirt's no doubt harder to move around in than shorts. And it can't be significantly cooler, nor does it provide better protection from the elements. A woman would never choose to wear one while backpacking alone in the wilderness."

"Okay," she said, seemingly amused at my quirky thinking.

"So skirts are foolish and impractical."

"Rick," she said with a smile. "You're being ridiculous. A skirt's simply the appropriate thing to wear for certain occasions. It makes the right impression on people. So it's a very practical part of a woman's wardrobe."

"Then you have to admit it's as crazy and impractical as wearing a tie," I insisted.

"Rick, you just don't get it, do you," she said, showing her frustration. She and I were butting heads because *practical* meant different things to us. For me, practical had a very narrow meaning. It meant physically functional—no frill, no fluff. That was my style. For my roommate, practical took on the larger meaning of being physically or *socially* functional. For her, the idea of a skirt or a tie for a job interview was practical, while I saw it as cultural fluff that shouldn't really matter.

There was a simplistic purity to my vision, but ultimately I only hurt myself with such thinking, like not always wearing a tie to work in places where it was expected. Through experience, I've come to see the wisdom in Judy's ways. I now realize that, day to day, most of us live and work in a world dominated more by social than physical concerns.

It's rather ironic I chose to fight the Battle of What's Practical over skirts rather than ties. In retrospect, it seems I had an extra incentive for putting them down, because deep inside I longed to wear one myself but knew I couldn't—like the fabled fox who couldn't jump high enough to snatch the grapes off the vine, so he dismissed them as sour.

Although a lock on my door gave me privacy, Judy out of town for Christmas vacation gave me something I hadn't faced in years, availability, i.e., an empty apartment fully stocked with women's things. After spending Christmas day with my family back home, I flew back to Beantown for a night to pack my gear for a five-day winter-backpacking trip with the Appalachian Mountain Club. The trip was to be my hardiest ever: ice axe, crampons, snow caves, and temperatures well below zero.

Although excited about my trip, I couldn't rid my mind of the fact that there was nothing and nobody to stop me from trying on any of the thrilling things in my roommate's drawers or closet. I was overwhelmed with temptation yet conflicted by how wrong it was to mess around with someone else's stuff, let alone her underwear. I tried to go around the apartment minding my own business, all the while my hands were shaking and my heart racing. After an hour at best, I succumbed to my old foe, Compelling Curiosity. I didn't like it. I didn't understand it. But how could I pass up this once-in-a-lifetime opportunity?

Preferring not to disturb Judy's clothes too much, I started with the hamper. I tried on a bra and stuffed it with socks. I found some frilly panties and couldn't put them on fast enough. I couldn't believe my erection. I moved on to raid her bedroom. I had to know how it felt to wear pantyhose. Because she was much smaller than I, I pulled one pair up my right leg and another up my left leg so I didn't ruin them. I tried on a dress but couldn't pull it over my shoulders. So I put on a blouse, without fully buttoning it, and a skirt, without fully zipping it.

Suddenly I froze. Were those footsteps I heard coming up the stairwell? My heart rose in my throat. Could Judy possibly still be in town? She couldn't be? But if she was, she could *not* see me this way, I would just plain die. I couldn't imagine my future beyond that terrible moment of discovery. With my heart pounding in my ears, I scurried over to the front door and tensely prepared to hold it closed against anyone who might try to enter.

My whole body relaxed with relief when the footsteps abated. They were probably those of our neighbor Mike returning to his apartment downstairs. But in case it was still somehow my roommate or perhaps landlord making a surprise visit, I thought of chaining the door. But—god damn it—we didn't have one, so I schlepped a heavy night table in front of the door, all the while shimmying around in Judy's way-too-tight clothes. Now feeling more secure, I was eager to try on more things, like her bikini.

First I took off her blouse and skirt and put her underwear back in the hamper. But her blouse became a problem. Where exactly did it come from? Did she hang it next to the other shirts that looked like it? Or did I take it from that place the hangers looked freshly pushed apart? Yikes! My skin was all goose bumps, and my hair stood on end, as I took my best guess. Would she notice? And if she did, what would she think?

After a frantic search, I found her little bikini and sat naked with it beside me on the couch. As I fastened the top, chills shot down my spine. As I pulled the little bottoms up, I got so intensely aroused that all I had to do was pull them a little to the side and barely touch myself to trigger a breathtaking orgasm and spurt like a fountain into a handy paper towel.

Coming down from it, I took my roomie's bathing suit off and looked it over carefully. No spots, no stains, no traces. As I pulled my shirt and pants back on, I tried to pack my unnerving adventure into some kind of palatable package with some of the usual strategies. *Wouldn't any guy be curious?* I thought. *It's not that I wanted to try on her clothes so much; it's just that I couldn't say no to the opportunity. It's really just the novelty of it all that's exciting.*

Returning from the windswept mountains to our still empty apartment, I came up with a new strategy: Make It Mundane. On that occasion, plus the next time Judy was out of town, I hung around in her underwear for hours and didn't let myself masturbate. You could call it behavioral therapy. Picture how absurd it must have looked—me roaming around the apartment in tiny panties with an equally tiny bra strapped over my hairy chest, trying to forget my arousal and concentrate on my homework. Unfortunately, the strategy backfired, because it broke the ice between me and lingerie without making the stuff any less intoxicating. Maybe someday women's underwear would feel mundane, but for now it was as frightfully exhilarating as ever.

I don't know if it was the build-up of pressure from my own gender confusion, but when it came to women I was more than ever determined to find the hands-down gorgeous girlfriend I'd longed for since the beginning of college. Someone whose bones I'd want to jump every time I saw her. I knew my taste was shallow but figured I was just like any other guy my age. Or in a more introspective moment, I might think, *So I have a few twisted turn-ons. What does it matter, if I find a wife who ignites me like no one and nothing else? Then I'll feel normal, even virtuous, as I race home to enjoy the pleasure of her company, night after night.*

Back when Judy and I had moved into our apartment. I had made friends with Keith, a rather congenial, skinny redhead, and his girlfriend, who had been moving out. I hung out with them from time to time and let them know that I was single and looking. Now, in January, in my second year of med school, he called to say that I simply had to come by his ad firm to meet his friend Betsy, who—he'd just recently learned—was now available.

The next day, I got home early from class to drop my books off and spruce myself up. On a lark, I decided to keep one of my medical texts on me to let a little of my catch-appeal show. I met my pal at his desk, and we sauntered over to Betsy's office. Although her door was open, he rapped lightly on it, poked his head around the corner, and cleared his throat. "Uh, Ms. Nakata?"

"Yes, Keith," a cheerful voice responded.

"Do you have a minute?"

"Sure, but I may have to kick you out when the Schweppes people call."

I followed Keith through the door, and my heart skipped a beat, as I beheld a radiant Japanese-American woman with shiny dark brown hair and perfect skin. Her eyes sparkled as they shifted over to meet mine and her lips parted ever so slightly in a magnificent moment of chemistry. She was slender, well dressed, and killing me with the way she crossed her legs.

"That's fine," Keith replied. "I just wanted to introduce you to my friend Rick."

"Nice to meet you, Rick." She seemed so gracious, especially because it didn't look like he had given her the heads-up about me. "How do you guys know each other?" she inquired, seeming interested in starting a conversation.

As my copper-top friend explained, she stole a quick glance down at my hands.

"That's a funny book to carry around," she teased. "Never know when you might need to bone up on your orthopedics, eh?"

"Well, I just popped by to see Keith after class," I replied, pleased that she had noticed.

Just then, her phone rang. She answered it, then covered the receiver with her hand. "I have to take this," she whispered, pleasantly shooing us away. "Thanks for dropping by, Keith. It was really nice to meet you, Rick. I hope I'll see you again sometime." And from her expression, I knew she meant it.

Wanting to strike while the iron was hot, I called her up the very next day and asked her out. We met for a drink after work, and I swear we must have sat across from each other with stars in our eyes, because I don't remember a thing we talked about, except that she had this funny burst of civic pride about coming from Milwaukee. It was peppy and endearing and reminded me of how my mother could get all abubble about Buffalo. Like me, Betsy now hailed from Boston's South End and lived a mere four blocks away. Soon I was calling her up for dinners, movies, and parties. Somewhat old-fashioned, she rarely called to ask me out but was always thrilled to hear from me and every bit as eager as I was.

She seemed to be the yin to my yang. I was a squarish doctor-to-be with great potential but no passion. She was a stylish account executive with fun ideas and a wide circle of friends. At parties, she could fend well for herself and even fend for me if I started to tire out. Always upbeat and courteous, she made a good impression on almost everyone. To me, she represented glamor. As we left a movie theater arm in arm, I whispered to her that the only difference between her and Michelle Pfeiffer was that she'd chosen advertising instead of acting.

We moved along in a whirlwind of romance. We couldn't get enough of each other. Within a week we slept together, and within a month we spent every night together, either at her place or mine. We held hands even in the supermarket and started to meet each other's friends and family. I loved every little thing about her, from the funny knock-kneed way she often sat to the carefree way she giggled on the phone with her girl friends. I barely noticed when she took a dislike to Judy. I didn't get it but figured, *Who understands women anyway?*

Her femininity was energizing and inspiring. I wanted nothing more than to do things for her, take care of her, and please her. Everything she wore, from her shoulder-length hair to her pointy-toed shoes, seemed to say, *I love being a girl.* We were tremendously attracted to each other and had great sex nearly every night. Her skin was so smooth and her body, so soft. She was supremely snuggly. While making love, I would look down and admire her beauty and ethnicity. I would push myself over the edge with the notion that I was *plucking* the loveliest of flowers.

As Betsy and I set out on our first car trip together, I made my way out onto an open stretch of highway and sighed, "You know, I haven't been this happy since my days with Fiona, back in high school." I felt warm and expansive. She, however, fell oddly silent. "Did you ever have somebody like that in your life?" I continued, eyes glued to the road.

"Oh, I had some silly crushes just like everyone else. But I do not appreciate hearing about your old girlfriend," she replied with an unexpected edge.

"But it's all part of my life."

"Fine, but let me tell you, no woman wants to hear about her boyfriend's old girlfriends," she explained, practically spelling it out for me.

"Oh," I replied, accepting her scolding. "Well, who really cares anyway?" We moved on, although I was troubled to see a brittleness to Betsy I hadn't seen in other women.

A big fan of fashion mags, she'd no doubt encountered plenty of pop psychology and one night in bed was surprisingly inquisitive. "You're so calm and controlled. Don't you have any vulnerabilities? How about fantasies?"

For starters, I didn't know what a vulnerability was, despite having plenty: a fetish for female clothing, a blinding attraction to beautiful women, and an occasionally quite painful social awkwardness—to name a few. At the time, though, I was a typical guy, who never thought about his life in terms like *vulnerability* or *feelings.*

Fantasy was a word I knew, but I wasn't about to mess up a perfectly good night by telling Betsy about my sexual fantasies. So I simply said, "When it comes to sex, there ain't nothing like the real thing, with a real fine girl like you." I wasn't willing to open up Pandora's box just because she happened to ask. Besides, I presumed my fantasies were fast becoming a thing of the past, so *no one* needed to know about them anyway.

The fact that my girlfriend was Japanese-American added to her mystique. Bored with my own Jewish roots and Rust Belt background, I had always yearned for diversity in my friends and experiences. Perhaps because I couldn't see the richness within me, I had always gravitated toward people and places that were excitingly different. I appreciated how someone like Betsy might link me to an enchanting foreign culture all the more, now that I'd entered the domestic grind of a career in medicine.

"Fuckin' Gus Gober!" I complained to her about the intern I'd been assigned to, from a payphone outside Saint Elizabeth's Hospital on a cold December night.

"What now?" she asked sympathetically, but sleepily, as if she had just woken up from a nap.

"That guy had sworn up and down that I should do a full physical exam on every patient."

"Yeah."

"Well, I just got in trouble with the attending surgeon for doing a one-hour physical on this sweet little lady the night before her gallbladder operation."

"Jeez, you're just trying to do what you're told. Have you eaten? There's a roast chicken in the fridge for you, if you like."

"Great. Hey, did you manage to tape *Thirty Something*?"

"I did. Aren't you proud of me?"

"You're the best, Bets. Let me just hop on my bike, and I'll be home before you know it."

"Please be careful, Anjin-san," she said, turning her *l*s into *r*s in a pretend Japanese accent.

Just that weekend, we had rented the miniseries *Shogun,* and afterward around the house, I had become the English sailor Anjin and Betsy'd become the lovely Lady Mariko. I reveled in the romance of it all, though I sensed she might not be as ecstatic about her heritage as I was, despite inheriting a Japanese-like eager-to-fit-in affability from her father and a less-is-more elegance from her mother.

Just as I was in love with my fantasy of Betsy, she was in love with her fantasy of me. She felt insecure about her origins and seemed invested in the idea of me as a white knight sent to carry her away from it all. She didn't like hearing that it was any more intricate than that—like the fact I'd had a love life before her. As a girl, she had struggled to overcome weight problems and ultimately turned into a remarkably beautiful woman. Perhaps in concentrating on her appearance, she never developed a high regard for who she was on the inside and was looking to draw her sense of self-worth from the kind of man she might attract.

On the surface, I must have been perfect for her. I was a handsome, well-educated young man from a good family, a conscientious medical student whose primary joy was doing whatever I could to make her smile. Was it wrong for her to want a white knight? Was it wrong for me to want a graceful geisha? No, we're all entitled to our joyful illusions. But could our love last as we discovered ourselves to be more complicated than our starry-eyed dreams?

Her enthusiasm for the holidays that year—Christian and Jewish alike— was childlike and infectious. Her eyes would light up each time she found the perfect new ornament for our little Christmas tree, and I'll never forget how irresistible she looked that spring getting all giddy over Easter eggs. It felt like we were beginning our own family traditions. We even toyed with names for our future children.

Meanwhile, in the thick of my third year of med school, I was busy rotating through the major specialties, hoping to find one that would be fulfilling without being overwhelming. Radiology fit the bill and seemed to combine the allure of science with the satisfaction of patient care. Unfortunately, it appealed to a lot of other med students too, so I knew the pressure was on. I made extra efforts to better my chances and began to think about what city I might like to do my residency in—assuming I would have any choice in the matter.

By now, Betsy and I had been together a year and a half and had become very attached. I couldn't imagine my life without her, perhaps all the more so because I wasn't especially close to anyone except Judy. In the meantime, she had been getting more serious with her boyfriend, and our lease was coming up at the end of the school year.

One Saturday, at the end of a long week at the hospital, Betsy and I were running around the neighborhood catching up on errands and stopped for lunch at a local Chinese restaurant. After settling in and ordering, I leaned back in my chair. "So what should we do about next year?"

My Mariko looked askance at me, as if I'd said something inappropriate, then softened. "Honey, you're the *man*," she said. "Tell me what you'd like to do."

Her formality made me apprehensive, for I was hoping to discuss the idea of moving in together in a way that was casual and collaborative. "Well, it just doesn't make sense," I explained, "for us to have separate places, when we spend all our free time together anyway."

"Yeah, but I do *not* believe in moving in together without getting engaged," she insisted.

"That's crazy. But it doesn't really matter, because we want to be together and I can't expect you to move away with me when I finish med school next year without getting married."

"This isn't the way it's supposed to happen," she said, as her face registered both elation and dismay.

"Can't we just relax and figure things out" I implored, scared to see the stakes escalating. After a tense pause, I tried a different tack. "Hey, what kind of ring would you want? I'll find a nice way to surprise you with it later on."

She smiled amiably, and peace was restored. I proposed to her a few weeks later, on the way to my college roommate Colin's wedding, and presented her with a stunning sapphire ring. I have to admit I was proud of the way it looked on her hand.

We leased a high-rise apartment and had fun setting it up together. She liked to furniture-shop and decorate. I was handy and enjoyed assembling things. Despite our limited finances, I felt we put together a pretty nice living/dining room, with Venetian blinds hanging from a big picture window, a paisley-print futon-couch, and a chunky wooden table from Conran's (think IKEA).

Halfway through my last year of medical school, I reached a point where my month-to-month grades would no longer be reported to the residencies I was applying to, so finally the pressure was off. I now had the chance to catch my breath and contemplate the reality of my situation at home. From the beginning, I could always answer the question *Am I happy with Betsy now?* with a resounding yes. But when I shifted gears to *Will I be happy with her forever?* I felt uneasy and started to worry about things I had never before paused to ponder.

3

Crisis

Knowing that my sexual future belonged to Betsy, I took a few tentative steps to see what little extras she and I might enjoy in the bedroom. I asked if she would like to come to bed sometime in a lacy black bra, garter belt, and stockings, and she seemed to like the idea. But somehow she lacked the true enthusiasm to ever make it happen. I couldn't believe it. *If I were a woman,* I thought, *I'd love the chance to be a sweet little sex kitten in my fiancé's arms.* Neither, could I understand how her sex drive was so profoundly affected by her various moods and aches.

To be fair, she was puzzled as to why I wasn't more excited about planning a wedding and getting to be a groom. She seemed to think that if she had been born a boy, she would have dreamed of the day when she could be a groom. Clearly I was more complicated than your average man and had many reasons to be less than thrilled about being a bridegroom. Nevertheless, our feelings were typical of many young couples. *He* can't understand why *she* doesn't care more about sex. *She* can't understand why *he* doesn't care more about weddings and romance.

Still, I hoped I could mix my fantasies into my love life with Betsy. Perhaps I could ease her into them with a laugh? Once, while she was in the bathroom before sex, I jumped into the bra and panties she had left behind on the floor. When she returned, I sprang up from bed and flexed my muscles. "Look, I'm a weight-lifting woman."

Betsy stopped dead in her tracks and glared at me from the doorway. "What the hell are you doing?" she growled, without waiting for an answer.

33

"That's not funny. Take that stuff off now, and don't ever do it again." Maybe it was wrong to surprise her like that. But what if she could have been more open-minded about my little stunt? Would that have kept me from what I was about to do? Perhaps not, but at least it would have made me feel more fully loved and less confined by our fast-approaching nuptials.

An innocent experience on the road hammered home my impending loss of liberty. By that January, I had started to interview for the internship year that loomed ahead of me in July and the four years of radiology residency that would hopefully follow it. While checking out a residency in Seattle, I made friends with a woman who was also interviewing there. Because we were staying at the same hotel, we decided to have dinner together, and I had to admit, as I looked at her across the table, she was rather tasty. *Maybe I should act now and enjoy my freedom while I still can?* I thought. But while she was away at the ladies' room, I reconsidered. *No, that's stupid. You've been with plenty of women.* So I let the opportunity slip away. Still, the notion of *Speak—or at least act—now or forever hold your peace* remained in the forefront of my mind.

Is there anything I need to try while I still can? I asked myself and in so doing awoke the demon child I'd safely locked away for so long. I let my imagination roam freely over possibilities I had never before dared envision. I imagined going to a gay bar and getting picked up by a man. I'd wear a bra and panties to bed with him and do everything a girl does for a guy—and allow everything a guy does to a girl. Once I saw myself in that scenario, I shuddered with an otherworldly exhilaration that seemed to say, *You will never rest until you know how that feels.*

Of course, this fantasy didn't come out of the blue. Ever since sex ed in seventh grade, I'd been uneasily curious about anal sex and tried my best not to think about it. Just meeting a few gay guys in med school had made me think, *I'd really like to try it, but of course I can't because of AIDS.* By now in 1990, people were well aware of the AIDS epidemic and the suffering it caused in the gay community. Because there were still no good treatments, HIV infection was a death sentence. Although I'd been right to fear it, I'd been using my fear as a powerful new way to keep the lid on my curiosity. It was a strategy that had worked well throughout medical school but now yielded to the pressure of *Act now or forever hold your peace.*

Hoping to be as safe as possible, I went to a pharmacy to buy some condoms. The notion that I wasn't going to use them but that *someone else* would use them on me was dizzying. I was consumed by the combination of titillation and self-hate.

"Uh, Sir," the store clerk interjected, "Did you want those?"

"Um, yeah, yeah," I replied, a little embarrassed at my spaciness on top of everything else. The anticipation was killing me. I had to just do this thing and get it out of my system. It sickened and confused me to think I might be a guy who liked dressing up in women's underwear and having sex with men. And if that weren't disgusting enough, could my desire to feel like a woman mean I was destined to be gay or even transsexual? How could I live with that? I was the mountaineering medical student, the sailor from *Shogun*, a proud masculine man. That's how I saw myself, and that's how everyone else saw me.

Though I showed no outward signs, I was deeply troubled and couldn't think of a soul to turn to. I could barely admit my secret to myself, let alone breathe a word to anyone else. The clash between my desires and my image was excruciating. Dearly I hoped that, by acting them out, I might demystify them and free myself from their painful grasp. As my stomach turned to knots, I fell back on Try It and Hope You Don't Like It.

Because I'd have sooner died than approach one of the gay guys at school with what I had in mind, I decided I'd go to a gay bar on my next trip out of town and sought the counsel of the only other homo I knew, Mike, the swishy brunet who lived downstairs from the apartment I used to share with Judy. After dinner at home with Betsy, one weekday evening in late January, I excused myself to go out and replenish our supply of coffee.

Like Alice in Wonderland, I chased my white rabbit—and it led to Mike's door. Because I had ostensibly come over just to buy some of the gourmet coffee he sold, I was very pleased to see that he was interested in talking for a while in his living room. His taste was clearly very different from anyone I knew. There was a provocatively dressed female mannequin in the middle of the room and all sorts of other whimsical touches, like bright red homemade chiffon curtains. He offered me a glass of wine, and we started to chat.

He knew I had always been a bit curious about gay life, so he bubbled on about a conversation he'd had recently with some friends. I was intrigued by how they would talk to each other and say things like "Girl, please!" and "Oh, Mary!" Mike would occasionally call one a *queen* and refer to him as *she*, as in "I just don't know what to do about Kevin. Ever since the break-up, *she* just sits around watching old Bette Davis movies." It would be a long time until I understood his chatter and where it fit in with who I was and what I liked, but for the time being, it was chilling and made me think I might not be so different.

Finally, I drew a deep breath and told him, "I've always been curious about sex with a man."

"Really," he replied, as a smile spread across his face.

"I was hoping to pick someone up at a bar, and I'd like to get your advice."

Mike was pleasantly surprised and freely offered his two cents. Then picking up on my urgency, he stunned me with a proposition, "You know, you're totally hot. You could experiment with me if you want to," he offered in a relaxed take-it-or-leave-it tone of voice.

"When?" I stammered.

"Whenever."

I wasn't ready for this. But it was too good to be true. So what if I didn't have a bra and panties with me to put on as planned. I suddenly had the chance to get my whole experiment over and done with fast. "How about now?" I suggested.

"Why not!"

I'd never encountered such a casual attitude in all my experience with women. Not even the boldest among them had been near so easy and breezy. I had just stumbled across an international border, the border between the female attitude of *Sex? Why?* and the male attitude of *Sex? Why not!*—between *I need to be persuaded* and *I'll even persuade you.*

Mike insisted on pouring me a little more wine, then took my hand and led me back into his bedroom, which he had just proudly adorned in a very of-the-moment Southwestern motif. He put his arms around me, and I met his lips in a kiss that felt forced and unnatural. More surprises were soon in store. His body felt strangely different from any woman I'd ever been with. Women had always felt soft and pliable, like a mold of Jell-O. My former neighbor felt bony and stiff, like a bundle of sticks. Because of that, his body didn't mold into mine. Instead of feeling cuddly, our embrace felt awkward.

I didn't even find him attractive. Not that I found any man appealing, but Mike, in particular, was weak-chinned and scrawny. I had to will myself to make out with him so that we could move on to bigger and better things. After pulling each other's shirts off, he started doing the darnedest thing. He was pinching my nipples. *I guess they do that on his planet,* I thought, but it was just too weird for me. "No, no, don't do that," I murmured, as I knelt down by his feet.

I was on a mission with two major objectives. Feeling his bulge, I pulled down his pants, opened my lips, and eagerly engulfed his ever-growing organ. Of course, I had never done that before, and *that* was objective number one. Pretty soon he had us both on his bed doing sixty-nine, but I couldn't really enjoy it, because I was impatient to move on to objective number two.

As soon as Mike was hard enough, I put a condom on him, but he lost his erection. We gave it another try, but it was no use. "What if I fuck you first?" I suggested. Though it wasn't anything I craved doing, it seemed my best bet to get him aroused enough to return the favor. With his okay, I pulled a condom on and entered him. Resentfully I thought, *Why can't you just do what I'm doing?* His anus felt more or less like a vagina, and before long I came.

His penis again stiff, I rushed to put another rubber on him. Then I lay back, spread my legs, and waited for him to make me a woman. He tried but soon went soft again. I was young and had never heard of anyone struggling to get it up. Frantically I tried to revive him with my hand and mouth. *I can't believe this is happening,* I fumed. *I can't believe I've cheated on Betsy and let things go this far without getting the one thing I need the most. God help me if I have to do this again!*

"You masturbate don't you?" I asked bluntly, looking up at Mike from his flaccid phallus. He nodded. "You must know what it takes to get you hard. Just do it."

"Okay," he replied and soon restored his erection. "Do you want to just do it without a condom?"

"Have you ever been tested for AIDS?"

"No, but I'm sure I can pull out before I come."

He had always seemed like a nice enough guy, so I had no reason to doubt his word, or at least his intentions. Nonetheless, I was aware he might be infected and might ejaculate inside me. Yet I was under horrific pressure to live out all my womanly dreams in this one window of opportunity. So I pushed ahead. "Okay, do it."

Do it, I thought on a rational level. *It's worth the risk just this once to end all my wondering. Do it,* I felt on an emotional level. *Maybe some real chance of getting AIDS will teach me to think twice before giving in to my depraved fantasies again.*

Again I lay back. This time I felt the tight discomfort of Mike pushing himself into me. But I was determined and urged him on. Finally, as he slid inch after inch inside me, I heard myself moan. Moan with the satisfaction of a longing built up over decades. Moan with the fulfillment of a desire as strange, yet as natural, as the nipples on a man's chest—a sound neither pretty nor ugly, but real—a memory that would stick with me, no matter how much I wanted to forget it and conclude I hadn't enjoyed myself.

Although I loved the idea of what Mike was doing to me, the act itself continued to hurt. Nevertheless, I wanted him to keep going so that I would never have to wonder again. He got more and more into it and then all at once stopped, rolled me over onto my hands and knees, and entered me from behind. He did me some more and pushed me down onto my stomach. I felt like I was doing *nothing.* I was just lying there taking it, absorbing, and waiting. He pumped faster and his body grew tense. He pulled out, and before I could twist around to see what he was doing, I felt a warm, thick fluid spurt onto my skin.

Believe it or not, my whole walk on the wild side hadn't taken more than a half an hour, before I returned home to Betsy, with a pound of coffee in hand. For the next couple days, I felt a bit sore and tingly "down there," but it was my own little secret. I continued on with my life, busy learning the practical skills I would need for internship and preparing for more interviews.

Other than a few stray thoughts, I wasn't tempted to hook up again with my scrawny new friend. Though happy I had experimented, I concluded it was exciting in fantasy, but uncomfortable in reality. That's how I put the lid back on the box and kept from feeling perverted and unfit for a normal life. The fact I had cheated on my fiancée didn't weigh too heavily on me, because I figured that I had done what I had to. I had acted now rather than risked adultery and a broken family later.

I suspected that if Mike had leaked a little before coming, then there might be a very slight chance I could get HIV and even pass it on to her. It was a dreadful thought, but I didn't know what to do about it. Getting tested right away wouldn't be helpful, because HIV wouldn't show up for another five or six months on any of the tests available back then. Betsy was on the pill, so I couldn't exactly start insisting on condoms without setting off an alarm. As I saw it, I had no choice but to keep silent. As long as we both seemed okay, what did it matter? A few weeks passed quietly, including several interviews and a few days skiing with Colin.

Days after I got home, she got another one of the urinary tract infections she was prone to. This time, however, her gynecologist put her on a new antibiotic, and soon she developed vaginal itching and discharge. From a medical standpoint, I knew that starting a new antibiotic might cause a yeast infection. But my better judgment was drowned out by the panicky feeling that I had done something terribly wrong and she was paying for it. She and her doctor needed to know that sexually transmitted diseases were a possibility.

She was able to get an appointment for the very next day. So that evening, as we finished dinner in our apartment, I made a partial confession. "Look Betsy, I'm really, really sorry, but there's something you need to know."

It took her a moment to realize I was serious. Then she froze like a deer caught in the headlights.

"I fooled around with someone when I was on the road."

She screamed in agony and looked like she was going to pull her hair out.

"Hey, I'm just trying to do the right thing."

"It's a little too late for that," she said sarcastically, while I listened, knowing I deserved it. "I can't believe this is happening to us. How can I ever trust you again? How can I look forward to our wedding? You've ruined everything!" She grabbed one of her shoes and whipped it hard against the wall. It dented the dry wall with a thud, then fell to the floor. "Who was she?"

"Nobody. She was just someone I met at a bar in Seattle."

"So you don't know anything about her. How could you endanger my health and our future?"

She's right, I thought, as guilt tore through me and I fumbled for something to say. "I don't think I did, because I used a condom. But I care about you and want to be on the safe side, so I want your doctor to have all the information she might need," I said, sorely regretting every last half-truth.

We slept fitfully that night, she in the bed and I on the couch. Fortunately we learned the next day that her symptoms were simply due to a yeast infection from the recent change of antibiotics. Nevertheless, she continued to be stressed out by my infidelity, and I encouraged her to reach out to her sister-in-law Sandra.

That evening, in a foul mood, she confronted me in the apartment. "God, I hate you. You're no better than Ryan." He had been caught having an affair, while his wife, Betsy's cousin, was pregnant. "That," she had said, "was the lowest of lows."

"Listen," I countered, feeling unfairly compared to a common cheater, "I did what I had to do to get something out of my system before we got married—"

"Just shut up!" she spat. "You really blew it. And it's gonna take me a long time to get over this."

"Please just leave it be. I'm suffering enough inside. Believe me, nothing good will come of belaboring this."

"Sandra said I might have periods of feeling okay followed by periods of feeling angry. And you'll just have to deal with it." Day after day, true to her word, Betsy's rage simmered, then boiled, and then simmered, even seeming to go away for a while, before boiling up again.

I tried to understand what she was going through, but not only had I never cheated before, I had never been cheated on either. And imagining myself in her position didn't help much, because I was not an especially jealous person; I always cared more about a woman's long-term loyalty than her absolute exclusivity. But the fact I had so terribly upset the woman I loved was bad enough. And I experienced her rage as a series of gut punches that could come at any time or place.

Under barrage from without and within, I started to come apart at the seams. If only Betsy knew that there were such extenuating circumstances, that I had conducted a necessary experiment, not a reckless betrayal. She had been my sole source of joy and human contact, and now I had virtually none. I drifted through each day in gloom, helpless to pull myself out of it.

We continued to have sex in the wake of my revelation, but I insisted we use condoms until I could absolutely rule out the chance of her getting AIDS from me—although in the dark recesses of my mind, I had begun to mull over the fact I might have been HIV positive for a month or so and already given it to her.

After two weeks, Betsy had cooled down enough to see the anguish on my face one Saturday morning and ask how she might help. I explained that I needed to get something off my chest, though I wasn't sure it was worth going into. "You can tell me," she assured me, as we sat on the edge of the bed, her hand gently stroking my back. "I just want to see you feel better."

"Do you promise not to blow up?" I asked, my hair on end in an intense mix of hope and dread.

"Hey, we're supposed to be there for each other."

"I can't shake this fear that I could've picked up AIDS," I said, averting my eyes in shame, "because the fling I had was with a man."

"Who, when?" she stammered, her eyes wide with terror.

"It was—It doesn't matter who it was. It was a one-time thing."

"How *could* you?" she asked with her jaw clenched tight.

"I had to know what it was like before making my mind up forever."

"What a crock of shit," she scowled, as she rose to her feet. "What kind of *man* are you?"

"Like I told you—"

"Shut up!" she demanded, as her outrage turned to despair. "It would have been better if you'd told me you'd killed someone." With that, she began to cry, threw her engagement ring down on the ground, and stormed off down the hallway of our apartment building.

I took off after her, desperate to keep my life from getting even more chaotic. I grabbed her in the hallway. "Hey, I know I've got problems, but I love you. We don't have to give up hope."

The notion that I was guilty of something as bad as murder fueled my darkest fears. I couldn't stop worrying I'd be responsible for Betsy's death as well as my own. I broke out into sweats and chills and even had some diarrhea. This all scared me even more because I knew it was typical of the flu-like Acute Viral Syndrome people get 3-6 weeks after infection with HIV. I feared I was infected and knew it would be a death sentence.

But more than an early death, I feared a disgraceful death. Back when I was in medical school, the only high-risk groups for AIDS were homosexuals and Haitians. "What's the worst part about having AIDS?" we guys used to joke. "Having to tell your mom you're Haitian." The joke being that we all knew—without having to say it—that having to tell your mom you're gay was *unthinkable*. But even more than a disgraceful death, I feared a despicable death. What if I'd not only infected myself, but Betsy too? How could I live with that possibility? Desperately I sought information and reassurance.

I thought of one Dr. John Calabrese, who had spoken to our class about gay people and their healthcare concerns, and scheduled an appointment with him as soon as I could. At the office, he was every bit as short, round, and outgoing as I recalled. Once we were safely behind the closed door of his examination room, I began, "Dr. Calabrese, I'm a fourth-year medical student with a big problem, and you're the only one I could think of to talk to."

"Why me?" he asked.

"I remembered you from the talk you gave. You're a gay man who knows a lot about sexually transmitted diseases."

"I never actually said I was gay."

"Oops, sorry. I guess I just assumed it."

"I guess I'm more obvious than I realize," he grinned.

Moving on to the matter at hand, I explained, "I'm engaged to be married, but I felt like I had to first experiment with a man. I didn't like it, but I'm afraid I might have exposed myself to HIV."

Brows raised in a look of both concern and curiosity, he loosened his tie, hit the intercom, and said, "Giselle, I'm going to need a little more time in here with Mr. Novic." Then he turned to me. "Now tell me exactly what happened."

"About two months ago, I . . ." I was so glad that Dr. Calabrese was gay. I was able to admit the whole truth of what I had done, by repeatedly reminding myself, *I'm sure he's done far worse.*

He had a number of technical questions: "Do you know Mike's HIV status?," "What kind of discomfort did you feel when he put himself inside you?," "Did he use lubrication?," "Do you remember bleeding afterward?"

I wanted to crawl into a corner and die, but I did my best to remain seated and answer all his questions before pushing on to my chief concern. "I'm real scared by these sweats and chills and occasional bouts of diarrhea I've had over the last week or so. Do you think I might have the Acute Viral Syndrome?" I suddenly became aware of sounding like a woman who was afraid she might be pregnant, and part of me liked it. I winced, *God, am I twisted.*

"Have you had any fevers?" Calabrese inquired.

"No, I've never been able to document a temperature."

He checked my vitals, gave me a brief physical exam, and then concluded, "I think your symptoms sound more like panic attacks. You don't have the classic fever of the Acute Viral Syndrome or swollen lymph nodes of AIDS Related Complex."

"But I've *never* had panic attacks. I'm not even sure I believe in such things."

"Well, believe it or not, these things happen, and you're going to need to know about them as a doctor. But the most important thing is that you were possibly exposed to HIV-positive pre-cum. On that basis, I think your risk of seroconverting is extremely small. I do think it's worth getting tested, but unfortunately you'll have to wait at least another three months to take a meaningful HIV test."

Shaken by the implications, I replied, "That means I won't be able to get tested until a week before my wedding and a month before internship. How will I ever be able to think about anything else until then?"

"Let's meet again at the beginning of next week. I have a few ideas that might be helpful."

Dr. Calabrese appreciated the agony I was in and went out of his way to help me. He asked for Mike's number and called him later that week to persuade him to get tested. If he were currently HIV negative, then I would only have to worry about the chance that he had been recently infected and passed it directly on to me. Mike, however, refused. If he were HIV positive, he insisted, he would just as soon not know.

For me, *knowing too much* had never before been a problem. In difficult times, the more I could learn, the better. But now, extreme duress was pushing my needle into the red zone. I couldn't handle knowing that swollen lymph nodes would be a bad sign. Several times a day, whether at work or at home, I would stick my fingers into my armpits and feel my lymph nodes. Because I didn't know their normal size, I worried they were enlarged.

From there it was off to *How would I ever deal with getting AIDS?* Because I couldn't come up with any decent way of breaking the news and coping with it, I would swirl into another of what I hoped was just a panic attack, all the while keeping it to myself. No one saw the inner chaos, merely the distraction and dejection. Normally, in a pinch I'd ask myself, *What's the worst thing that could possibly happen?* Then, once I had figured out a plan for it, I could relax. Yet I could devise no plan for the possibility of a disgraceful and despicable death.

One day, I started to spin out like that while trying to focus on nephrology consultations at the VA hospital. I scrambled to find a phone that offered any sort of privacy and settled for one of the phone booths in the front lobby. I called Dr. Calabrese's office and waited on hold for him.

"Hi, Rick," he said in a pleasant, slightly patronizing tone.

Nervously, I looked around to make sure no one I knew was in the adjoining booths or anywhere in the vicinity. "Dr. Calabrese, I'm so sorry to bother you, but I wanted to make sure I had told you that Mike and I also had oral sex, in case that affected my chances of . . . bad news."

"As long as he didn't come in your mouth, then we're still dealing with the issue of pre-cum and my assessment would remain the same."

"He didn't," I replied.

"Then your chances of becoming HIV positive are very, very small."

"How small?"

"How small? Let's say less than the chance of dying in an airplane crash. Do you worry about things like that?"

"Well, no," I answered emphatically.

"Then try to think of it that way."

"I will. But is that your real assessment, or are you just sugarcoating it for me the way we doctors sometimes do when someone has terminal cancer and we want to preserve hope?"

"Rick!" he exclaimed, straining to maintain his professionalism. "Do you realize that you're beyond human reassurance? Let me phone some Xanax in for you. You can take it when you start to panic." Although I had never before taken a mood-altering medication, I figured the time had come.

The good doctor then ended our conversation with a surprising initiative. He suggested that we talk sometime without having to rush or worry about privacy and invited me to come by his condo that Sunday.

Over the next few days, I told myself, *The risk is one in ten thousand, just like flying—or driving, for that matter.* But for some reason, I couldn't keep my mind off the chance I would get AIDS. Fortunately Calabrese's medicine calmed my nerves and kept my disaster scenario at bay. Of course, I made sure my betrothed knew what I was doing.

As we came back from dinner together that Friday night, I started to spin out again, but my pills weren't where I had left them. "Betsy," I inquired, "have you seen my Xanax?" She hesitated suspiciously. "Betsy?"

"I just don't think you should be on a drug like that."

"You took my Xanax?"

"I'm just afraid you'll get addicted," she said in a way that felt manipulative and left me wondering whether she thought I should be suffering more for my offense.

"Damn it, the doctor prescribed them for me because he thinks I need them. I'm only gonna use them when I have to." Reluctantly she produced the bottle from beneath a stack of towels.

Sunday afternoon, I arrived at Dr. Calabrese's quaint Commonwealth Ave. condo, not knowing exactly what to expect. He greeted me at the door and insisted I call him John. As he walked me in, he introduced me to his hunky boyfriend, who was friendly but soon on his way out shopping. We sat around a mahogany coffee table in the living room. Though a little dark, the room seemed elegant—and perhaps professionally decorated—with old porcelain lamps and an oriental rug on a hardwood floor.

John poured a Perrier and lime for both of us and explained, "I wanted you to come over here to see how Peter and I live so that you'd have a better sense of gay life. I didn't want you to think we were all like Mike."

"Thanks, but I don't think that."

"You know, I want to share something with you about what it was like for me growing up," he began. "I didn't always know I was gay. I knew I always liked Superman and Batman, but didn't everybody? Back in high school, I used to fantasize about being with the jocks, even fucking them. But I told myself that was the only way a little squirt like me could get to be with the girls." I shot him a puzzled look, and he proceeded, "If the jocks fucked the girls and I fucked the jocks, then I'd be fucking the girls through the jocks. I didn't realize that I was gay until I got to medical school, and by then," he chuckled, "I was working so hard that it almost didn't make any difference." He stopped and looked at me as if to say, *Your turn.*

I matched his essay with a short answer. "I needed to know what it was like to be with a guy before getting married and losing that option forever."

"But why?" he asked, while I grew uneasy. "Did you ever fantasize about it? What do you think about when you masturbate?"

"I've wondered what it would be like to be a woman in bed with a man," I admitted at great pain, my face growing flushed. But I stopped there, unwilling to say, *I'm turned on by bras and panties* or *I'm insanely curious about everything female.*

Figuring that I must be some sort of gay or bi man with a taste for being on the bottom, he said, "Do you ever feel anything when you see someone like Christopher Reeve?" I explained that I didn't, and ultimately he got frustrated and must have concluded I was holding back on something, for after fielding a few more questions about HIV, he wrapped our conversation up with "Maybe worry is the alcohol that keeps you from looking into why you wanted to be with a man? Maybe you should explore this with a psychiatrist?"

"I'm not crazy. Wouldn't anybody be bothered by what I'm going through?"

"Just think about it."

In retrospect, I can see that John was on the right track. Worrying about AIDS kept me from dealing with the shocking results of my experiment: It had made me feel like a woman, and I'd loved every inch. At the time, though, all I could see through the haze of my HIV fear was that I had disgraced myself as a man. What I had done made my masculine qualities and achievements look like a ridiculous sham. I figured, if any guy I knew heard the story, he'd have a good laugh at my expense and agree. Men would look down on me like I was some closeted freak.

Although Betsy and I were trying to move on, she agreed with Dr. Calabrese, "You need serious help." If I ever were to lose her, I assumed other women too would see me as highly damaged goods. Once, in an unrelated conversation, my sister Laura spelled out exactly the kind of reception I feared, "I don't understand this bi thing. If a guy's had sex with a man, forget him. He's gay, period."

I continued on in my own private hell. How could I talk about what I'd done? I felt like a drunk driver who might have killed someone in a hit and run—or a woman who had been date raped and felt stupid for allowing it to happen. Because Betsy and I were struggling with my anxiety and her anger, we had to back out of a much-anticipated vacation with my family so that we could "work on our relationship." My parents were dumbfounded, and when they came to Boston for a medical conference afterward, my father asked if I would like to go to a Red Sox game so that we could have some time alone.

Because he was an internist, like Dr. Calabrese, I hoped he could offer further reassurance that I wouldn't turn out to be HIV positive. We sat side by side, speaking softly while staring off at the game. I told him virtually the same story I'd originally told my fiancée: I feared AIDS from a one-night stand I'd had with a floozy out of town. "Though I know I didn't take too much of a risk," I explained, "a month or so later, about the time I confessed to Betsy, I started to get strange sweats and chills, which I'm afraid might represent the Acute Viral Syndrome."

"Did you have a fever or a rash?" my father asked, following my lead and sounding like we were simply two doctors discussing a case.

"No, but I'm concerned I might have swollen axillary lymph nodes."

Being a practical man, Dad rose from his seat and motioned toward the aisle. "Let's check it out."

I followed and soon we found a relatively secluded spot behind a flight of stairs.

There he stuck his fingers up into my armpits just like Dr. Calabrese and fortunately wasn't impressed by what he found. "The overwhelming odds are you didn't catch anything," he concluded. "I think you're just wracked by guilt. You shouldn't feel so terribly bad. You just wanted a last piece of ass."

I couldn't bear telling him I wanted to be that last piece of ass. Sadly the taboo nature of my troubles kept me from giving my predecessor any real chance to help.

Days passed slowly, and I still couldn't concentrate nor sleep very well. I took no pleasure in food nor anything else, for that matter. The prospect of

AIDS wouldn't go away. If I got it, I would hope like hell I hadn't given it to Betsy. If I had, I would devote the rest of my life to taking care of her as best I could. Or perhaps I would do my best to apologize and then jump off one of the high bridges in town.

I had failed miserably as a man. I wished there was a war going on so that I could volunteer for hazardous duty. At least then, I'd have the chance to redeem my honor. I felt like I was fighting something unspeakably horrible that I could never defeat because it existed inside me, like a cancer in my brain. Although Jewish, I had never put my heart and soul into it. Now I longed for something to believe in.

After a month of the worst misery I had ever known, I found my religion—and her name was Demetra Burnett. I was assigned to work with her on a cardiology rotation that April. She was a tall, thin woman with a big head of wavy black hair, which—like her first name—came from her Greek mother. She was six years older than me and had a funny little mole on the tip of her nose, though I got the sense she was beyond caring about such things.

Without realizing it at first, I began to feel a little less wretched whenever she was around. There was something soothing about the way she measured her words before speaking. She was also refreshingly open about being separated from her husband and helping a girl friend through a painful break-up. It seemed to fit with the fact she was going into psychiatry and had an interest in psychoanalysis, the traditional form of talk therapy originated by Sigmund Freud. Doctors who were formally trained in it were known as analysts, and in 1990 they still represented the most tried and true way for people to learn more about themselves.

Trying not to pester Dr. Calabrese with more requests for reassurance, I asked Demetra for some time to talk one on one, and she invited me over for dinner after work. As she opened the door to her apartment in Beacon Hill, it seemed a bit small and congested, but her living room had a lovely way of extending out to a balcony, where she apparently tended flowers. Her accumulation of books and photographs and even her black lacquered home entertainment unit reminded me of how grown-up she was compared to me. As we chopped vegetables, she explained that things had been going well with her husband lately and that he would probably be moving back in by the end of the month. We brought the food out to a small table by the balcony and sat down to eat.

"I'm surprised to hear you've been hurting so badly," she began. "I thought you were just a naturally brooding kind of guy."

"Maybe so, but not like this. I've done some terrible things." Her eyes widened. "Oh, nothing you need be frightened about." Nervously I confessed that I had experimented with a man, that I was afraid I might have become

HIV positive, and that I was horribly ashamed I might have passed it on to Betsy.

She seemed to find my story compelling and allowed me to tell it comfortably, even expand on it. When the phone rang, she let the answering machine pick it up. She never got riled up or rushed the conversation in some direction of her own, but neither was she amused if I tried to joke or stall. Once I was back on track, she seemed to use her imagination to get a whiff of what I was feeling each step along the way. Emotion after emotion registered across her face.

Strangely, I felt like I had come home, although no one back home had ever been like Demetra. So I dared go further. "The whole reason I bothered experimenting was that I needed to know what it felt like to be a woman. I've been turned on by lingerie and troubled by this kind of thing for years."

Her jaw dropped a little, and she looked like she might be about to say something.

"Listen, I *know* this is really fucked up," I assured her. "And that I made things worse by acting out. And that exposing Betsy to danger like that was very, very wrong." Finally, I stopped to see what she would say. I felt like some kind of pathetic movie-villain, but I was trying to come clean and ready to accept help. Would she rise to her feet aghast and promptly show me the door?

"I feel bad for you," she said softly. "You've got some serious psychological baggage that you tried to work out on your own. Does Betsy know what you've done?" I nodded. "How did she take it?"

"She said it would have been better if I'd told her I'd killed someone."

"No wonder you feel so badly about this," she said with furrowed brow.

"I wish that was all there was to it."

"Maybe going through this will make you a better, more sensitive person."

"I'm already nice," I protested. "I'm probably the nicest of the four kids in my family."

"These things aren't fair," she said, clearly feeling my pain. "Sometimes it just sucks what we have to deal with."

Spellbound, I thought, *Who is this woman?*

She told me there was a richness to me that went beyond anything I was aware of. When I replied I was afraid I'd get AIDS and never get the chance to appreciate any of it, she let me know that she had just finished working at an AIDS clinic and thought I was going to be okay; it was not my time to go.

"I feel like such a miserable freak," I admitted, unable to rein it in. "I walk by people on the street and think, *I'd trade places with him or him or him.*"

"The only normal people," she replied, "are the ones you don't know very well."[10]

I laughed. I couldn't believe it. I actually laughed. The idea was funny and comforting. "You know, when I talk with you," I confided, as our chuckles abated, "I forget about the sweats and chills for a moment." When I saw that she too was moved, I asked, "Can I hold your hand?" She held out the hand nearest to me, and I grasped it and teared up.

"You know, you should really think about psychotherapy," she pleaded. "It could help you in much the same way."

Soon we both got up to clear the dishes. As we said goodbye, she promised to be there for me. And I held her like she was my last bridge to happiness and sanity.

For the first time in my life, I had known the burden of having something horribly heavy on my mind and having to bear it in isolation. Now I had experienced the invaluable intimacy of being able to talk about whatever I needed to with someone who took the time to understand. Naively I hoped Betsy could be as comforting.

"You know, given everything I've been going through, I wish you could be as supportive as Demetra," I begged, as we got ready for work the next morning. I knew my timing was awful, but I just had to say something.

"What do you mean? Of course, I am," she fired back. "That's all I ever do these days is worry about you."

"Gee, thanks," I replied, shaking my head. "A lot of good that does me. I'm going through a crisis that's worse than anything I've ever seen before and probably worse than anything I'll ever see in the future. And whenever I look to you for solace, all I get is anger."

"Well, how do you think I feel?" she said trembling. "It's very easy for Demetra to be all sweet and supportive. She's not the fiancée you cheated on. You're not the only one in crisis."

"You can't just say you're in crisis just because I'm having a crisis," I objected. "What if I do that to you later in life when you're having trouble with something?" Although I argued on for a while, I saw her distress and sensed the severity of what she was going through. Fighting for survival had handicapped my empathy for her.

Meanwhile, I continued to find solace in Demetra and inspiration from the extent of what we shared, though from the start our friendship was unequal. Although she turned to me with some of the angst she felt over her bad back and credit card debt, she didn't need my compassion the way I needed hers, and there must have been moments when she experienced me as nothing short of overwhelming. I could never get enough time with her and tried to savor our contact as best I could. For days, I would look forward to any plans we made. Afterward, I'd reminisce again and again about our last conversation. I would remember every word she had said, whether she was helping me through my emotional morass or just talking about the movies she liked. Although I didn't have any overtly sexual feelings for her, in so many other ways, it felt like I was falling in love with her—perhaps like the love a patient might feel for his therapist, or a parishioner for her priest.

Once, Betsy and I had Demetra and her husband over for dinner, and I managed to take a snapshot of the two women together. I secretly carried it in my wallet afterward, and in my bleakest moments, I'd pull it out, gaze on Demetra, and recite a version of the "Salve Regina" that had somehow stuck with me and quieted me when I needed it the most.

> *Salve Regina mater misericordiae,*
> *Vita, dulcedo et spez nostra,*
> *Salve, salve Regina.*
>
> *Ad te clamamus,*
> *Exsules filie Hevae,*
> *Ad te suspiramus, gementes et flentes,*
> *Oh clemens, oh pia.*
>
> Hail Queen, mother of mercy,
> Our life, sweetness, and hope,
> Hail, hail Queen.
>
> Unto you, we clamor,
> Exiled children of Eve,
> Unto you we sigh, burdened and weeping,
> Oh merciful one, oh holy one.

I could never stay tranquil for too long, however, because Betsy could be very tense and unpredictable. If I ever seemed too easy on myself, I might run into an unpleasant reminder of "what you did to me." Or she might pull out of something like the year-end med school banquet at the last minute or go along with whatever it was but spoil it with a foul mood. Still, at other times, we were able to avoid our troubles, stroll out to dinner in Back Bay, and snuggle up in front of a video afterward.

Maybe it's unrealistic, but I wish she could have couched at least one of her reminders of "what you did to me" with "even though I know you weren't trying to hurt me," because I began to resent the often intentional way she lashed back at me for the unintentional harm I had caused her. While my actions may have been deliberate, my intention was always to experiment quietly and avoid hurting her in the process.

Crazy as it seems, we still tried to plow ahead as planned to our wedding day in June. Betsy immersed herself in the details of wedding invitations and bridesmaids' dresses, while I planned our honeymoon.

Both Dr. Calabrese and Demetra had recommended I build a group of people around me for support. But I wasn't comfortable reaching out to anyone in my family. Although my parents and sisters were concerned about me, they had never shown any real interest in talking about life's ordinary woes, let alone anything as atrocious as homosexual experimentation.

The only people I could think of confiding in were my fiancée's warmer, fuzzier older brother, Lee, and his wife, Sandra. They were an obviously good choice and an obviously bad choice. He wrote for a newspaper, and she practiced family law. They were hippie-ish and friendly, and routinely talked about things like drugs, divorce, and therapy. They were my kind of people and part of my family-to-be. On top of it all, Betsy was already in touch with them about what had happened, so I wouldn't have to make any startling new revelations. But of course, looking to them for support was complicated, because they were *her* brother and sister-in-law and would always have her interests at heart.

They lived in Detroit, and I called them up, late one afternoon, before she came home from work. Although it was hard to talk with them about experimenting, they were as wonderful as I hoped they would be. Instinctively, I was more comfortable broaching the subject with Sandra, but the fact I could speak at all candidly with Lee surprised me.

Like Dr. Calabrese, he helped me open up by telling me some of the things he had struggled with. "I don't know if Betsy ever told you," he explained, "but for years I couldn't resist dallying with women outside my relationship with Sandra."

"I didn't know."

"Eventually I got the crabs but didn't realize it until we were both itching like crazy and couldn't figure out why."

"What a nightmare!" I remarked, impressed that he would share such a thing with me.

Soon he switched the conversation over to me and asked, "Why did you do what you did?"

"All I can tell you," I explained, "is how can you know for sure if you want a life of vanilla ice cream, if you've never tasted chocolate?"

"*I've* never been curious about chocolate. I don't think most people think much about it. I'm not saying you're gay, but it sounds like you have some issues worth looking into."

"You think so?"

"I do. I think it's about time you joined the Therapy Club. Sandra agrees. She and I have been members for years."

Betsy had liked the idea for a while now, although she seemed to like it more in the spirit of court-ordered rehabilitation. But now, with all five confidants in favor, I was prepared to do something no one in my family had ever done. I agreed to see a psychiatrist.

Because my wife-to-be needed our car for work, I asked Demetra's analyst if he could refer me to someone near the hospital I'd be interning at, and he suggested Dr. Posner. I was two months away from my HIV test and barely able to think about anything else. Desperately I hoped Posner could relieve my worries and rid me of my sexual baggage.

Two parts of me were locked in a bitter struggle: the I'm-turned-on-by-pretending-I'm-a-girl side and the this-is-disgraceful-for-a-man-like-me side. Battle raged between what turned me on and what I thought of it. Although both sides were overpowering in their own way, the disgraceful-for-a-man-like-me side had typically dominated so soundly that I experienced the other as something foreign that would seize hold of my mind from time to time. Like catching a cold, it was a nuisance that would take control and run its course. It would lead me to imagine this or try that until I could wash it away with action and orgasm. It was a disease I was vulnerable to, but one that had never interfered with the peaceful and productive flow of my life, not until now. Now my dark side had led me to act out and cause great pain. It had ground my life to a halt and may have sewn the seeds of my death. It was a cancer; I wanted Posner to root it out.

He worked out of his house in an attic that had been specially renovated for the purpose. He was a lanky man with frizzy brown hair, glasses, and a beard, a Jewish Abraham Lincoln. He greeted me cordially, and although he was an analyst complete with a couch, he directed me to a leather chair opposite the one he sat in. It took nearly the whole first session to explain my predicament to him, at the end of which, he recommended that I see him twice a week and we negotiated a fee.

The next few times I came to see him, he spoke less and less and I found I had to carry on about 95% of the conversation. I would bare my soul to him, and he would just sit there with nothing to say. When I would stop to ask him a question, he would usually respond with "Why do you ask?"

I wondered what I was paying him for and would've quit if it hadn't been for Demetra. "He's just doing what Freudian analysts are supposed to do," she explained.

"What, sit there like some kind of strange, silent robot?" I interjected.

"Just be patient. It'll be worthwhile in the end."

Being a strict analyst, Dr. Posner gave me very few kind words and little reassurance, and never spoke about himself. His exclusive aim was for me to focus on my feelings rather than gloss over them with my usual coping strategies. He even encouraged me to access unconscious feelings through free associations, memories, and dreams.

Generally, he would only break his silence to ask me to clarify things he didn't understand. Though I was hurting and needed answers, he politely refused to answer all but the simplest of questions. He didn't ask many either, with one notable exception. He asked if I could hold off on the wedding, which was now a mere two months away. "People in therapy," he explained, "often make important discoveries about what they want in life. So I generally recommend putting off any long-term decisions until we've worked together for at least six months."

Of course, I was unsure whether Betsy and I could be happy together. But our current crisis was the first we had ever faced. I was fully mobilizing to meet the challenge, and she had started to see a therapist of her own. I didn't know how our relationship would work out, but I remained hopeful.

Still on my best behavior at home, I made spaghetti for dinner and set our table in the living room. As we ate, I casually inquired, "How do you like therapy so far?"

"It's okay," she said, tightening her grip on her fork.

"How do you like Dr. Graham?"

"She seems like a nice enough lady."

"My therapist is kind of creepy. Are you learning anything about yourself?"

"I guess I'm a pretty emotional woman," she replied, looking a little cross. "But that's o-kay."

I nodded approvingly.

"I also have a fear of abandonment, but I'm not sure how much longer I'm gonna need therapy. How's *yours* going?"

"Well, it seems like experimenting sexually was more connected with my childhood than anything else, and—"

"But how do I know you're not gay?" she interrupted.

"I assure you I'm not. I've never been attracted to men. In fact, if we ever broke up, I wouldn't go looking for a man. I'd try to find someone a lot like you."

"How can you say that?" she said, looking wounded.

"I was trying to prove a point. I thought it was a compliment." We both sat there frustrated for a moment, before I broke the silence. "Dr. Posner suggested we postpone the wedding, while we work more on our issues. What do you think?"

Now utterly flabbergasted, Betsy rose from her chair. "That would be like telling everybody we have problems," she said with unusual deliberateness. "It would be humiliating, and you're the one who's caused this whole mess in the first place."

"Okay, okay. Fair enough." I echoed sheepishly. "But it just doesn't seem like the right time for us. We could get married later."

"Either we get married in June, or we end it," she said with finality.

"Okay, then June it is," I replied, trying to conceal my trepidation. I couldn't bear being torn from her and having to tell everyone the news, let alone having to field questions about it. So to get the spotlight off us, I figured, I would marry her. Then after we had some peace and quiet, we could sift through our uncertainties, before making any lasting decisions—like when to have children.

I don't know why Betsy was in such a hurry to commit to me given how scared and angry she was, but she wasn't a woman who spoke freely about how she felt inside. Instead, she tended to push the less pleasant things out of her mind and trust that no one had the bad manners to bring them up. If I had been in her shoes, I would have postponed the wedding to get a better sense of what was going on sexually with my fiancé and find out why he was falling apart in front of me. But maybe she had her own desperate fear of ending up alone and clung to me for survival the way I clung to her? Maybe only the promised permanence of marriage made all of our troubles worthwhile? At the time, though, I was so thankful that she still wanted me that I didn't dare push my luck and ask why.

Meanwhile, my HIV fears raged on through late April and May. They would recede into the background when I could talk with someone like Demetra, Lee, or Sandra, but would jump right back to the fore when I returned to Betsy. Still, I hoped that someday she could forgive me and I could feel as safe and open with her as I did with the others. As my HIV test approached, just days before our wedding, I tried not to worry her about it, as she flew back to Milwaukee to make preparations. Instead, I called Demetra. "In case of bad news, can I stay with you and sleep on your couch?"

"Of course," she replied with such warmth that I felt she was right there by my side.

Back in 1990, most HIV testing was done anonymously at city-run sites, because people were afraid they would be scorned by friends, family, and employers if word got out that they were infected. I arrived at the Fenway site shaking with fear, even though I knew there was only a small chance of bad news. According to protocol, I met with a counselor in a little office with a desk and chairs that looked left over from the '40s to get my results. Right away, she noticed I wasn't just another patient coming through. "Are you okay?" she asked. "You look white as a sheet."

"I'm terrified."

"Do you think you might be HIV positive?"

"I don't know, but I don't know what I would do if I was."

"Are you close to anyone?"

"I'd prefer not to go into things too much. But if you don't mind, maybe you could say a prayer for me before you open the envelope."

"Sure," she said, "May the Lord protect and keep you. May he sustain you in this, your time of need. Amen."

She opened the envelope and handed me the result . . . I would live. I was negative!

As I hugged her and thanked her, I tried to process the good news. It looked like Dr. Calabrese had been right all along. Maybe the sweats and chills and other things going on with my body had been symptoms of panic? I had a new lease on life and could now stop worrying and begin the long process of investigating my disaster and figuring out what to do next.

4

Aftermath

Two days later, I flew to Milwaukee to get ready for my wedding. There I informed Betsy and then Lee and Sandra of the good news. None of them had been nearly as concerned as I was. With guests on their way and a world of troubles still between us, Bets and I looked to them for guidance, and they were a godsend. "Act as if everything's fine," Sandra advised, "and enjoy the day. You'll work your problems out in due time."

Nonetheless, I needed Xanax to get through our wedding "festivities," which were held at a lush green country club with far too many people there for my liking. As we recited our vows, I was struck by how delicate and pure Betsy looked and ever so sincerely hoped I would never have to hurt her again.

At the reception, we greeted people as a couple and then individually. As each approached to offer his or her congratulations, I became all too aware of how we should have postponed everything. "Good god, man, she's gorgeous," my cousin Phil proclaimed, "You two must be so happy."

Not right now we aren't, I thought and instead replied, "Yeah, thanks, and we're totally psyched to take off to Italy tomorrow. You were there recently, weren't you?" And soon he and I were safely talking travel tips.

Ill at ease with each other from the outset, our honeymoon got off to a rocky start, as we ran into the inevitable snags of European travel, like getting lost on the road, running late, and having to notify our *pensione* from a confounding old payphone. Rather than seeing these things as challenges, my bride saw them as "things *you* should have taken care of." I did my best to be patient and resourceful, and eventually she came around.

By the end of the trip, peace had been restored. We sat for dinner on a bougainvillea-lined terrace on a cliff overlooking the Mediterranean. Betsy looked tanned and resplendent in her soft white halter dress. Although she had decided to spend the day in town shopping for gifts, she seemed genuinely interested in my visit to Herculaneum. Looking at her across our candlelit table, I felt a flicker of my old affection. Going with it, I gazed into her eyes and said, "I love you."

"I love you too," she replied, as her eyes grew dewy. She grabbed my hand across the table and continued, "Hey, I want to show you this beautiful beach at the bottom of the cliffs." After dinner, we enjoyed a romantic walk—and a passionate tumble.

Within days of returning from the Amalfi Coast, we moved to a high-rise apartment building closer to my new hospital and I started internship. Although I had been fortunate to secure a spot in radiology, first I had to do a year of internship in internal medicine. It required long days and nights away from my new wife. From the get go, I was immersed in responsibility for people's lives and the need to learn as I went along.

Although my first year of post-grad training was grueling, I liked it. I was more cut out to be an M.D. than a medical student attached to one. Call me a little masculine, but I just didn't make a graceful tag-along or a cheerful do-bee. I preferred the decisions and duties of patient care to the politics and nuances of keeping a boss happy. Now I could just do my job and watch my fellow interns' backs, and they would watch mine.

Although riddled with doubt as a husband, I was thorough and decisive as a doctor. I carefully reviewed all health concerns with each patient, taking the time to ensure that he or she understood how we planned to address each problem. Whenever the nurses called a code on my floor, I was quick to respond, confident with my CPR, and eager to soak up more advanced cardiac lifesaving skills. There's nothing like a few life or death situations to take your mind off your woes and put your nervous energy to good use. Internship made me feel like the American economy of the 1940s, devastated by the Great Depression but rising to the challenge of World War II.

For a while now, Demetra had felt inundated by my need for her as a confidante. So when her own world war started across town, she soon had very little time for me, whether in person or over the phone. On top of that, she was well aware of how fond I had grown of her. Though she knew I'd never make a pass at her as long as either of us was married, it still must have been awkward for her to keep in touch with me.

Meanwhile, internship and marriage made it easy for me to put off any more decisions until I made progress on my issues in therapy. As I told Dr. Posner about my sexual habits, he broke his silence with, "Why didn't you come for help sooner?"

"I don't know," I explained. "I guess up until my crisis, I didn't know there was anything wrong with me." He gave me a quizzical look. "How do I know what other guys think about when they masturbate?" I muttered. "For all I know, everyone might be turned on by women's underwear or curious about sex with a man."

"I don't think so," he said in a confident, but kindly manner.

"You know, my brother-in-law said the same thing. But how can a man not be curious about what it's like to be a woman,"

"Most men are *not* curious about such things," Posner replied, "at least not like you are."

I had to admit I had been consistently curious for a very long time. "You know, I always thought I might be messed up like that. But even then, it's in such a small, embarrassing way that I'd never want to bring up with anybody."

"Can't you see you're trying to minimize your problem? And before that, you were trying to universalize it so that you didn't have to own it and feel it." By cutting away at my defenses, Dr. Posner introduced me to the concept of feelings and strategies for coping with them. The term *defenses,* in fact, refers to the more superficial strategies. Stripped of mine, I had to face the fact that I was freakishly interested in what it's like to be a girl. I assumed it was a hideous problem, and Posner never suggested it was anything less.

He was very good at letting me know how abnormal and in need of his services I was. He wasn't near as good at reminding me how basically healthy and functional I was. As he pushed me to explore the "perverse" fantasies that fueled my problem, I started to feel more and more defective. Gravely, I emptied my savings to pay for my therapy and worked assiduously at it.

I read about the classic case of Daniel Paul Schreber. He was a judge who had bouts of believing that he was a woman who had been visited and impregnated by God. Despite the best efforts of one of Freud's colleagues, these bouts came with increasing frequency until the judge finally lost his mind. I let Dr. Posner know that Schreber seemed eerily similar to me, and he nodded. That's all, just nodded—not bothering to point out that Schreber also had *schizophrenia,* something he knew I didn't have and sure could have told me.

Although experimenting with a man had triggered my crisis, I soon put aside that part of it to focus on the more fundamental problem of why I wanted to feel like a woman. Don't think my homosexual experience didn't bother me. It did. I thought homosexuality was weird and unnatural, but fine—for other people. For me, sex with a man was interesting in fantasy, but awkward and a bit painful in reality. That's all I had to say about it. I had bigger fires to fight.

Over the course of one session, I conscientiously confessed to all my sexual fantasies and activities from the age of eleven up to medical school, then stammered, "When Judy was out of town—" I looked down at the carpet. "I can't do this."

"Why is it so difficult?"

"You should know why."

"Tell me."

"You're gonna think I'm a pathetic laughingstock of a man."

"I'm not here to judge you."

"Okay, when Judy was out of town . . . I couldn't resist trying on her clothes: bras, panties, pantyhose, skirts, everything. I even masturbated in her bathing suit." I looked for Dr. Posner to say something. He was alert but still as a stone. "Well, that's basically it." Still, no response from him. "So what do you think of me?"

"What does it matter what *I* think of you?"

I looked at him with my mouth agape. I had made a courageous confession. I was looking for help, and he offered me a Zen riddle.

"What matters is how *you* feel about you."

Although over the years I would come to understand and appreciate Posner's riddle, at the time though, the only thing I could pick up on was that he was as repulsed by me as I was. And his silence seemed to indicate that my penance and rehabilitation were my own to figure out.

So, the very next session I tried to cut to the heart of the matter. I pulled a Victoria's Secret catalog out of my briefcase and pointed to a picture. "For crying out loud, when I see a woman like this and face whatever comes to mind, I don't just want to have sex with her; I want to be her. It's like *Fuck her. Be her. Fuck her. Be her.* It's maddening." Posner rubbed his beard. "At the very least, I want to feel like her. I want to be admired, desired, *required.*"

Not only was it difficult to voice these thoughts, but I had no words to describe them. I had never thought of myself as a transvestite and had never heard the word crossdresser. Of course, the Master of Silence didn't help much here either. So I ended up referring to all this stuff as the Beautiful Woman Fantasy or sometimes, grimly, just the Fantasy, much as if I were saying the Curse. Rarely could I bring myself to say *my* Beautiful Woman Fantasy.

Why was *beautiful* part of it? Why not simply the Woman Fantasy? That's because I didn't fantasize about being any old woman; I fantasized about being a *beautiful* one. I tuned into an envy of women that followed the same lines. I didn't seem to covet anything more than the mere fact that they got to be sex objects—you know, drop-what-you're-doing, stop-and-stare, dying-to-touch sex objects. Because my imagination was so focused on having the sex appeal of a woman, I thought I was dealing with a very specific fantasy rather than a more general gender issue. I didn't realize that nearly all crossdressers and transsexuals long to be beautiful women; so do nearly all natural-born women, for that matter.

I began to see how my curiosity blended into my fantasies and feelings of envy. Though I hated to admit it, I finally started to own long-repressed feelings like wishing I could go prettily about my day in a skirt. These feelings clashed completely with my image as a rough-and-ready, no-nonsense kind of guy. Something had to give. What gave was my lifelong sense of who I was. My sense of self, as familiar as my face in the mirror, shattered. Who was I? How was I going to live?

Because Dr. Posner seemed convinced that I would need a lot of treatment, I asked him some basic medical questions. "What's your diagnosis?" He wouldn't give me a straight answer. "Is there cause?" He declined to answer. "Is there a cure?" Again, no answer.

I discussed my frustrations over the phone with Demetra, who replied, "He's not supposed to provide answers. He's supposed to spur you on to find your own."

"Well, whatever he's doing. It's not getting rid of my problem—just making me more aware of it."

"Often things have to get worse before they get better," she explained with such benevolence that I surrendered my skepticism in favor of my need to believe. In retrospect, I should have fired Posner and found a therapist who was warmer, more practical, and better informed on transgender issues. At the time, though, I was a medical intern with barely enough time to eat and sleep, let alone the energy it would take to find another shrink, figure out a way to get to his or her office without a car, tell my excruciating story all over again, and maybe get the same response.

Unwittingly, I had wandered into the misty borderlands of mental health and was facing questions that therapists themselves often don't face with sufficient humility. First, where is the line between diversity and disease? Were my transgender feelings part of a disease, like obsessive-compulsive disorder, or were they part of a difference, like being shy? Second, can people change? If I tried really hard, could I rid myself of the Beautiful Woman Fantasy? And third, can you help someone else change? Could Posner realistically help me achieve this goal?

Earlier that year, when Sandra had been concerned I was making myself miserable over the chance I might be HIV positive, she had comforted me with the Serenity Prayer.

> *God grant me,*
> *The serenity to accept the things I cannot change,*
> *The courage to change the things I can,*

And the wisdom to know the difference.[11]

-Reinhold Niebuhr

The Serenity Prayer had been helpful back then, but it took on new relevance now, as I wrestled with my Beautiful Woman Fantasy and troubled marriage. With all my heart, I hoped to change my desire to crossdress rather than lose Betsy and perhaps my chance of a normal life with any woman ever.

As a traditional analyst, Dr. Posner made assumptions that seemed reasonable at the time. For him, my transgenderism represented disease rather than diversity, and it was caused by problems in my childhood. Additionally, if he could help me process the feelings that had led to it, then I could recover from it, i.e., change.

Although I had always felt grateful toward my parents, I didn't just ooze with affection for them. So I couldn't brush off any notion of their culpability with a simple "What do you mean? They might not have been perfect, but they were great. I *love* those guys." One session, at Posner's urging, I followed my free associations back into my childhood in search of a cause for the Beautiful Woman Fantasy.

The first thing I fixed on was the time when I was seven and my parents had been so distracted with the rest of the family that they accidentally drove off and left me stranded at the downtown Holiday Inn. And dreadful though that was, perhaps it was only part of a painful larger trend. My father had spent nearly all his time at the office or hospital, and my mother had treated my three sisters and me as a batch. Being the only boy at home, I had often felt very left out.

Posner suggested that, by imagining I was a beautiful woman, I was trying to wash away the anguish of my childhood. "Yes," I thought aloud, "if I was a woman I'd be a real member of the batch, a first class citizen. If I was a *beautiful* woman, I'd be unforgettable, not ditched in favor of work, not left behind in downtown Buffalo." Suddenly it all seemed to make sense and—god damn it—I was furious with my parents for raising me in a way that could lead to such a crippling fantasy.

The next time I saw them, I took them to task on their failings. Ironically, it was when Betsy and I came home for Thanksgiving weekend. I cornered my mother alone in the kitchen and let her know I had been damaged because she had been too scattered to treat us as individuals. She denied it and started talking about other parents who "truly didn't pay attention to their kids." She also kept changing the subject until I finally gave up on getting the apology I had hoped for or even the admission I'd have settled for.

By the next day, when I approached my father alone at his desk in the den, he had been forewarned. "Did you ever think you might have spent too much time on work and not enough on your family?" I asked.

"Well, it's what I needed to do to support and educate all you kids," he replied. "Besides, we always had dinner together as a family. And your mother and I never took separate vacations like lots of the couples we knew."

"But what about when I used to approach you to play chess or toss a football? It didn't take me long to learn that your answer would always be no."

"Why do you dwell so much on these things from the past?" he said with upturned palms. "You have a pretty good life. Why can't you get on with it? What are you learning in that therapy?"

"I've discovered that you and Mom were negligent in the past and that that has caused me serious problems in the present."

"Of what kind?" he asked with knitted brow.

"Sexual baggage," I replied looking away, "that's too horrible to mention."

"What kind of baggage?"

"All I can say," I grimaced, "is that, being a decent person, I'm disgusted with myself and what I have to deal with."

"Well," he frowned. "I don't know what that therapist is telling you. But your mother and I are very hurt by these allegations. I don't know if we'd ever disown one of our children, but this business has to stop."

Already uncomfortable with the conversation, I backed down but continued to hold a grudge. If only I could have seen my Beautiful Woman Fantasy in a more positive light, then I might have let my parents off the hook.

Hoping to use it in the service of my sex life, one night back in Boston, I asked Betsy, "Do you mind if I pull your panties onto one of my ankles, while we make love?"

"You want to *what*." She made me repeat myself.

"Can I pull your underwear around my ankle?" I mumbled fearfully.

"No, you may not put on my panties!" she boomed loud enough for the neighbors to hear, seeming to draw strength from the fact that surely they would side with her.

I understood her feelings all too well at the time and still do. However, looking back, I also realize that she served as an emotionally armed and dangerous soldier guarding the frontier of Judeo-Christian culture, taste, and prejudice with regard to what was desirable or disgusting in a man. Unless her attitude changed, there would be a serious limit to how okay I could get with what I fantasized about and who I was. But perhaps I was just as much to blame, because she was a soldier of my choosing. Maybe I had gravitated toward such a conformist as Betsy—rather than a temptress like Deborah Collins—because I knew on some level she'd help keep me in line.

I couldn't blame my wife for being so disappointed in me. I was turning out to be frightfully more complicated than the simple outdoor-loving young doctor I thought I was. I understood how I had shattered the trust between us and, in my own fumbling way, strove to be as forthcoming as possible.

"I love you," she offered, one night as we were walking arm-in-arm back from a movie.

Although I wanted to, I couldn't say it back to her just then, because a scene from the film had reminded me of the time when I was panic-stricken and she had hidden my Xanax. Instead, I held her close and replied with as much warmth as I could muster, "We had a really great day together, didn't we?"

Crestfallen, she backed away and protested, "Why can't you say you love me?'

"I want to save it for when I feel it," I explained, trying to be as open and honest as possible.

"I can't believe this!" she cried. "And why don't you feel it?"

"I can't forget some of the nastier things you did last spring to lash back at me. Maybe if you could apologize for some of that, it would help me feel more loving again."

Although it was around ten at night, she stormed off in a huff, determined to find her own way home. Back at the apartment, I eventually soothed her, while she reluctantly admitted, "Yes, I lost control of my anger at times. I'm sorry."

"I want you to know you're in no way responsible for my problem," I assured her, "and I'm sorry you were hurt by it. It's a strange envy of women that began in my childhood." With that, we wrapped our bodies around each other and drifted off to sleep exhausted.

"A strange envy of women," that's how I referred to my gender *mishugas* with Betsy, although to me it was still the Beautiful Woman Fantasy. I realized that acting it out with lingerie made me a transvestic fetishist, but I didn't know whether that made me a crossdresser. By now I'd at least heard the word though I don't know where, and it would still be months before I decided I was one.

Could I have become a crossdresser because of being raised in a batch of girls? It sounds possible. A pure scientific answer would involve running my life over again from the beginning, except this time with my father around. Obviously it's impossible to do such an experiment. A statistical scientific approach would involve finding a hundred or so young boys and splitting them into two groups. One group would grow up surrounded by women, and the other would grow up in more balanced families. Twenty years later, we could evaluate the boys and see what percentage from each group grew up to be crossdressers. I can't see too many parents volunteering their sons for that kind of experiment, so that option is out as well.

With more rigorous scientific data lacking, I can at least draw on the case series of men I've known professionally and personally who grew up surrounded by women. The overwhelming majority of these men *did* not become crossdressers. And only a small minority of crossdressers actually grew up surrounded by women. So was I justified in blaming my parents? Absolutely not, but only later would I see that I had been wrong. Was I justified in my frustration over being batch-processed as a kid? Yes, but that's a different matter. Nonetheless, there I was, blaming my parents for my crossdressing, while barely knowing anything about it.

It seemed to be something men did guiltily in private for a cheap thrill or wretchedly in public for god-knows-what reason. Though I wanted to learn more, my rather expensive psychoanalyst wasn't able or willing to recommend any books or organizations. So one bleary-eyed morning after a night on call, I decided to do my own research. Unfortunately it wasn't going to be as easy as doing an Internet search from the privacy of my own apartment. Back in 1990, the Internet was not in widespread use, or at least not wide enough to reach me. I was an overworked, underpaid physician-in-the-making with no money to buy a home computer and no time to learn how to use one. So my search couldn't be done quickly or privately. I'd have to rely on daring and dumb luck.

Discreetly, I slipped into one of Harvard's lesser-used libraries and found a computer terminal that could do a subject search on all the books present in the university's libraries. I searched under *transvestism*. What I found was *Boys Will Be Girls: The Hidden World of the Heterosexual Male Transvestite* by John T. Talamini.[12] Wow, direct hit. It sounded intriguing and perhaps even hopeful. But I would have to fill out a request form and later pick the book up at Widener Library, smack in the middle of campus.

Meanwhile, I stewed and prepared. Thank god, I could sign it out as R. J. Novic, M.D. Even though I was strictly a *medical* doctor, the librarian might assume I was a psychiatrist studying up on my nutty patients. But maybe he'd be smarter than that. Maybe he'd start asking questions. Surely, I'd break down under the slightest scrutiny. I'd start to sweat, shake, and give myself away. If need be, I could drop the book and run. But no, I needed that accursed book. I would insist I was a shrink, whether he believed me or not.

I arrived at Widener, with my hands trembling and heart palpitating. Climbing the monolithic front steps, I felt like I was approaching a drug deal.

The hushed dignity inside only made me feel even more out of place. Greatly relieved to see no familiar faces, I stepped up to the front desk. "Dr. Novic here to pick up a book I've requested," I murmured, trying to suppress the quiver in my voice.

"What's the title?" the librarian replied.

I broke out into sweat. There was no way I was going to say *Boys Will Be Girls: The Hidden World of the Heterosexual Male Transvestite* or any part of it.

So I placed my copy of the request form down on the desk and pointed. "This one."

The librarian found it, smiled, and explained, "You'll have to have it back in two weeks."

Boys Will Be Girls turned out to be an immensely interesting book and the first of many I would read about crossdressers and others in the transgender community. First and foremost, it let me know that there was an underground of crossdressing men. And fortunately Talamini was a sociologist content to report on these secretive people without making them out to be ill. He simply described how they existed in most major cities, dressed up at each other's homes, and even had some sort of national organization.

Secondly I learned that many of them were heterosexual, as opposed to homosexual as I might've imagined. Because I suspected I'd want to wear more than just lingerie, I feared I too was a transvestite but was relieved to think I could at least be a straight one, like the men in this book, because I was in no way willing to give up my love for women and hope for children. In fact, studies show that 72-97% of transvestites identify as straight.[13]

Boys Will Be Girls filled my mind with a sense of mystery as I rushed around the hospital, a busy intern in the winter of '91. What was going on behind the picket fences of suburbia? What was going on downtown where the gay people go? What was going on—or not—in the bedrooms of the people I worked with?

At about that time, a rough-and-tumble man came to the hospital with a strange spinal infection that turned out to be advanced AIDS. Though he denied being gay, he worked as a bouncer at a bar and was very vague and touchy about the details. Late one night, an odd teenager came to the emergency room with severe diarrhea. He took his shirt off to be examined, and there was a ring hanging from his right nipple. The little hoop passed right through a hole that had been pierced into him. *Freaky,* I thought, as I inquired about the strange device.

"It's a tribal thing," the youngster replied with a shrug.

All of the sudden, Boston was no longer familiar, American, and boring. Danger and drama, novelty and wonder lurked behind every door. I even looked at the offering of books at our local Barnes & Noble with new eyes. I picked up a copy of *The Kinsey Institute New Report On Sex*. I was surprised that Betsy let me get away with it, but I suppose the book looked sufficiently sober. I wanted to learn more about all aspects of sex, but especially about men who found pleasure in women's clothing.

Slowly my thinking started to shift. I still thought of putting on panties as an illegitimate sexual turn-on, but I also realized that it was something I enjoyed. *God damn it*, I thought, *Why does it have to be this? I never would have chosen to want this. Why can't I just love weekends of golf or blowjobs from my wife or something else wholesome like that?*

I had hoped that if I found a reason why I had such an unsavory interest in women's wear, then maybe it might dissolve and be replaced by more savory pursuits. But even when I found a reason—like being raised in a batch of girls—nothing changed. In fact, the more I learned, the more my appetite grew, and the more problematic my pursuit of happiness became.

Meanwhile, there were some noteworthy developments in my love life. Once, when Betsy and I were having sex in the missionary position, she reached down and squeezed my balls hard just as I was reaching orgasm. Timing it as she did, I didn't feel any pain, just a mind-blowing intensity. I wasn't sure why she did it, but it really worked for me and her too. We called it the Oochy Trick, and I began to request it more and more.

Slowly she became more tolerant, and occasionally she *would* allow me to take her panties off and pull them up onto one of my legs. Then with an extra head of steam, I would push her onto her back and ravish her to her heart's content. As we lay together in the afterglow of such passion one night, I felt open and relaxed. "You know, I'm learning all kinds of interesting things about myself in therapy," I confided.

"Yeah," she said uneasily.

"I guess that, growing up, I felt left out and developed this perverse envy of my sisters."

"I'm sorry," she said while stiffening and pulling away a little.

Trying to keep things from getting too somber, I explained, "It doesn't have to be such a big deal. I was talking to Demetra the other day about football." Betsy winced, while I went on, "And she said she would love to be Jerry Rice for a day so she could know how it feels to catch a touchdown pass. I told her I'd like to be Cindy Crawford."

"Um hmm," my wife replied in a schoolmarm-ish tone I had heard before. "It's just what they call a little gender dysphoria," I said, trying to intellectualize it.

"Um hmm."

Not exactly the response I was looking for, but it felt good to express myself. Remaining hopeful I explained, "You know, I never really found men attractive. I only experimented because I wanted to know how it feels to be a woman."

"God, how can you say this?" she burst out, looking like I'd mentioned the noose in the house of the hung. "You're really fucked up. I can't hear any more of this." She pushed me away and began to cry.

"Honey," I said, reaching out to comfort her, trying to keep a handle on the situation.

"Get away from me!"

I slept a few fitful hours on the couch, then awoke to her stroking my arm. Tears streamed down her precious face, as she choked on her words. She didn't know what to say, so I held her and said, "Listen, I'm working hard on this stuff with Dr. Posner. We don't have to talk about it anymore," and in so doing aborted my attempt to let her know I might be a crossdresser.

Meanwhile, I didn't have to worry too much about my appetite for the more feminine things in life, because I wasn't free to pursue anything. I was either working long days at the hospital or spending my few spare hours at home with my wife. I didn't have to worry too much—*except* for those weekends when she went out of town on business or to see family. Then, once again, after three years, I found myself alone in an apartment full of temptations. Everything was available to me: lingerie, pantyhose, dresses, lipstick, even eyelash curlers. It was all so intriguing. There was no way I could risk going to a local store and buying these things myself. I couldn't even order them from a catalog. Betsy would be suspicious of any unexplained packages arriving for me. Like a live-in cop, she kept me from any questionable uses of my time (or money). But while she was off duty, her own pretty things beckoned.

Still, I didn't want to be the kind of man who snuck into his wife's panty drawer. So I developed—what turned out to be—one last strategy: Starve It of Resources. I would allow myself very little time or money in the pursuit of crossdressing or anything connected with it. Typically I'd make plans to get out of the apartment whenever my love left town. But often my friends weren't available, because they were also interns who spent most of their time off with their families or just plain sleeping.

One particular Saturday arrived with no Betsy and no plans. Although exhausted from a night on call, I was anxious to look things up in my *Kinsey Report*—without having to face her scrutiny. The section on transvestism was fascinating and listed two national support organizations. By a stroke of incredibly good luck, I noticed that one of them, the Tiffany Club, was based just outside Boston. My heart raced as I called the number listed. A kindly older man with a put-on female voice answered. *She* (remember anyone presenting as a woman gets referred to as a woman) let me know they were having a meeting that night and encouraged me to drive out for it. "Will I be able to wear a dress?" I asked.

"Yes, but you'll have to bring your own."

"Wow! Will I be able to try on makeup?"

"I think I could let you use some of mine."

"Will you show me how?"

"I suppose. You're an eager one, aren't you?"

"I guess so," I replied, feeling a bit embarrassed.

I took care of a few errands, then got ready for a nap. But first, I laid out what I'd be wearing later on: Betsy's black bra, matching panties, and stretchy gray T-shirt dress. *How could this be real?* I was so overcome with anticipation that—fatigued as I was—I couldn't get to sleep without taking a Xanax. When I awoke, I put my wife's lacy underthings on and felt my head spin, as I pulled a shirt and pants on over them.

The notion of driving off to meet a group of transvestites felt about as bizarre as blasting off to visit a neighboring star system. Forcing myself to concentrate, I prepared a cover story for Betsy, or anyone else for that matter who might call the next day and ask how I spent my Saturday night. As I made my way out of town on the old interstate, the bitter cold January air felt bracing, as it whistled by my open window. I felt alive and free and bound for adventure.

My instructions were to rendezvous with a club officer in the parking lot next to an old library in a little colonial town outside Boston. I drove into the dark, empty lot and placed a call from the payphone there as directed. In ten minutes time, another car arrived and pulled up alongside me. It was a real live transvestite, perhaps the kindly older one I'd spoken to on the phone. She rolled her window down and said, "Rick?"

"Yes."

"Hi, I'm Laura. Come on in," she said, motioning me toward her passenger seat. The plan was for us to talk for a while in her car before she would take me to the clubhouse. "How long have you been interested in women's clothes?" she inquired.

"Since I was eleven," I replied in earnest.

"Why do you want to meet other crossdressers?"

"To meet people I might have a lot in common with."

After a couple more questions like that, Laura decided I was for real and told me to get back in my car and follow her to the club. As we entered a modest old home at the end of a wooded cul-de-sac, she explained that others would be arriving soon. I could put my dress on in the basement. Then she would come down to do my makeup. She even had a pair of ladies' shoes that might fit me.

I couldn't believe what was about to happen. I was going to be a girl for the first time! I threw Betsy's dress on and couldn't wait to get started. I didn't want any other guests to arrive and distract my hostess from making me up and answering my questions about cosmetics and about a *million* other things. Once we finished my face, I walked over to the full-length mirror, as the doorbell rang and she scurried up the stairs to answer it. I looked at myself in a dress and high heels and was surprised by what came to mind. I imagined I was laying down the law to my three sisters: *It's my turn. After twenty-seven god-damn years, it's my turn!*

I looked ridiculous with hairy legs and no wig. But back then, I assumed I would look like a freak. I was just thrilled for the opportunity to wear a dress and makeup and hang out. By the time I got upstairs, there were five or six people milling about the living room. Laura was fixing a glass of water for another friendly transvestite in the adjoining kitchen. As soon as I entered the room, she asked, "What's your name?"

I couldn't believe she had already forgotten, and I didn't want to broadcast it all over this place, so I murmured, "Uh, Rick."

"That simply won't do," she insisted. "You don't look like any Rick I know, all dolled up like that. You need a *woman's* name. Don't you have one?"

"No, there's never been a reason for me to have one."

"Well then, you'll have to choose one."

"Uh, well I feel like I've arrived in Wonderland, so I guess that makes me Alice?"

"Then *Alice*, it is," she pronounced playfully.

The whole idea of it felt right to me, and I've been Alice ever since. Nowadays, a budding crossdresser, like I was, will typically first meet others and choose a female screen name over the Internet. Many will even try out one or two before settling on another.

Thank goodness, everyone was amiable at the Tiffany Club, because I was super-nervous and had no idea what to expect. Soon all eight of us settled into the sofa and chairs in the living room. We were a tremendous variety of people: old and young, lovely and scary. We took turns introducing ourselves and sharing a bit about our lives. Each of the "girls" referred to herself as either a crossdresser or a transsexual and many talked about being straight or bi. Some were incredibly candid and interesting. Some seemed pretty messed up. Some were uptight and unwilling to say much—like me.

Afterward, we hobnobbed informally. People talked about going to stores and restaurants and bars. It all seemed so daring. Soon three of the younger, prettier girls dashed off to a nightclub downtown—the name sounded like

Jocks. One of the older ladies told me that the Tiffany Club was involved with a national transvestite magazine named *Tapestry.* I was impressed by how professional and intelligent the older gals were, but when they started to sit around the kitchen and talk state politics, I got bored.

So I took off my makeup and put my pants back on. I thanked Laura and the two other crossdressers she was chatting with. Although they might have expected a hug, I gave them each a farewell handshake. One of them had seemed flirty with me earlier on, and she tickled my palm with her middle finger as we shook hands—I wasn't sure *what* that meant. The other said, "You're so lucky to be coming out at the age of twenty-seven."

Who said I'm coming out? I thought, at the same time not knowing exactly what *coming out* meant in this context. But I was itching to go, so I bit my tongue. My hostess then walked me to the door and welcomed me back whenever I could make it.

Although I could not have been more warmly welcomed, I was nonetheless relieved to be out of the club and on my way home. For some reason, I didn't fully relate to the people I had met. I didn't think I belonged among them. I felt like Phil Donahue, just an inquisitive guy who had done a talk show with these zany, but nice, people from a strange secret society. Just like I did after experimenting with Mike, I told myself, *I've faced one of the things I feared I'd like the most. And it wasn't all that great.*

Again I was trying to rush to a conclusion, but back in therapy, Dr. Posner didn't buy it for a minute. "I'd encourage you to process the experience," he cautioned, "rather than simply renouncing it."

"I can't deny I'm turned on by women's clothes, but that doesn't mean I'm a transvestite," I said, clinging to my confusion rather than facing the shame of who I was. "A transvestite is someone who likes dressing up from head to toe. Maybe I am? Maybe I'm not? But I've only tried it once."

Nowadays, I define transvestite, or crossdresser, more broadly. If you're turned on by the idea of wearing women's clothes, then face it, honey, you're one of us. You're a crossdresser. If you just fantasize about it or if you like to masturbate in your wife's lingerie, then you're a private crossdresser, but a CD nonetheless. If you like dressing up and going out, then you're a public crossdresser. Most public crossdressers start out as private crossdressers and through experiences like mine at the Tiffany Club discover there's more fun to it than the simple orgasm it can bring.

From the folks at Tiffany and the pages of *Tapestry*, I learned the traditional wisdom about crossdressers, transsexuals, and drag queens and how we all made up the *transgender community*—even if we didn't always get along. Although people outside the community may have used the word transvestite to refer to all of us, people inside liked to be more specific.

A *crossdresser* was typically a married man who was turned on by women's clothes but didn't dare to fully dress up until later in life, like when his kids left home. Whenever the term *transvestite* was used, it seemed to refer specifically to crossdressers. A *transsexual* was someone who felt like a woman trapped in the body of a man. She dressed up to express her inner identity and was eager to go on hormones, get her beard removed, live full time as a woman, and go for sex-change surgery. A *drag queen* was typically a gay man who dressed flamboyantly as a woman for the sheer spectacle of it. Although I had met crossdressers and transsexuals at Tiffany, there'd been no drag queens, and no one had said very much about them.

Not only were there many types of transgendered people, there were even more abbreviations to refer to them (for future reference listed in a glossary at the end of this book). Crossdressers were CDs or occasionally TVs. (Maybe soon we'll be DVDs?) Transsexuals were TSs and drag queens, DQs. TG, or tranny, could refer to anyone in the transgender community, whether CD, TS, or DQ. That made me a TG, or t-girl, or transgendered girl, as opposed to a real girl, or genetic girl, who would be a GG. Often we crossdressers referred to GGs as real girls but needed to be careful around transsexuals, who might resent the implication that they somehow were *not* real girls.

Without a wig at Tiffany, I had felt like Rick with makeup on. Everyone had told me how a head of hair could be almost magical in its ability to change you from man to woman. So I was now incredibly curious to see what it could do for me. I bought a cheap wig from a costume shop by the hospital, hid it away, and anxiously awaited my next opportunity.

With Betsy again out of town, I put on her foofiest, poofiest Christian Lacroix dress, though I could hardly zip it, and tried to cover my hairy legs with pantyhose I'd purchased for the occasion. I did the best I could with her makeup and lipstick, threw my wig on, stepped in front of a tripod-mounted camera, and snapped. I was dying to see how I looked. But where on earth could I get my film developed? What would the person printing the pictures think when he saw this macho guy sneaking around in his wife's little tutu? Although I didn't reveal my private parts, would my pictures be seen as pornographic and against the law? Maybe they'd be handed back to me with a menacing sticker and a stern warning from a smirking store manager.

Nonetheless, I *had* to see them, so I went to a pharmacy in another neighborhood and submitted my film under a false name. A few days later, I could barely wait for work to end so that I could rush over to pick up my pictures. The drugstore clerk then handed me my envelope, as if it was . . . just another envelope of pictures. Phew. I raced down an alley to look at them. There I was, as a woman, and I looked . . . hideous. I was a woman with a beard and mustache. Despite a fresh shave, I still had a five o'clock shadow that showed through my wife's makeup like it wasn't even there. Would I always look like a freak?

The next time she was out of town, a group of us dashing young doctors planned to go to a Red Sox game and I was tempted to *underdress* for the occasion. I had learned that some crossdressers routinely wore women's underwear under their male clothes, like I had done on my way out to the Tiffany Club. It was called underdressing, and the idea seemed sexy to me. Although it sounds like a weird, kinky thing to do, I'm sure a lot of women could relate if they really thought about it. In fact, *Chic Simple Women's Wardrobe* begins its chapter on lingerie with—of all things—the thrill of knowing that, under your jeans and comfy sweater, you have on the kind of satin and frills usually reserved for antique dolls or harlots.[14]

I put a white bra and panties on under my shirt and jeans and Gore-Tex jacket and drove off to the ballpark. Although it was quite a thrill, I kept worrying that my bra would somehow show through my clothes. Finally, I couldn't take it anymore and made a beeline for a bathroom stall to take the accursed undergarment off before meeting my friends. Which turned out to be a very good thing, because the first thing my best intern-buddy did was to give me a hearty handshake and a slap on the back. Whoa, how's that for narrowly avoiding disaster? His hand would have landed right on my bra strap. Still rattled, I watched the baseball game in panties, but I couldn't get comfortable or stop worrying about being discovered.

Following up on a lead from the Tiffany Club, a few weeks later, I visited Vernon's Specialties, a clothing shop specifically for crossdressers. I went there to take advantage of an amazing opportunity. In the privacy of the store basement, they offered Complete Transformation. All you had to do was bring your own razor. Vernon would dress you up, make you up, lend you a wig if need be, and take snapshots.

The experience was spine tingling and fun. God, it felt great to wear a red polka-dot dress. And I was only too eager to buy the black brassiere and panties the convivial shopkeeper picked out for me. My girl pictures turned out better than the ones I had taken on my own, but even Vernon couldn't make my beard go away. Sure, I'd made progress—from freakish to silly looking. Nonetheless, I loved seeing myself as a woman and treasured the pictures for years. I still have one of them around today.

Flouncing around the tranny shop was so exciting that I threw caution to the wind and freely played with fire. I bought myself a black negligee, stockings, and a vibrator. Why not if it would make me happy? I was so curious that I quivered with anticipation on the drive home. Once behind closed doors, I gave in to my desires, never mind what they said about me, never mind I might only yearn for more. My heart rose in my throat as I slipped into the silky negligee. I couldn't believe how filmy and slippery it felt, as it fell to my thighs. I wrestled with a garter belt and stockings for the very first time, then stared with apprehension at the electric phallus buzzing in front of me. And moments later, I was hating how much I loved it.

I was doing things no self-respecting man should ever think of and turned to Dr. Posner for help making sense of it all. "Because all of your acting out occurred with Betsy out of town," he surmised, "I think it has to do with missing her. And because your trip to the Tiffany Club occurred while I was on vacation, you may also be missing me."

"I don't think so," I replied rather directly. "My adventures took place with her out of town, because that's the only time they could take place. Besides, I know what missing feels like. I've been missing Demetra all year long. I don't have those feelings for Betsy or you—not that I don't appreciate your services."

Later on, I would see how Posner's comments had come more from his psychoanalytic training than any special knowledge of what was going on inside me. For the time being, though, I gave him the benefit of the doubt and assumed he was right on some deeper level I couldn't yet comprehend. As we continued working together, he offered more such explanations of my behavior. Eventually I confronted him, "You seem to have developed an understanding of why I've grown up to be a crossdresser. Do you mind sharing?"

"Why is it so important to you?"

Frustrated, I fired back, "Because I've poured my heart out to you for a year. This isn't some sort of game. I'm a real person, with a real problem, and I think I deserve an answer."

"Okay," he conceded. "I think your Beautiful Woman Fantasy is connected with missing your father and growing up with no real male influence."

"Then what's to be done about it?"

"I think it's a serious problem that requires something more intense than weekly therapy. What you really need is psychoanalysis."

"Full-blown psychoanalysis?" I exclaimed in disbelief, my hands gripping the sides of my chair, while Posner nodded. "You mean *daily* therapy on the couch for *years?*"

"Well, at least four times a week."

I gulped. Could I be that messed up? Composing myself I replied, "Well, that's just not possible, at least not while I'm still an intern."

Meanwhile, my covert operations continued. Following up on another lead from Tiffany, I discovered that "Jocks" was really Jacque's, a gay club in Bay Village. And I drove down to see the drag show there.

Once through the door, I suddenly felt nervous I might run into someone from the hospital. I'd have to explain what I was doing out on my own in a gay bar but figured I could say, "My wife's out of town, and I'm bored. So I'm here to check out the show."

I ended up sitting at a table with a couple of preppy-looking men in polo shirts. One seemed in his late twenties like me, and the other appeared in his early thirties. Friendly, they introduced themselves as Greg and Joe and broke the ice with a little banter, before Greg asked, "Are you here by yourself?"

"Yes," I replied.

"I'd think a guy like you would have a boyfriend."

"Well, actually I'm straight, or at least I think so." Just like with Dr. Calabrese, I found myself surprisingly at ease with these men, especially in *this* environment.

Just then, Joe, the older of the two, leaned in and began to take a keen interest in the conversation. "Really?" he remarked.

"Well, I've only ever liked women, but I have these troubling fantasies about wanting to dress up like a woman and do all the things a woman does."

"Wow!"

"I even experimented with a man once, but I didn't like it very much. Does that all make me gay?"

"I don't think so," he said, "Being gay is about being a man who's attracted to other men."

"Then what about this perverse fantasy and this fetish for women's clothes?"

"In our community, we call these things gifts."

I stared back blankly. "What are you talking about?"

"People in the gay community look favorably on anything that helps a guy get more fired up about his sex life—whether it's leather or lace, handcuffs or comic books."

Now it was my turn to marvel. "Really?"

He gestured at his boyfriend. "If Greg here wanted to dress up as Scarlett O'Hara and meet me at the bottom of the staircase," Greg let his jaw drop, pretending to be shocked, "then I might have a lot of fun playing the part of Rhett Butler." He looked me straight in the eyes. "So, you see, it's a gift."

"I only wish my wife would see it that way," I said as lightheartedly as I could, while Joe flashed a wry smile, as if to say, *Hey, what can you do?*

Soon the drag show was underway. It was the first one I had ever seen. It was mysterious and exhilarating, and I found two of the performers especially enticing. I totally bought the notion they were women—and rather sexy ones at that. After the show, my freethinking friends wished me well, while I stayed on to flirt with my two favorites. A-man-duh readily brushed me off, but Sharon Cher-alike thought I was "utterly scrumptious" and welcomed me to join the girls and their gang at an after-hours bar in the Combat Zone.

It was a lively scene in a scary part of town, and the night didn't end until Sharon and I were making out in the front seat of her car. Before she could do anything about it, I snuck a quick grope up her skirt. Oh, my god, she really was a man. It only made we want her more, but ultimately neither of us had the nerve to get any wilder, because she had a boyfriend and I, of course, had Betsy.

Though troubled to know that I had again been unfaithful, I focused on the more immediate matter raised by my mischief with Ms. Cher-alike: What did I really want sexually? Clearly I was attracted to anyone who could look like a pretty woman. And the idea of a drag queen like Sharon bringing me to her bedroom and suddenly turning the tables on me was the most erotic thing I could imagine. Maybe I wanted to be a man outside the bedroom, but a woman inside? Maybe I had always secretly felt that way?

So far, I had conducted all my adventures in complete isolation. All the while, I'd longed for someone with whom I could share the wonder and sift through the confusion. I longed for Demetra, but still busy with her own internship, she only rarely had time for me. I cherished those occasions, and her listening and understanding remained invaluable to me.

"I'll never forget all that you've done for me," I told her over coffee, when I realized I might not get to see her again before I left Boston. "If there's anything I can do for you, anytime, whether that's in three years or thirty, please let me know."

"I'm just happy I was able to be there for you when you needed me the most," she replied, in a manner both gracious and knowing.

I wondered what it would be like to be married to someone like her and found the notion powerfully appealing. The intensity of my feelings for her restored my confidence in my masculine, woman-loving side at a time when my feminine side was emerging and rocking my most basic assumptions. When all my defenses failed to hold back the fire of my transgender desires, at least my longing for Demetra declared itself to be an equally potent force. The way I felt just talking with her was like no other intimacy I had ever known.

Yet, she was drifting out of my life. I *had* to find someone like her. Just then, I saw *The Last of the Mohicans,* and a scene from it shook me to the core. Under dire circumstances, the hero has to part ways with the woman he loves. He urges her to stay alive, no matter what happens. He will find her, no matter what it takes or how long.

I would look hard to find Demetra in Betsy and do my best to nurture those qualities. Betsy lacked Demetra's sophistication, but she was six years younger. Maybe it would come with age? With each challenge we faced, I hoped for her anger to abate and her character to shine through.

5

Three-Ring Circus

As I completed my internship in June 1991, Betsy and I packed up our belongings and moved to Chicago, where I began training in radiology. We had chosen the Windy City because it combined first-class teaching hospitals with proximity to her family, just over the border in Wisconsin. And following up on one of her father's leads, she found an in-house advertising position at a large corporation headquartered in the Loop.

Unfortunately, I soon found radiology far less satisfying than my internship experiences in internal medicine and emergency medicine. I had hoped it would combine science and patient care. I began to suspect, though, that for me it was neither. As a radiologist, I felt trapped in a barren middle ground between the physicians (whom people came to see with whatever ailed them) and the physicists (who developed the tools to diagnose those ailments).

That was all I needed, ambivalence in another major area of my life. What the hell was wrong with me? Would I ever be satisfied with anything? I was already uncertain whether I wanted a life with Betsy and how I should handle my Beautiful Woman Fantasy. Now I was facing a veritable three-ring circus of professional, marital, and personal problems. Over the next three years, I would spend hours pondering my predicament as I jogged along the lakeshore through the extremes of Midwestern weather, before returning home among the concrete canyons.

In life as in running, I preserved my peace of mind by pacing myself. I stayed focused on my gender issues and marriage. Any career changes could wait. In the meantime, I'd give radiology a good long look before making a final decision. Besides, I appreciated its lighter workload and wasn't sure what specialty or career I would want to switch into.

Knowing I needed more help, I called up a psychoanalyst Demetra knew and through him found Dr. Joshua Adler. He was a slightly built man of about forty who always wore a jacket and tie and had a neat head of dark, curly hair dusted with a little gray. He worked out of an airy office in an old skyscraper and insisted I call him Joshua. Like Dr. Posner, he wouldn't allow me to shrug off my uncertainties about my wife and about myself. As he learned more about me, he suggested, "You'd be better off thinking of your Beautiful Woman Fantasy as your Beautiful Woman Side."

"It feels like you're expanding the size of my problem," I replied, somewhat alarmed.

"No, just encouraging you to honor and own an important part of who you are." Because I had begun to like Joshua and trust his judgment, I followed his suggestion.

Unfortunately though, like Dr. Posner, he had an insidious tendency to steer my therapy toward a search for the childhood origins of my gender issues. He and I, however, came up with a theory based more on my mother being scattered and absent than on my father being workaholic and absent. The idea was that, if I couldn't have my mother's attention, then I could at least be my own version of her. The idea felt plausible for a while—although I now wonder what I would've come up with if I had played the blame game a third time.

I knew women were said to have penis envy and wondered whether I was dealing with the flip side of it? What exactly was penis envy anyway? From Demetra, I learned that it was a theory Sigmund Freud had developed to explain the envy many women felt of men's status and career opportunities— as if such feelings required a theory, especially one with such a provocative and misleading name. It makes you think of women who would want a penis and consider surgery to obtain one. Basically, it makes you think of female-to-male transsexuals, but penis envy was never meant that way.

It's ironic that analysts spent so much time talking about penis envy when there are so very few women who would actually want a penis. All the while, there's a significantly larger number of men who really would want a vagina. *Vagina envy* would have been a very accurate term to describe male-to-female transsexuals. Nonetheless, traditional analysts never recognized transgendered people of either variety nor spoke of vagina envy.

I knew that I had always envied a woman's body and the powerful effect it could have on people. I admitted that I had vagina envy—or, as I preferred to say, Venus envy.

"So I have Venus envy, which is no doubt part of my Beautiful Woman Side," I acknowledged in a subsequent session with Joshua. "Still, what in the world am I to do about it?"

"You might integrate your female side into your traditional male life and end up a more sensitive man," he suggested.

Interesting idea, I thought, as I bicycled home from his office. *Why can't I be a sensitive man for the '90s, like Alan Alda or perhaps . . . Joshua?* He was an intelligent, soothing, somewhat effeminate man. I thought he might be gay, but then I noticed his wedding band and didn't know *what* to make of him.

The next time I saw him, I treaded lightly but told him, "I don't want to mix my female side in with my day-to-day life, because I don't think it's attractive for a man to do things like tilt his head tenderly or get all excited about a friend's new purchase from the mall. If I allowed myself those liberties, I'd come off as gay, catch flack from Betsy, and risk alienating my friends." Nevertheless, I kept my eye out for tasteful ways to weave some of my softer side in with how I conducted myself as a man.

As late '91 turned into '92, I wondered if all I really needed was something akin to women's liberation. After all, women had been liberated from a life of skirts and housework to a life full of choices. Were we men still stuck in a life of pants and breadwinning? It seemed right that women could wear skirts or pants, so maybe it was okay for a man like me to also have a choice.

Perhaps society was backward and unfair in this respect—just like my parents had been in how they had distributed chores between my sisters and me. Maybe we needed *men's* liberation? Naively I figured all my angst over crossdressing would be solved if men were simply allowed to wear women's clothes. Basically, what women's lib did was to stretch the things a woman was allowed to do in our society while still being thought of as a woman—rather than some sort of oddity, unfit for marriage and motherhood. A comparable men's lib would allow a man to do (or wear) more things and still be thought of as an able-bodied man.

Helpful as that might be, I eventually realized that it was not what I ultimately yearned for. Looking back, I see that I've always been captivated by the notion of *turning into a woman*. Being a man in a dress was never an end in itself, only something tangible I could do to bring my fantasy to life. This distinction came into focus as I first contemplated crossdressing in public and was repelled by the idea of being seen as a man in women's clothes. Whether I could pass perfectly or not, I needed to feel like a *woman* in women's clothes. So, I realized that for me it was not fundamentally about liberation; it was about *transformation*.

Though men's lib might make my life easier, I wouldn't want it to go to the extreme of making all clothes unisex. What if we lived in a culture where men and women all wore the same button-down shirts, pants, and short hair? Then we crossdressers could only transform ourselves by covering up our five o'clock shadows and wearing breast forms under our shirts. In that case, we might also need another name, because we'd no longer be *crossing* by dressing, and people in Button-Down Shirt Land would have to look very closely to see that we were trying to transform at all. We would lose all those satisfying symbols that scream, "Think of me now as a woman."

Even if men's lib made it socially acceptable, I wouldn't want to mix a skirt in with whatever else I was planning to wear to work Monday morning. Very few of us crossdressers are interested in presenting ourselves as odd mixtures of male and female. It's just not a pretty sight. For me to feel good in a skirt, it has to come with a cute top, heels, hair, and makeup—the total package—because, of course, it's all about transformation.

And transformation isn't just about dressing as a woman dresses; it's about doing as a woman does. Though Mom had taught me men and women were "the same in every way that matters," I'd learned that wasn't such a safe assumption. Where before I'd been oblivious, now at twenty-nine, I became fascinated by the differences between men and women. I read articles and books based on scientific studies, like *The Evolution of Human Sexuality* and *You Just Don't Understand: Women and Men in Conversation.*[15] I asked questions and listened closely. But more than what people said, I watched what they did. I aimed for accuracy rather than political correctness.

Ever since the advent of feminism, most progressive men and women have stressed the similarities between the genders in order to liberate women oppressed by social constraints. However, we equally, if not more, oppressed transgendered people highlight the *differences* between the genders in order to transform from one to the other. Who says women and men can't be different-but-equal? Who ever decided that a militant denial of differences was better than a healthy respect?

At the time, I didn't know why I became so curious about gender differences. It just flowed as I got more in touch with my feelings, and it seemed to connect with my lifelong fondness for women. Perhaps as my perspective shifted from having a Beautiful Woman Fantasy to a Beautiful Woman Side to simply a female side, I began to wonder, *Just how much woman am I? And how can I transform to express that part of me?*

Of course, to answer these questions, I would have to look for the differences. To this day, anything new I notice that distinguishes women from men is immediately interesting—from their distinctive clothes to their relative difference in size and shape; from their distinctive speech to their relative difference in behavior and underlying priorities.

On some level, a conscientious crossdresser (not to mention a conscientious single person of either gender) needs to know male/female behavior the way a poker pro knows demeanor around the card table. For example, studies have shown that 71% of the time when an unsophisticated player brings his fingers to his mouth while placing a bet, it means he is worried about his hand or bluffing.[16] With his chips down and livelihood at stake, do you think a poker pro would dismiss this fact as a "meaningless stereotype"?

For the record, the problem with most stereotypes, like "Few Jews are great athletes," isn't that they're false. After all, most aren't complete lies and do exist for a reason. The problem with a stereotype (or any other tool, for that matter) is that it can be abused, like when an individual, like a Jewish kid at a college-football tryout, is swiftly dismissed with no real chance to show his merit.

I think a lot of people understand male/female differences on an unconscious, intuitive level. Thus, they can make decisions based on that knowledge without being aware of the rules of thumb (i. e., stereotypes) they are drawing on. I lack such intuition. I have to process my experience more explicitly to find patterns that can help me be better informed next time around.

Now if you'll excuse my informality, I'll take you for a lighthearted stroll among the sacred cows of typical male and female behavior as I began to see them. Of course, there are plenty of exceptions, most notably gay and transgendered men and women, whom I'll discuss later.

Let's begin with sex. Generally speaking, men want it. Women don't, not the way men want it, not near as much as other things, like romance or, better yet, marriage.[17] Women want commitment. Men trade commitment for sex. Women trade sex for commitment.

Women have sex appeal. Men have catch appeal. A woman's appeal is based on being beautiful, youthful, and warm. A man's appeal is based on being wealthy, accomplished, and strong.[18] Men work hard to get an appealing woman to the bedroom. Women work hard to get an appealing man to the altar.

Back then, in the early '90s, I saw how Donald Trump and Marla Maples fit these profiles perfectly. He bedded her, she snagged him, and America couldn't seem to get enough. Of course, these tendencies are lowest common denominators, which any particular man or woman may stray from or rise above. Nevertheless, these are the themes and those are the variations, as I've seen them—again and again.

As a boy in high school, I had learned that getting a woman to bed was like baseball. Now I realized that, from a woman's perspective, getting a man to commit was also baseball. You get to first when he asks you out. You're awarded second when he agrees not to see anyone else. You've made it to third when he says he loves you. You've reached home plate when he puts a ring on your finger and proposes. You can score the engagement and register for the china.

A man's success may be measured by professional achievements. But for better or for worse, a woman's success is still often judged by having a good husband and nice children. Retro as it may sound, men are better adapted for risk-taking and action, women for empathy and communication.[19] At leisure, men tend toward competition, whether participating or watching, whereas women prefer decoration, whether adorning themselves, their homes, or their children. Women like decorating things to make them beautiful. To men, women *are* what makes the world beautiful.

When it came to the women in my life, Betsy was typical in most respects, whereas Demetra was very much her own person. Unfortunately, the only way in which my wife wasn't typical was that she didn't like to talk about us and our relationship. I longed for a super-close, share-everything relationship with her. But week after week, I was discovering how difficult it would be to find a soul mate in someone who had no interest in matters of the soul. "Why do we have to talk about *everything?*" she would often sigh. "Can't we just live and be happy?"

"Maybe she'll grow out it," I thought aloud, one day with Joshua.

"Maybe she will, but in the meantime, don't let her push you to have kids," he warned.

"Believe me, I won't."

"Don't gloss over your frustration," he continued. "You need to understand it so that you can either work on it with her or move on."

Maybe Betsy's reluctance to share stemmed from how wounded she still felt by my infidelity, because she wasn't a shallow person. She was always loving toward her family, loyal to her friends, and admired by her colleagues. Although she had said that she forgave me, her flare-ups showed that deep down she might never, and her tension showed how terrified she was about who I was turning out to be. Yet, for reasons she couldn't articulate, she remained committed to staying with me. While her commitment was absolute, mine became increasingly dependent on whether we could be content as a couple, even if still handicapped by the whole mess I had created by experimenting.

Hoping that we could share more of the things on our minds, I tried to lead by example by going into some of my mixed feelings about being Jewish, one morning at our favorite little breakfast joint. "So that's why I had such a hard time in med school when I met so many Jewish guys who wore gold chains and went on and on about sports cars," I explained.

"I see," she replied.

"How about you? Have you had any issues with being Japanese-American or coming from the Midwest?" I inquired, trying to get her to open up.

"No, not especially."

"Aw, c'mon. How come whenever I mention anything I don't like about Chicago, you get all bent out of shape?"

"Wouldn't anybody?"

"No, not your friend Wendy," I replied, striving to stay patient. "I must have told her a couple things I liked about Chicago and a couple things I didn't, last night. And she couldn't have cared less."

"I don't like it when you compare me to people," she objected.

"All I'm saying is you're a little insecure about being from the Midwest."

"There you go again with your labels," she complained. "It's so insulting."

Though committed, Betsy was becoming increasingly brittle. When it came to conflicts like the one we were having that morning, her approach was painfully simple. She would restate her position with more emphasis and more volume, as if that would remind her how right she was and, at the same time, drive her point through my thick skull. Any effort to understand my point of view or to consider a possible solution would come hours to days later. When we were able to reach an agreement, I ran into another vexing frustration. She seemed to feel absolutely no compunction to live up to any pact she made with me. I felt she should have come with a fine print that said: *Please be apprised that, in the heat of the moment, all prior agreements will be considered null and void.*

At my wits end, I turned to Joshua for ideas, "I just want to feel as emotionally intimate with her as I do with Demetra or with you," I pleaded.

"Well, then you'll have to be able to talk about what's most on your mind with her," he replied.

"But all too often, that's crossdressing."

"Well, then you'll have to be able to talk about crossdressing."

"Or else never feel close?"

"I'm afraid so," he frowned.

"So every other guy gets to feel good if he can talk about his divorce or his mother in a nursing home." My hands balled up into fists. "But I can't feel close, unless I tell people I like to wear women's clothes. That just isn't fair."

"No, it's not," he said succinctly, but compassionately.

"So I'll never feel intimate with Betsy or any other woman unless I tell her I'm a crossdresser?" He nodded. "I think she'd hit the roof . . . But I suppose I need to know whether I can talk about that stuff with her."

"It sounds like nothing else has worked. Maybe she'll feel like you finally let her in and she'll begin to let her guard down."

"I doubt it, but I guess I have to give it a try."

"You do, if you really want the kind of relationship you say you want."

Outside it was drizzling, and I trudged back home up Michigan Ave. feeling like I was marching off to be slaughtered. I got back to the apartment and found Betsy snacking on celery in the kitchen. "I have something important to tell you about me and my issues," I began.

"Okay," she replied hesitantly.

"It's not just that I'm envious of women, but . . . I'm a crossdresser." I could see her tense up, yet surprisingly she kept her cool.

"What does that mean?"

"It means I'm turned on by women's clothes."

"Putting them on?" she asked, looking like she'd just tasted sour milk.

"Uh, yeah," I murmured.

"How long have you known?"

"In some ways all my life."

"How can you tell me this now?" she demanded.

"Because I want us to be soul mates, because I want us to feel like we can tell each other everything."

She eased herself down on a stool, befuddled.

"I'm so glad we're able to talk about this," I said, trying to put a positive spin on things and lead her into some kind of comfort zone. "How do you feel?" I inquired tentatively.

"I don't know how I feel. I guess as long as you're working on it in therapy, it might be okay. But I do *not* want you to be one of those husbands who run around airport hotels in wigs and dresses."

I didn't know how she knew about such things but wasn't in the mood to ask. "I don't think I'd want to be one of those guys either," I said, then added in a funny Groucho Marx voice, "but I don't know if I'm ready to swear off that option forever."

Not especially amused, but still sincere, Betsy asked, "Is there anything more you'd like to say?"

"No, that's all," I replied as I approached and gave her a warm hug. I didn't think this conversation was over, but we had at least gotten off to a reasonable start. The very next weekend, she flew off to Detroit to see Lee and Sandra. They continued to be the people she looked to for guidance.

In the meantime, I called Demetra long distance. "I told Betsy I was a crossdresser, and I'm feeling guilty I didn't do that before we got married. What do you think?"

"You hadn't admitted it to yourself until recently," she reminded me. "Nonetheless, I think you were courageously forthcoming about your sexual confusion, months before you got married."

"So I can feel okay about what I've done?"

"*I* think so."

"As you well know," I said with a sigh, "that's always been good enough for me."

Days later, Betsy returned from Detroit with a sense of clarity. Her brother had said that being married to a crossdresser was like being married to an alcoholic. Simply put, crossdressing was an addiction as destructive as alcohol; it had to be renounced and carefully avoided. Was he right? I wondered. Should I find a twelve-step program so I could bravely admit my failings and strive to make it through each passing day without reaching for a bra or a panty?

Lee had some experience and insight into these issues. He had written an article in which he compared his own struggle with pornography to alcoholism and recovery. Posner too, back in Boston, had seemed to assume my female side was something dark and sexual—perhaps not so different from an obsession with pornography? Earnestly, in my next therapy session, I asked Joshua, "What do *you* think?"

He gathered his thoughts for a moment. "I think being a crossdresser is much more like being gay than being alcoholic," he said, taking me by surprise.

"Wait a minute," I bristled. "You should know by now that being a crossdresser does not make me gay."

"I didn't say it does," he explained softly. "Being a crossdresser is like being gay, just like being an orthodox Jew could be compared to being gay."

"Huh," I said, now more baffled than bothered.

"Nowadays, most people think of being gay as an unusual, but acceptable, alternative lifestyle rather than a disease or character flaw. Alcoholism, however, is still seen as more of a disease." The being-a-crossdresser-is-like-being-gay analogy was not one I would've come up with on my own. But I was open to it and in time understood it much more fully. Slowly but surely, it became the compass that guided me through the wilderness of ideas about gender, sexuality, and mental health.

Joshua inspired me to think a lot about the best way to view crossdressing. Clearly it's not normal in our culture. Normal things, like seeing the man next door in a baseball cap, rarely capture our attention and don't require an explanation. However, if we were to see him in a halter-top, we'd wonder what he was doing and might even ask.

Abnormal, or unusual, things or habits can be seen in a number of different ways, ranging from alternative to self-destructive to criminal. Behavior that's unusual but harmless is considered alternative, like an eccentric man who always wears a bow tie or a Jew who keeps kosher. Self-destructive behavior most commonly comes in the form of addictions or mental illnesses, which harm a person's home life, work life, health, or legal status. Criminality describes behavior that's against the law, generally because it hurts others.

Where does crossdressing fit into this framework of the unusual? Well, up until the late 1960s, it was against the law in most of the United States. Fortunately things have changed since then. Yet even today, many people, including many mental health professionals, consider it a mental illness or addiction, and so, it continues to be listed as Transvestic Fetishism in the *Diagnostic and Statistical Manual* of the American Psychiatric Association. Like the APA, I originally saw crossdressing as pathologic, but with Joshua's help I began to see it as quirky, colorful, and alternative.

"I *won't* handle your crossdressing like it was drinking," he proclaimed. "I'm *not* going to help you suppress it by reinforcing the guilt you've felt all along." Thank god, he saw what I could not: a clear distinction between weird and wrong. He saw that line and stood by it, even if that meant turning away work—because I probably would have been willing to pay him for untold years of psychoanalysis if it had seemed necessary to contain my compulsion.

Many people ask, "Is crossdressing a choice?" to which I reply, "Why does it matter?" Most of these people make the assumption that alternative behavior is only okay if it can't be helped. The truth is *It's okay if it doesn't hurt anybody.* That being said, for me, *crossdressing* is a choice, but *being a crossdresser is* not. The scary thing is I never would have chosen to be a "fetishistic crossdresser," but I began to see I was stuck with it.

"So I am this way," I admitted to Joshua, "then how am I to live? How is a *crossdresser* to live in our culture?" It was a question I would ask myself over and over again.

"I don't know," he replied.

"It's not like there are any public role models," I continued, while my new shrink remained silent. "Well, other than enjoying a little lingerie here and there, I hope to channel my crossdressing energy into my regular life."

Letting Betsy know I now considered myself a crossdresser had been a last-ditch attempt to connect with her, and it seemed to work. Over the next couple of months, she began to level with me in a way that was refreshing and hopeful, though at times followed by an irritable mood or a new health concern. As we approached Halloween, she made a remarkable gesture of acceptance. She suggested we go to a costume party as doctor and nurse. *She* would be the male doctor, and I would be the female nurse. I couldn't believe my ears.

As I asked for a scrub-nurse dress at the hospital, I felt like I was doing the most clever, most exciting thing in the world. I was taking full advantage of Halloween, the one day of the year men were allowed to dress up as women. It was like Trans Liberation Day. No questions would be asked, unless I did it again next year with the same people. I was going to jump up and snatch the permitted fruit, and the lady in my life was going to help me do it. Even though she had decided that crossdressing was like alcohol, maybe she was showing me that, at the appropriate time and place, I might enjoy a drink.

The next day, I came home with pantyhose and she came home with a headache. The following day, I appeared with a wig—which I had secretly just dug out of the closet—and she appeared with a box of tissue. By Saturday night, she had worried herself sick and it looked like neither of us would be able to attend the party. Finally, it became clear that, despite our best efforts, she and I just weren't meant for each other. If we continued to force it, we would make each other feel flawed and inhibited, miserable and unfulfilled.

But how do you divorce someone you still care about? Despite it all, Betsy and I were still a husband and wife who were attracted to each other and, most of the time, nice to each other. We continued to enjoy the simple pleasures of cuddling up on the couch, watching movies, and having sex. I used to live to make her smile, and I still tried to as much as I could. But boy, was I about to ruin her day, month, and year.

I simply couldn't bring myself to do it, until a small misunderstanding escalated senselessly into a fight one night and flared up again the next morning. As I returned home from work that day in December 1992, I approached our apartment door with dread. *Courage to change the things I can*, I told myself. *Courage to change the things I can.*

As soon as I walked in, Betsy approached me with a look of tenderness and remorse.

With perhaps the most somber expression ever etched on my young face, I held her off gently, but firmly, and informed her I was going to move out and begin a separation that would lead to divorce. She cried and protested.

"I need a kind of closeness and comfort we could never have together," I explained sadly, as I packed some essentials into a suitcase. I hoped like hell she'd be okay, as I walked with determination through the blowing snow to a friend's apartment. *She's got a good job*, I reminded myself. *Her friends and family are nearby.*

Even so, I hunched over with the gravity of what I had done to pave the way for happiness. To keep myself going, I drew strength from the words of our founding fathers:

> *When in the course of human events, it becomes necessary for one people to dissolve the political bands which connected them with another . . . they should declare the causes which impel them to separation.*

> *We hold these truths to be self-evident, that all men are created equal, that they are endowed by their creator with certain inalienable rights, that among these are life, liberty, and the pursuit of happiness . . .*

Whenever any form of government becomes destructive of these ends, it is the right of the people to alter or to abolish it and to institute new government.

-Thomas Jefferson,
The Declaration of Independence

At Betsy's behest, I did a session of couples therapy with her. "I love you and don't want to lose you," she despaired. "You're gonna have serious problems with any woman. So let's work on this together."

"We've been working on this for a while now with no real progress," I replied. "I know I have issues, and I'm sorry for the ways in which I've hurt you, but I'm not ready to give up my dream of a soul mate and a peaceful relationship. There must be some woman out there whose issues mesh better with my own."

Soon I found a lawyer and initiated a divorce, after five years with Betsy— two and a half of them married. "I have some unusual sexual baggage that might be used against me," I told him.

"Relax," he snickered. "Even if you're one of those guys who likes to parade around in his wife's panties, it won't make a bit of difference." Though greatly relieved, I did my best to keep a poker face and not let him know he'd struck the nail on the head.

I was surprised to find how little I missed Betsy. Perhaps I'd lost my fondness for her a long time ago and ended up feeling more trapped than anything else. I could now breathe easy, as I began to live on my own. I moved into a furnished studio in a funky old building with a friendly coffee shop on the ground floor, which featured rotating exhibits by local artists. I answered to no one, not my wife, not my mother, not even a roommate. With no one to watch over me, I was entirely free to explore.

I heard some gay men talk about a drag bar called Cheeks on the way back from the hospital I was working at. So when I finished call, late one weekday night, I stopped by to check it out. Though practically dead, I had the chance to hang out at the bar with a drag queen named Prima. Overflowing with curiosity, I asked her question after question about herself and her scene. She humored me and told me a lot about gay life but knew surprisingly little about transgender life. "Are you interested in anything more than investigative journalism?" she asked, batting her false eyelashes.

I blushed. "I like to crossdress in private." She arched an eyebrow. "And I have to admit I'm fascinated by the idea of dressing up as a woman and being made love to by a man."

"Sounds like fun. Maybe we should make a night out of it?"

"Okay," I replied, astonished to see an idea turn so quickly into a plan. We arranged for me to meet Paul, Prima's "other half" that Saturday night.

I arrived at the door of his North Side apartment, chilled by the December air and rather nervous, but I was on a mission, the same mission I'd been on back in Boston. But this time, I was going to do it right so that I'd never be tempted to live my fantasy out again.

The door opened on Paul, who—as opposed to Prima—looked short, scrappy, and boyish, but had the same devilish blue eyes. Although his apartment was very simple and unrenovated, he had given it a cozy feel with a sofa and pair of overstuffed chairs on either side of a wooden table. A fire crackled in the fireplace, and there were plenty of plants and a holiday flower arrangement—Paul was, after all, a florist.

He poured us each a glass of wine, and we settled into the two chairs. He eased me into conversation by telling me about an affair he had, in female form, with a very masculine construction worker. Although I wasn't especially attracted to him, I appreciated his hospitality and eagerness to please.

After the conversation swung back to me for a little while, I decided I was ready, and Paul was game. In the bathroom, I slipped into the bra, panties, and stockings that I had hidden away since my trip to Vernon's. Throwing my old costume-shop wig on, I stepped out into the dining room, where he showed me how to fill each cup of my bra with scrunched-up pantyhose. After helping me into a short black knit dress of his, he sat me down for some hair-and-makeup magic in front of a big antique mirror. He took my picture with the handy camera I'd brought along for the occasion and then let me play model while he shot the entire roll.

Afterward, he led me back to his bedroom. We stood opposite each other, while he put his arms around me and tried to kiss me. Sensing my hesitation, he let go. "Maybe you'll feel better if I do this," he said, nursing me along by closing the door and walking around the room turning off all the lights. On his return, he stood behind me, ran his hands adoringly down the sides of my dress, and slowly twisted me around. This time, I succumbed to his kisses and the pointy pressure of his . . . pants against my thigh.

Soon I was lost in the thrills and chills of fantasy made flesh. The next thing I remember I was on my hands and knees in Paul's bed, arching my rear end up in the air as he confidently slipped a condom on. He reached under my dress and pulled my panties down and entered me—ever so slowly.

Oh, my god, I thought, *this is it! I'm doing it: I'm having sex as a woman.*

He pulled back, then pushed into me, pulled back, then pushed in, several times, before finally pulling out. "I want you to see what I'm doing," he said, rolling me onto my back.

I spread my legs and watched as he again entered me. I played with myself as he plunged in and out. His pace quickened, while sensation overwhelmed me. I climaxed, and he collapsed on top of me. I could hardly believe it, but evidently he had just come at the very same time.

He asked if I wanted to touch up my makeup and go out to the bars with him. I declined because the idea sounded risky and I felt like I had taken this woman thing far enough. I didn't want to shock my system anymore that night, because after all, I had only been separated from Betsy for two weeks and was still adjusting to life on my own. So I changed back into male clothes and headed for home.

I was immensely pleased with the outcome of my secret mission. I felt like an Israeli commando after the stunningly successful raid on Entebbe. I realized the irony of such manly pride over such an unmanly endeavor, but that's how I felt. Queer as my objective was, I had achieved it in full, and this time, there would be no casualties.

I didn't freak out after this second experiment, for a number of reasons. First of all, I'd had safe sex with Paul. There really was nothing we'd done that I could wrap my mind around and worry about. Additionally, I felt less guilty about my desires. I'd grown a lot and no longer felt so bad about wanting to be a woman in bed. And finally, I no longer had to bear the psychological impact all by myself. I saw Joshua regularly, and he helped me process the things I was going through.

I had again played with fire. Though thrilled to be free of Betsy's constraints, I would now have to set my own limits, or else I might develop a taste for sex with men, which would hardly make me a more eligible bachelor. Although a man had a place in my fantasies, I still saw a woman in my future. I would experiment no more.

I remained focused on redirecting my crossdressing energy into my regular life and entered full-on psychoanalysis with that goal in mind. I was to see Joshua four times a week and borrowed money to pay for it. I was to lie down on the couch, and he would encourage me to free associate. I was to relax and verbalize the flow of ideas going through my mind, no matter how half-baked or humiliating.

At first, it felt very unnatural for me, a person who *always* thinks before he speaks. I lay on the black leather couch, looked up at the acoustic tiled ceiling, and began, "It feels like I'm on a backpacking trip, lying down on the ground, looking up at the stars with a friend." Then I continued, "Hey, this isn't too bad. I think I can handle this." However, it wasn't long before more troubling things came to mind. The idea of being alone in an intimate situation with another man made me worry I was going to think *Fuck me.* But I didn't want to admit it, so I stopped verbalizing my associations. Joshua urged me on, and I quickly found a safer tangent to follow. But as the session ensued, there it was again and again. Finally, I had to admit it, and he politely pressed me to say more.

I really didn't want this to be a big deal, I explained. Sex with men was okay, but only for guys who knew they were definitely and thoroughly gay. Bisexuality, I assumed, was some kind of excuse for people who couldn't make their minds up. Because Joshua never begged to differ, I ended up seeing myself as a messed-up straight guy who needed serious therapy. After all, I only fell in love with women, had my heart set on finding someone like Demetra, and was determined to clear up anything that could get in the way.

I wouldn't get involved again without admitting my crossdressing up front, yet that might frighten any gal away. First off, she'd probably assume I was gay, and I'd have to assure her that I was basically straight and working hard on any part of me that wasn't. Still, she might see me as perverted and scary or less-than-male and unappealing, each of which would be reason enough to move on and check out the next guy. I feared that that's how it would always go, even with one as open-minded as Demetra. I asked Joshua if he agreed.

"You might not be right for the majority of women," he said sympathetically. "But then again, you don't need to win an election. You only need to find one. Who needs to be right for everybody?"

"Okay," I figured, "let's say I'd only be acceptable to about 5% of women. That's still plenty to work with . . . But what about someone like Demetra?"

"Why not ask her?" he suggested.

"You know, she's married."

"I know, but still, who would know the instincts of someone like Demetra better than Demetra?"

So I called her up long-distance. We caught up a little, then I explained, "For a while now, I've had my heart set on being with a woman like you. And I would want to be open and honest up front. But what would someone like you think about a guy like me?"

"I think you'd be in the running."

"Really?"

"Sure, your crossdressing might come as a bit of a shock, but ultimately I'd see it as an issue for us to work on, rather than a fatal flaw."

"Is that right?"

"Keep in mind a gal like me isn't perfect either, and I'd need your support on my issues."

"Fair is fair. But you're married and unavailable. Would you really feel the same way if you were single?"

"I think I would. In fact, I'd introduce you to my friend Cary if you'd consider a long-distance relationship with someone in Boston."

"Well, okay then" I said emphatically, my spirits lifted by her very tangible vote of confidence.

Back on the couch with Joshua, I looked further into my yearning for someone like Demetra. She had arrived in my moment of direst need and seemed a revelation, a human being; unlike any I'd ever known. But could she be entirely unique? If there were others, how would I know a Demetra when I saw one? Where should I hang out to meet such a woman? Had I ever known anyone like her but not had the depth to appreciate her?

6

A New Woman

When I looked back on all the women I'd been involved with, I stopped when I got to Melissa Wrubel. *She* may have been very similar to Demetra. For starters, she'd been in therapy when we were dating and had been secure enough to talk about it. And hadn't she done oddly intimate things like breaking the conventional silence of sex by looking me in the eye and saying hi?

More than anything else, I remembered the way she had ended our relationship. I'd lost interest in her but didn't know how to tell her. She noticed the change in me and asked me directly about it. When I replied honestly, she was disappointed but civil, not hysterical as I would've expected. What then seemed like a weird way to handle a breakup, now seemed like *character*. Maybe she had been the first coming of Demetra, but I didn't have the eyes to see her.

Whatever happened to her? I wondered. Fortunately my sister Kathy had kept in loose touch with her and had some news. Melissa had left writing behind and now worked in the music industry in Los Angeles. Apparently she'd never married. She was dating but didn't have a serious boyfriend. *Would she care to hear from me? Would she possibly be interested in a long-distance relationship?* I had no idea.

Figuring I had nothing to lose, I called her on New Year's Day. I guess I was hoping that old acquaintances would not be forgot. When I discovered she was out of town, I let her roommate know that I was an old boyfriend, calling to catch up. Her pal relayed the message, so I learned, adding, "How come I haven't heard about this guy Rick?"

"Oh, he was no big deal," she replied. "Just a guy I dated for a little while, five or six years ago." Nevertheless, she rang me soon after she returned to town. "Rick, what a surprise to hear from you." Her voice was raspy and self-assured, definitely the voice of a woman, not a girl. "So you're married, right?"

"Yes, technically, but I've been separated for a month and I'm on my way to a divorce."

"I'm sorry for you," she said appropriately before blurting out something like "not so sorry for me."

Not sure if I had heard her right, I decided to play it safe, "Well, it's probably for the best."

"What happened?"

I told her that Betsy and I had had problems for a number of years, which had led us both into therapy. I ended up liking it and sticking with it, while my wife didn't think she needed it. Even though I may have contributed more to our woes, I felt she wasn't interested in talking about things and working on them, so eventually I decided to leave.

Melissa then updated me on her life. Tired of her old job in New York, she had snapped up an opportunity to move out to San Francisco and write for *Rolling Stone,* where she made a lot of friends in the music industry. People were quite impressed with her taste, and ultimately she was offered a position with a record label in L.A. Now she worked as an executive at Epic, with a mission to find and develop new talent. "In fact," she explained, "I thought you might have been calling because you had a CD you wanted me to hear. Do you have a CD you want me to hear?"

"Nope," I said lightening it up. "Hate to disappoint you, but no musical talent here. I'm much more interested in you than what you could do for me." After a relaxed little laugh on the other end of the line, I continued, "You know, when I looked back on all the women I've been involved with, I stopped when I got to you."

"I like this."

"I thought, *That Melissa was someone really special that I just couldn't appreciate at the time. I wonder whatever happened to her.*"

"Sounds like you're getting a lot out of that therapy," she joked.

"Yes, I am," I replied unabashedly.

"I've gone back into it myself. I'm even going for psychoanalysis," she said, sensing it was okay to stick her neck out.

"That's cool. I'm doing it too," I volunteered. Meanwhile, I wondered if I could handle someone whose issues might be as sensational as my own. Maybe she was secretly Cat Woman?

"How's your family been with you being separated?" she asked, and we spoke for about two hours about my family, her family, and whatever else came to mind. I was thrilled to see Melissa was the beautiful, soulful person I remembered. She didn't even seem to mind when I spoke a little about Demetra and what she meant to me. I called her again in a week, and we had another glorious conversation. It was clear we were both interested in being telephone confidants and possibly long-distance lovers.

I was still worried my secret identity might scare her away, but I'd be darned if I didn't give her my best effort. I would limit myself to lingerie and masturbation. Only if I was securely in a relationship with someone like her, would I consider dressing up any more than that. There would be no playing with fire, without a home and a hearth to contain it.

Though very excited by my prospects with Melissa, I hedged my bets and over the next few months surveyed the landscape. I wondered if there was a special type of woman who might be a better match for someone like me. From the back of an old *Tapestry* magazine that I had squirreled away, I learned about the Chicago chapter of Tri-Ess, the Society for the Second Self. Tri-Ess was—and is—a national organization that gives heterosexual crossdressers the opportunity to dress up and socialize. This would be my first time connecting with the community since the Tiffany Club. This time, though, I wasn't interested in dressing up, just looking for advice on dating and marriage.

Tri-Ess met in the conference room of a suburban Holiday Inn. I was screened by phone ahead of time and let right in by the girls watching the door, no cloak-and-dagger rendezvous necessary. Everyone was wonderfully hospitable, but no one was thirty and single like me. They all seemed to be forty-five and married, or if not, they were older and had originally come out at forty-five. Most of them had coupled up and had kids in their early to mid-twenties. Now that the kids had left home, Mom and Dad were free to ponder all the other things they wanted to do in life. And for these dads, that meant crossdressing.

The mentality of most of the people at Tri-Ess was different than I expected. Unlike me, they didn't care why they crossdressed, they were simply interested in how they could do it better. I mistook their approach for superficiality, when it truly reflected deeper acceptance. Susie, Naomi, and Deanna were warm and motherly. They weren't surprised by anything I said. Susie even gave me the sense I was like her when she was younger. I resented that. But you know what? It turned out she was right. I learned later that, despite our differences in age, ethnicity, and circumstances, we crossdressers have a surprising lot in common.

Naomi was the club president, and she told me I could call her at home if I needed to talk. She was a respected lawyer and I took pride in associating with someone of her caliber. As the well-informed club secretary, I sought Deanna's advice on how to find a woman who might be a good match for me. "What about women who crossdress as men?" I asked.

Deanna gave me a funny look, as if to say, *What planet are you from?*

"Why not?" I insisted. "It would be perfect. We could both do it together."

"Well," she said, hesitant to deliver bad news, "there are some female-to-male transsexuals. But I've never heard of female-to-male crossdressers."

"Never?"

"Oh, once in a while, you see a photo spread of Cindy Crawford or someone dressed up as a man, complete with mustache and stubble. But that's more of an arty experiment than anything else." Soon I would learn that numerous women in history had crossdressed and passed themselves off as men to escape their limited lot in life. But perhaps that was no longer necessary in 1993.

"Then who do you think would be a match for someone like me?"

She said she didn't know, but she could tell me that many Tri-Ess members had told their wives about their crossdressing. And 25% of the wives were sympathetic and tolerant, 50% were upset and barely tolerated it, and 25% forbade it and threatened divorce.[20] Most of the crossdressers Deanna knew came forward after several years of marriage and children. Their wives then had to deal with the shocking revelation of the crossdressing and the troubling possibility that their husbands had hidden it from them when they got married. She thought if I let a woman know what she was getting into from the start, she'd be more likely to be sympathetic. And even if she wasn't, then it would be better to learn that now so that I could try my luck with someone else or learn to live alone.

Finally she suggested a number of books, and her facts and advice were borne out by the studies they reported. I read those books and everything else I could find on crossdressing. Often I would read them while riding the El (elevated commuter-train) to work. I put white label stickers over their covers and spines so that the other riders wouldn't see titles like *Crossdressing, Sex, and Gender* or *My Husband Wears My Clothes.*[21]

I favored books that presented real stories or raw facts, rather than theories, because most theorizing in print at the time was unscientific or tainted with anti-transgender bias. I preferred to learn from personal accounts and statistical surveys and to draw conclusions on my own. I started to question the theory that crossdressing was a perversion caused by a bad childhood. It just didn't seem to match the stories I was reading and hearing. I was already skeptical about the theory that crossdressing was an addiction. I suppose for some people it can become one, but then again, for some people heterosexuality can be pursued to excess and become an addiction (repeated infidelities, lies, risks, neglect of responsibilities, etc.).

With my intelligence gathering under way, I was ready to hit the ground in search of women who might be a good match for me. Naively I thought that, if lesbians were attracted to women, then they might be attracted to peo-ple who could look like women. I befriended two lesbian women at work, let them know I was a crossdresser, and asked for their advice. Smart and sassy, Claire shared the details of her life with me and recommended movies, music, and sex toys she thought I might enjoy. Welcoming and fun, Peggy took me around with her to bars and parties.

Although my two chums couldn't have been kinder, it soon became clear that—guess what—lesbians like *women,* and preferably feminine ones. They have no special taste for anything less than a real woman, and that's all too often how crossdressers and transsexuals are seen. Even some real women struggle for popularity in the lez world if they come off as too butch. Claire thought that women who liked both women and men might be more inter-ested in someone in between, like me.

Where does one go to meet a bisexual woman? Maybe someone like Deb-bie Collins back in college? I sure didn't know. At about this time, Great Expectations dating service got my number and called unexpectedly. The woman on the phone explained that, with so many single women looking for eligible men in Chicago, she would be happy to offer me a discount if I signed up.

"Is there any way to be sure I'll be sexually compatible with the girls you fix me up with?" I asked.

"Hmm?" the woman on the phone drew a blank, as if to say, *You're a man. They're women. What more is there to say about it?*

"Well, you could say I'm a sexually adventurous kind of guy." I explained. "Is there a way you could set me up with a bisexual woman or maybe a dominant woman?"

"Sir," she answered uneasily, "I'm afraid there's no way we can do that."

"Okay, then no thanks," I replied, having confirmed that conventional channels had nothing to offer a person like me. Although I can't remember how, I discovered a very promising *unconventional* channel in THP (which stood for The Hitching Post). It was a social club for people of alternative tastes that ran a matchmaking service and hosted two dance parties a month at a nondescript assembly hall in an obscure Chicago suburb.

Despite the setting, these mixers were wonderfully festive, highly unusual events, which captured my imagination from the moment I first ambled in, in my inconspicuous jean shirt and khakis. *Thank god I'm not from here,* I thought then, pleased to see only strangers in line to enter the party room. At the front table, we were all asked our names and whether we preferred women, men, or couples. Then we were given nametags with pink, blue, or green stickers on them respectively. Though I simply wrote Rick next to the little pink sticker, some people used funny fake names, like Rod or Aphrodite.

Affixing my nametag to my breast pocket, I entered a softly lit split-level rectangular space, which had been made into a dance floor surrounded by an array of round tables with a bar and two couches at the far end. A handful of people cavorted around each of the tables, which were decorated innocently enough with bunches of colorful helium balloons.

After mingling a bit, I gathered that the club served three major groups. The first and largest were the swingers. They were playful married couples looking for a girl to join them in bed. Generally, the wife was bisexual and launched the initiative, but the husband sure didn't mind. Sometimes these couples settled for other couples for the purpose of swapping and perhaps all going to bed together. It seemed easier to find other couples than willing single girls. Such a girl was a precious commodity and had to be courted. "It helps to have a lot of money to sling around," one seasoned veteran told me, mistaking my curiosity for serious interest. "But whatever you do, don't offer to pay her."

I assured him I wouldn't.

The second major group the club served were straight people who were interested in S&M, consensual sadism and masochism. These folks would act out scenes right in the middle of the party. A man might crawl around like a dog on a leash and lick people's shoes. Or a "slave" might be scolded, tied up, and whipped in front of everybody.

The third major group were crossdressers who had found the solution to being all dressed up with nowhere to go. Such a girl could go to THP and be accepted by all and perhaps even admired by a few. *Very interesting*, I thought, but I still didn't own a single dress. And even if I had, I wouldn't have dared take a step outside my apartment door in it. I came to the party that night more as a surveyor than a sister. I might as well have shown up with an orange hat and a tripod.

There was a flutter of activity, as a DJ beckoned people onto the dance floor for country line dancing and stopped the music for a minute to teach them the Electric Slide. An effervescent black woman from the front desk borrowed his microphone to announce that she would pass secret love notes from person to person and was soon swarmed with requests. I looked down on the silliness and decadence, while knowing all too well that the very same existed deep inside me. Only vaguely was I starting to put it together another way.

Wait, who could that be over there? I thought. *It's Paul. Or is it Prima?* There he was in black vest, makeup, and bowler hat, like he just stepped off the set of *Cabaret*. He was friendly and asked me to dance with him after the line dancers were done. Not wanting to offend him, I said yes. *Dancing with a man*, I thought, *can it get any more humiliating?*

Just then, he pulled me in close. "Wanna get fucked again?" he whispered in my ear.

"No thanks," I replied, jerking back, not allowing myself an instant to think about it. I explained that I was more interested in women and soon excused myself to try my luck with them. I was gratified to get some of their attention too that night but still ended up in an ornery mood, figuring they wouldn't like me if they knew who I really was.

In a week or two, THP sent me a list of five women who said they'd like to meet a crossdresser. Raring to go, I began dialing and ran into a disconnected number, a no-one-home with no answering machine, and an irate boyfriend who insisted there was no one there by that name. Finally, I reached one woman who sounded okay, and we arranged to meet. I rode the El all the way out to her station, but no one showed up. After an hour, it was clear I'd been stood up.

Rita was the last name on my list. She wasn't in when I called, but at least she had an answering machine. I was thrilled when she called back. She didn't seem spooky or inappropriate. In fact, she had a nice mellow way about her over the phone. She was a Latin/Native American woman who identified as bisexual and had recently been involved with a pretty, young Latina from THP. She was divorced with a six-year-old son and, a number of years back, had served in the Marines.

She lived in a small town in northern Indiana and invited me to hang out with her that Sunday. Our only definite plan was that she would help me buy a pair of ladies' shoes. As my train stop approached, I was so eager to peer behind the picket fences and so unsure of what I'd find. She greeted me at the railway platform along with her son. She was about forty and a little round, but rosy-cheeked and pretty. After a relaxed lunch at Burger King, we dropped the little fellow off at a play date. It all seemed so homespun, so normal, so civilized.

We began our play date by sitting down on the sofa of her humble, but spotless, living room. As we made plans, she touched me casually on the forearm and then on the thigh, and soon I returned the favor. Instead of kissing, though, we kept on talking. The way we stroked each other and the explicit things we discussed were uncanny. I felt very comfortable opening up with her, which was a good thing given what was about to happen.

Rita suddenly got up from the couch and closed the curtains.

"Why did you do that?" I asked.

"Because if you're going to buy women's shoes, then you'll have to wear what every woman wears," she replied beguilingly as she walked over to a laundry basket on top of her galley-style kitchen counter and pulled out a bra and matching panties. "Because you seem like such a nice guy, I'll let you borrow mine." She thrust them at me.

"Really?"

"Yeah."

"Okay, cool," I replied as I started up from the couch to find the bathroom.

"Ah, ah," she protested as she blocked my way out of the living room. "I want you to put your bra and panties on in front of me."

"You're kidding?"

"Don't worry I won't attack you or anything. I'll just watch you from over here," she chuckled, as she backed off a few steps. "Oh, you're such a cute thing, even if you are a bit muscley," she commented, as I took my clothes off.

I might have been turned on if I hadn't felt so self-conscious and stupid for not making sure there was no one prowling around in another room. I toiled to find the leg holes in her panties and had trouble hooking up the clasps of her bra. Ironically, with bra and panties on, I felt far more exposed than when I was naked.

Rita smiled at me, apparently quite pleased with the scene she had choreographed. As I hastily covered up with my flannel shirt and jeans, she teased, "So you all ready to get your first pair of shoes, *girl?*"

O brave new world that has such people in it! I thought, surprising myself with a Shakespearean quote I'd learned back in high school.

By the time we got to Payless, I was swooning with anticipation. My Marine escort had to practically lead me by the hand down the aisle with larger size shoes. "Let's get you something sexy," she whispered. "You can try walking in them back at the apartment."

Although I couldn't describe them near so well at the time, I spotted some strappy black-velvet slings with stiletto heels in size twelve, the largest available. "These are perfect," I whispered back, as I anxiously handed her the box. "Can you buy them for me? I'll pay you back in the car."

We bonded on the way back, feeling like a kinky version of Bonny and Clyde. Rita said if I stripped down to my bra and panties and put on my new shoes, she would show me her sex toys. It didn't take much convincing to get me to traipse down the hall in her underwear, stumbling on my stilettos, clawing at the wall for balance. Following her into the bedroom, I saw a mysterious and menacing collection of vibrators arrayed *en masse* on her dresser. "I'd love it if you used one on me," I begged.

"I'd be happy to . . . if I could tell my friends about it at work," she said, knowing I'd agree to just about anything at this point.

"Sure, as long as you don't use my name."

She picked up a long bullet of a vibrator and cleaned it and lubricated it, right in front of me. I bent down on all fours as she gripped it powerfully in her right hand and pulled my panties down with her left. I flinched a little, as I felt its cold, wet, buzzing tip advance between my cheeks. But after overcoming my initial shock, I decided it was a rather exhilarating invasion.

What happened next was even more remarkable. Removing the vibrator, she twisted me over onto my back, straddled me, and reached for something that looked like a small white baseball bat. It was attached to a cord, which she plugged into the wall, and it started to buzz. Then she touched it to her clitoris. Thirty seconds later, she tensed and shook.

"What was that," I asked.

"An orgasm," she answered, real relaxed and low-key.

"No way."

"Sure, want to see me do it again?"

She did it a second time and then a third time. I had never seen anything like it. She explained that vibrators were much more stimulating up against a woman's clitoris than in her vagina. The one she was using was actually marketed as an electronic back massager called the Hitachi Magic Wand. I could see why, but I didn't know which was more impressive, the vibrator or Rita herself. In my experience, female orgasm had always been a time-consuming hit-or-miss proposition. "You're amazing!" I exclaimed. "What's your secret?"

"I can't really say, except that things have gotten better and better as I've gotten more comfortable with who I am and what I like."

Although I was concerned about us coming from such different walks of life, I called her a couple days later to see if she wanted to get together again. Somehow she made it clear that, although she liked me very much as a person, she was generally busy and basically looking to get back together with her ex. It seemed like having an adventure with a crossdresser was something she had done on a lark, which for now was fully satisfied. Because Rita seemed so unique and not at all interested in a relationship with me, I came away from our tryst with a fresh sense of all that might be possible between me and a woman, but no better notion of what kind might suit me best.

Through it all, I continued to see my feminine side as something sinister. I was a beer and football kind of guy who knew that, somehow deep inside, he was the Princess of Darkness. Though suspicious of all things edgy, maybe it was my fate to haunt the *demimonde* in a demi bra? I read in the *Chicago Reader* how some men went to professional dominatrixes to live out their most hideous fantasies. Cautiously I set out to learn more by attending a lecture by nationally renowned dominatrix Eva Taurel. As I sat there hanging on every word, I saw the world turned upside down. Instead of a tyrant, I found an actress, instead of a tormentor a teacher, instead of darkness light.

Mistress Eva described and at times demonstrated how creative she could be when it came to sex. She could play with power; she was confident and commanding. She could play with control; she was devilishly clever with ropes and restraints. She could play with pain, cracking whips and applying nipple clamps. She could play with urine, feces, just about anything. Costumes and scripts, it was all possible. Of course, she could play with gender. And it went without saying that she could play with money and for money. She was a professional after all.

I went up to chat with her after the lecture, and we made plans to stroll through Boys' Town the next day. I overflowed with questions for her and practically took notes on her answers. I was becoming very informed and tolerant of people's sexual tastes—including my own. So why shouldn't I find out what it was like to be forcibly feminized at the hands of a pro like Eva? She, however, was only in town for one busy day, so she referred me to her colleague Susanne, who worked locally.

Mistress Susanne hurt me and humiliated me. She forced me to wear a bra and lipstick while she immobilized me and had her way with me. The experience was everything I had hoped for, yet oddly unsatisfying. I couldn't shake the fact she was only bothering with me because I paid her. Afterward, I asked, "How can I find a girlfriend who's into S&M, a dominant woman like yourself? Are there certain bars or social circles?"

"Grow your own," she replied. "There are so few sexually adventurous women, and the ones I know are either taken or busy getting their asses kissed. I suggest you find a girl you love for all the good old-fashioned reasons. Then if you introduce kinky things gradually and playfully, you might be pleasantly surprised."

Already very hopeful and excited about Melissa, I was pleased to hear those words of wisdom and finish my survey of alternative women. There was no special kind that made the perfect match for a crossdresser like me. My best bet was to follow my heart and try to work it out with Melissa.

Throughout my search, she and I had continued to exchange long-distance phone calls at least once a week and had grown very fond of each other. We would call each other at the end of the day and often talk into the night, once for more than four hours. We'd even have to stop our conversations from time to time so that we could go to the bathroom. We began to share the things that made us more complicated and needy—and to look to each other for support.

Although Melissa didn't turn out to be Cat Woman, her issues were no less real and difficult for her than mine were for me. She was a worrywart and would drive herself crazy worrying about all the bad things that could possibly happen. Often she could control her anxiety about a thing by learning more about it or simply airing the anxiety out with someone she trusted. But still, she feared she might be too much of a handful for anyone.

Though I knew what irrational anxiety felt like from my panic over HIV, I was generally calm and levelheaded and didn't tend to catch other people's panics. In this regard, I was well suited for her and able to handle her anxieties with reassurance and pragmatism. But on the flip side, I would be giving her a whole host of new things to worry about. I eased her into it over the phone. "I'm sexually odd, but in a harmless way."

"Are you like Jerry Lewis?" she wondered. "They say he liked to get shat on."

"Hmm, I've never given it much thought."

"Are you into pantyhose?" Suddenly the pressure was on.

"I don't want you to guess," I improvised. "I'll tell you soon enough."

In April, after three months of a rather auspicious telephone relationship, we decided to see if it could work for real. Although we had dated in the past, six years had gone by and we no longer knew what the other looked like. From the phone, I knew I was so attracted to her emotionally that all I needed physically was a spark. Well, as Melissa bounded through the gate at O'Hare, I could see right away, there'd be plenty. She was slimmer than I remembered, and her new hairstyle took her from curly and crazy to full and sexy.

This was to be the weekend I would tell her I was a crossdresser. But first, I wanted us to get used to being with each other face to face. We took in the sights of Chicago by day and relaxed over romantic dinners by night. We shared my bed and started to get it on for the first time in what we thought of as the modern era. I had to show her I could be a man before telling her I also liked to be a woman.

Sex was very satisfying, and I noticed something new about Melissa. She was a woman with a great sex drive. I mean she really liked it, not like my ex-wife, who could take it or leave it. She truly had shades of Rita and happened to find me very attractive, not just as a catch, but as a sex object. And to top it off, she was rather impressed by my performance, mostly by the fact I could bring myself to the edge of orgasm and then linger there, thrust after thrust, for as long as she wanted. In this regard, I thought I was normal. Melissa considered me a "swordsman."

Because I didn't want to risk spoiling our fun, I didn't come out to her until Sunday evening, when we returned to my little apartment after Chinese food. "I suppose it's time I shared my secret with you."

"Uh oh," she said, as she braced herself against the back of her chair.

"I'm a crossdresser," I said nervously, but proud to be doing it the right way.

She gulped and thought for a moment. "Of all the things I worried about with men. This is something I never even thought of. What exactly does it mean?"

"It means I'm turned on by women's clothes and generally curious about all things feminine."

"Where do you do it?"

"Generally, here in the apartment as a way to relax and get off before bed."

"Would you ever go out in public?"

"No, because my whole fantasy is to be a beautiful woman, not be seen as a freak." I cringed as I saw myself at the local supermarket in a dress and lipstick. "Even the few times people helped me dress up, I still looked like a man."

"Are you gay?"

"No, and I know what I'm talking about. I've experimented twice, and I'm glad I did." She raised her eyebrows. "Even though I've never been attracted to men, being a woman with a man was an exciting extension of my fantasies. Nevertheless, it didn't come naturally. The body-to-body contact felt weird, hardly the warm cuddly feeling of being with a woman."

"Really?" she remarked in amazement.

"So anyway, I can't deny that I'm a crossdresser, but I'm a basically heterosexual one."

"Okay," she said with a little skepticism.

"Believe it or not, ninety-five percent of crossdressers are heterosexual, and we have organizations that represent us in almost every major city." I told her about the Tiffany Club and Tri-Ess and that I might want to dress up for a meeting sometime—though I didn't consider that being out in public. She asked me about the kinds of people I had met at these places, then seemed to take a breather. *Well, there it is,* I thought, *I've just dropped the crossdressing bomb on her.* I felt vulnerable. "Are you still interested in me?" I asked, leaning forward.

"I don't know. I'll have to think about it," she replied, pulling back. She remained pleasant and somewhat affectionate that night though she no longer felt like having sex. Although I had fallen in love with her and hoped she'd be okay with who I was, I didn't know what else to do but cross my fingers.

Melissa flew back to L.A. and called me a few days later. We exchanged greetings, while my heart began to beat faster. "How are you," I inquired, "in the wake of that bomb I just dropped?"

"I'm all right," she said, as I allowed myself to feel hopeful. "I talked to my shrink about it. Who else can you talk to when you find out the man you're seeing is a crossdresser,"

"Good question," I replied anxiously.

"Of course, she didn't tell me what to do, but she was very helpful. I'm gonna have a lot more questions about your crossdressing and we'll have to see how it goes, but I think, I'm okay with it."

I sighed long with relief. I wouldn't lose Melissa. I wouldn't have to try my luck with another woman and maybe lose her too. *I might not have to spend my life alone.*

Perhaps I had expected my crossdressing to be an instant deal-breaker, for that's how women would have seen it in college or even medical school. But a lot had changed since I'd been a single man in my early twenties, and forces in the dating market had shifted dramatically. Back then, the focus had been on sex, and there had been plenty of guys desperate for it and not too many girls who felt the same way. But now, at the age of thirty, the focus was on marriage, and there were plenty of women yearning for it and not too many men who felt as strongly about it.

In college, a woman like Melissa might have immediately discarded me upon learning I was a crossdresser and moved on to one of her many other suitors. But now, at the age of thirty-two, she had struggled with dating and was willing to consider me as a still rather appealing man despite this one flaw. Although she preferred to revel in my positives rather than dwell on my negatives, I didn't have to guess which category my crossdressing fell into. From experience she knew that all men have issues and appreciated that I was at least working on mine. Still, she remained realistic and chose to be with me based on who I was, not who I hoped to be.

Though she would have preferred me without it, she found that my fondness for things female did have a few fringe benefits. Right away, she noticed that talking to me offered the kind of comfort and depth she could usually only find in a girl friend. We assumed it was due to me being transgendered. But perhaps it was also because I was by nature a good listener and had by now become more sensitive through therapy and life experience.

A more substantial advantage was that by accepting me, crossdressing and all, she straightaway became one of the most significant people in my life. Her tolerance filled me with goodwill and a burgeoning sense of loyalty. Sensing that we were building something extraordinary, I soon resolved to work out any problems that arose between us rather than think seriously about anyone else and was eager for her to meet my family.

Although I had continued to join them for vacations and holidays, it had felt like the Cold War. Now that I no longer felt cursed to a life alone, I could give up my grudge against my parents. And with Melissa by my side, I was delighted to see how well we all got along on a family trip to Turkey. Afterward, she and I settled into a long-distance relationship consisting of warm, fuzzy phone calls each night and steamy romantic visits every third weekend or so. Meanwhile, I began to allow myself a little more leeway.

Deep down, my mind seems to operate in accord with Maslow's famous Hierarchy of Human Needs.[22] I think of my basic needs as a house with three floors. The first floor consists of my most pressing needs, those for safety (from physical or legal threats) and health (my own and my family's). The second floor consists of my concerns for the security and happiness of my relationships, work life, and financial life. Only when the first floor feels solid, can I work on the second. And only when the second feels safe, can I get work done on the third, which consists of fully expressing myself and living up to my potential.

As my affiliation with Melissa felt increasingly secure, my second floor became solid enough to support work on a third floor that might have some space for crossdressing. Privacy and the freedom it offered were becoming less terrifying. I was actually glad I could now buy and keep some women's clothes without having to worry about an outraged wife or nosy roommate.

So after work one unseasonably warm day in May, I set out for Victoria's Secret in Water Tower Place. Trying my best to keep my cool, I poked around the store until I found a pretty white bra with matching panties, then pulled a salesclerk aside. "I'd like to buy some lingerie for my girlfriend," I said softly, trying not to attract too much attention.

"What size is she?" the lady replied, naturally.

Oh, my god, bra and panty sizes? I thought, as I broke out into a sweat. *Should I just back out now as gracefully as I can?* Instead, I stood my ground and explained, "Well, her breasts are about . . . medium size and her hips are on the narrow side."

"What about her back?"

"Her back? Her back is a little bit broad, not terribly different from mine." I felt a flash of heat. *Now I've gone too far,* I fretted. *She knows I'm one of those panty perverts. What's gonna happen next? Is she gonna call the manager? The security guard? But wait a minute. I'm not breaking the law. I can always stick by my story—unlikely as it may seem.*

"That sounds like about a 38C with maybe a size 6 panty," the saleslady was saying in a business-as-usual tone, as she plucked the items off the rack. "May I gift-wrap them for you?"

"Uh, sure," I responded, a little slow on the uptake, as we walked over to the counter.

"Would you like to pay by credit or cash?"

"Cash," I replied, not wanting to leave behind any paper trail that might suggest Dr. Richard Novic liked to wear women's underwear.

For a while, I thought we crossdressers were unique in the way we carried on about things like bras and panties. Then I read a darling book for adolescent girls called *It's A Girl Thing: How to Stay Healthy, Safe, and In Charge*. In it, a woman recounts how embarrassingly eager she was as an eleven-year-old to try on her first bra, how she reveled in its look and smell, how she enjoyed dressing like Mom, and how she loved wearing it so much that she slept in it for the next two weeks.[23]

Wow, I thought, everything I experienced in my Victoria's Secret bra was right there: the embarrassment of wanting it, the delight in every last detail, the excitement of feeling like a full-grown woman. I even slept in my new bra the first few nights just like the girl in the book. Maybe I wasn't so abnormal after all! The only thing different was that I was moved to the point of orgasm. But maybe the girl in the book would have been too if her testosterone level had been as high as mine? (Though commonly thought of as the male sex hormone, women have it too—although in much lower levels—and it's the main hormone responsible for their sex drive as well.)

Although lingerie shopping had been an adventure, I yearned for my first dress and couldn't deal with the idea of walking into Bloomingdale's and asking for one in *the largest size available*. And even then, there would be no guarantee the darned thing would fit when I got it home. Catalogs, though, were everywhere, and I soon learned how easy it was to order women's clothes over the phone. I suppose the Internet would have been even easier, but I still couldn't afford a computer and had no pressing need for one.

The first dress I ordered was a tailored hound's-tooth sheath in size sixteen. When it finally arrived, however, I was frustrated to find that it just didn't fit; there was no way I could zip it up in back. Though disappointed, there was still a part of me that was relieved to think that maybe I was just too big for women's clothes. Perhaps that's why I didn't even think of looking for something stretchy, like that T-shirt dress of Betsy's I had worn at the Tiffany Club.

I shared my frustration with Melissa, who suggested I try a blouse and skirt. Bless her heart for not saying, "Tough luck, guess you'll just have to stick to lingerie." The next time she was in town, we went to Marshall Field's and she helped me put together an outfit. Wow, did I love her for that. As soon as we got back to the apartment, I excused myself to try my purchases on in the bathroom. The silk blouse was fine. The plain black skirt, however, was a little tight on my waist and fell straight down along my boyish hips and butt. Still, I could wear it. Though down the road I'd learn to create better curves, for the time being my new outfit worked. I felt lovely. I felt sexy.

By now, my Starve It strategy had evolved into a less severe Deprive It strategy. I would deprive myself of time by pursuing crossdressing and related things only after I'd taken care of all other conceivable priorities. In this way, I would rid myself of opportunities for dressing, or at least force it to be rushed and unrelaxing. This strategy was an overly rigid application of my—otherwise sensible—hierarchy of needs. It was like stopping all work on the third floor if there was any dusting to be done on the second.

I would deprive myself of money by agonizing over every potential purchase. Would buying a corset *really* be worth it? Was this one really my size? What if I *still* couldn't fit into a dress? And would I really have that much use for a *dress?*

If I had any doubt (and I always did), I would decide that I couldn't justify the expense. Much later, I realized that, when you're getting into any new area of interest, whether it's bicycles or breast forms, not all your purchases will pay off. If you're not making a few mistakes, then you're not trying enough new things. Experimenting is a vital part of learning and growing.

America may have experienced a sexual revolution with the arrival of the birth control pill in the '60s, but I experienced one with Melissa in the '90s. True, the first shots were fired with my multi-orgasmic bisexual friend Rita, but Melissa was the woman I loved. For a bright but conventional Jewish girl, she turned out to be a blast of fresh air.

She was remarkably playful and open-minded. She was up for almost anything, except bringing in other people. And she wasn't horrified by that either—she just said no thanks. She showed me sensuous ways we could stimulate each other's entire bodies. She was comfortable with masturbation and had no qualms about either of us throwing it into the mix. This simple act of tolerance gave us tremendous flexibility. We could show each other what we liked, and if one of us was tired or worn out, he or she could participate by caressing and whispering while the other found added bliss.

She let me introduce her to vibrators and toys of all sorts. We were free to talk during sex; sometimes we'd get silly and sometimes white hot. We explored erotica and porn. We embraced all the embarrassing little things that turned each other on. We truly saw these things as *gifts*, not fetishes, perversions, or addictions. We played on each other's bodies and minds like pianos, and the results were breathtaking: sex for hours, multiple orgasms, simultaneous orgasms. I opened up to her fully and felt like I could trust her with anything.

She didn't mind me doing feminine things in bed as long as I also did the masculine things she liked. I couldn't believe it when I was allowed to wear my new bra and panties to bed with her. I felt so exposed and excited. We even figured out a new position, which allowed me to be on my back with my legs spread and her on top thrusting. Ooh la la! Still nervous and hesitant, I asked her if we could take it one step further—complete role reversal. With a little urging, she said yes in theory, but not for a while.

I wanted to learn more about being a woman, and the three times I had dressed up, someone had always done my makeup for me. *Could Melissa teach me? Wouldn't it be fun* to *play dress-up together?* Although my soul mate had seen me in lingerie and taken me shopping, she thought twice about seeing me fully dolled up. "What if I get grossed out and lose control," she explained on the phone, "then you might resent me for my lack of support. Or maybe I'll never again be able to see you fully as a man, and you'll be forever tainted in my mind."

Because I suspected this was her worrywart side talking and because I wanted nothing more than to spend a few hours dressing up with her, I pushed hard for it and she agreed. So on her next visit to Chicago, we cranked up the air conditioning one sticky summer day and gave it a try. Melissa seemed tense as she showed me how to apply concealer under my eyes. But by focusing on the technicalities of makeup and clothes, she was able to stay positive and even nurturing. Then, after snapping a few pictures we called it a day. Strange as it may sound, I felt like a plant that had finally pushed its way up through the dirt and was now basking in the warm rays of the sun. Surely now, I would be able to grow and maybe even blossom someday.

We were able to talk about all aspects of my female side, and I loved Lissa's inside take on what it's like to be a woman. I had so many questions for her that at times she needed me to give it a rest. Our conversations were lively and not always harmonious. Often I would envy some advantage of being a woman, and she would either deny it or say yeah-but. If she denied it, then I'd go to great lengths to prove my point. If she said yeah-but, then I'd counter with "You only think of the extra hassles, because you take your advantages so much for granted. What if you weren't allowed to get all excited and emotional? What if you weren't the one who gets to give birth?"

For instance, once in a rental car on our way to my uncle's second wedding, I commented, "Women are lucky. You get to have real sex appeal."

"What do you mean?" Melissa replied from the passenger seat.

"You could just walk into a party or bar and find sex whenever you want."

"Well, I," she put her fingers to her chest, "went to plenty of bars with my friends, and no one came up to me."

"Oh, they didn't, did they," I said facetiously.

"No, they didn't."

"Well, did you separate at all from your girl friends?" I cross-examined, while doing my best to keep my eyes on the mountain road.

"No, we all—"

"Did you say hi to any of the guys?"

"Just the ones I already knew or was introduced to."

"Then it doesn't sound like you were trying too hard."

Melissa fell silent. It seemed in part because she knew I was right and in part because she couldn't believe how worked up I had gotten about it.

"If a nice-looking woman like you were trying at all," I said, trying to take a gentler tack and reaching over to touch her thigh, "you could find yourself a one-night stand before you knew what hit you."

Meanwhile, as a divorced man living in a strange city, I'd had to build a social life from scratch. Fortunately Jack and some of the other guys at the hospital were happy to include me in things. Soon I found myself part of a large group of tie-dye-wearing, volleyball-playing single people. With nothing to do one night, he and I met at a restaurant. We both felt uncomfortable about being two guys out for dinner on a Friday night. Ever the joker, Jack brought it out into the open. "Gosh, this feels so gay," he proclaimed, as we both erupted in nervous laughter.

Why can't two men get together for something other than sports or drinks? I began to think. *Why not coffee or dinner? Society sure doesn't give straight guys too many chances to sit and talk.* Though I liked Jack a lot, I thought it would be great to be friends with a gay guy, who'd be more comfortable hanging out one on one and maybe even hearing about my female side.

Ever since I had become aware of my gay classmates in medical school, I had been very curious about them. On the surface, I was heebie-jeebied by the thought of two men kissing, but deeper down, I was intrigued by gay people. I admired the free-spirited way they seemed to live outside the straightjacket of acceptable male behavior. For a while now, I had wondered what they were like and how much I had in common with them, and my experience with Dr. Calabrese had shown me that they might welcome me as part of the family.

So I pursued a friendship with my co-resident Liam, who was gay but quiet about it at work. He was happy to have a new bud, and we got off to a great start. Not long after he came out to me as gay, I came out to him as a crossdresser and we had a wonderful time telling each other about our different lifestyles. There's nothing like having a buddy in the same boat—or at least in a very similar boat. He was interested in the things I needed to talk about, and I was fascinated by the things he talked about. Occasionally, we would have lunch or even dinner together. Though still aware of the fact that strangers might look at us and assume we were both gay, I began not to care. After all, it would only mean I was like Liam, and he was a pretty good guy. From him, I learned that coming out is a real process that begins by coming out to yourself (i.e., admitting that you're gay) and continues by coming out to partners and peers (other gay men), friends, family, and perhaps coworkers. It generally proceeds in that order, but can be different for each person. The point is to go from being tense and secretive to being open and relaxed.

As crossdressers, we too have a coming out process. We just don't take it as far. It begins by admitting to yourself that you're a crossdresser. After coming out to yourself, you might come out to other crossdressers over the Internet or telephone or in person. Later, you may find a way to tell your wife or girlfriend. Most of us don't go on to tell our friends, family, or coworkers, because it's not worth the trouble for something that's private and relatively infrequent. However, transsexuals who are about to go full time must come out to these people if they want to keep their families and careers.

Sometimes we ladies of the cloth will treat coming out as if it's a single event rather than a process and ask, "When did you come out?" What we mean here is "When did you start dressing up and getting together with other crossdressers?" And in this regard, I came out and stayed out at the age of thirty, when I made my second trip to Tri-Ess, in early August '93.

I splurged on a rental car and headed out to the Holiday Inn. Tri-Ess had rented a hotel room down the corridor from their meeting room for those of us who needed a place to change. There I took my clothes off, squeezed into my skirt and blouse, and put on my makeup and wig. The thrill of it all raced through my body, but shame filled my mind when I looked in the mirror and saw   a man in a skirt, a man who should know better. How could I leave the room? But how could I stop after going this far?

I headed down the corridor alone, feeling like I didn't have a stitch of clothing on. My chest tightened, and I felt like I'd have a heart attack if I ran into a single other soul. How could I explain what I was doing? And what if I ran into parents with young children? Fortunately, I didn't encounter anyone, so I didn't have to deal with it—this time. Once I got to the meeting, I felt safe, a man in a skirt among many other men in skirts.

I was happy to see the familiar faces of Susie, Naomi, and Deanna. Once I re-introduced myself, because I had met them before only in male mode, they each opened their arms to give me a womanly hug and kiss. *Who are we kidding?* I thought. *We know we're all really guys.* Nonetheless, I went along with it, although I wasn't sure if I should kiss each one on the cheek like I would with my women friends or I should present my cheek to be kissed like my women friends would with me? On top of that, there was the whole matter of makeup. After fussing so much with mine, I really didn't want to mess it up, nor mess up theirs. Even now, I'm not sure I've figured all this out.

Anyway, this time I looked to these ladies for a different kind of advice. I asked questions like "Do you do your own makeup?" and "Where did you get those shoes?" I had to laugh at myself, eagerly engaging in the kind of hobby talk I had scoffed at, the first time I had come to Tri-Ess. Thank god, I had kept my feelings to myself. For some reason, I didn't make a third visit for quite a while, but in the meantime, I assiduously followed up on my leads and pored over Jo Ann Roberts's *Art & Illusion: A Guide to Crossdressing.*[24]

Over the late summer and fall of '93, I bought a new wig to replace my old costume-shop one and experimented with pantyhose, very pleased to see my leg hair nearly disappear beneath a black pair. I took advantage of Halloween by dressing up at my apartment and then waltzing right past the doorman to catch a cab and join Rita and her girlfriend at THP. Afterward, I decided to invest more in my crossdressing and finally bought that corset I'd had my eye on. Soon I was teetering around the apartment for hours in my tight corset and heels, trying to get used to them both. I'd also stand in front of the bathroom mirror and apply eyeliner and lip liner the way Melissa had taught me, then remove them, then apply them again, until I was convinced I was making progress.

With her moral support, I again splurged on a rental car so that I could go to the Tri-Ess Christmas Party. Like back in August, I arrived early to dress up in the changing room. Piece by piece, I put my new look together. With my corset pulled tight, I finally fit into my first dress, a red silk taffeta sheath with short sleeves. I stepped in front of the mirror and bent my head down into the cap of my new wig. I flipped my long brown hair back and bang. There was a *woman* staring back at me.

Wow, she's hot. I thought, instinctively tucking my tresses back behind my ears. *I'd do her in a heartbeat.*

I couldn't believe it. I had thought I would always look like a freak, but now as luck would have it, I was pretty. For a while, I supposed it was all in my head, but I began to see my appeal that night in the way people treated me. And it made me smile. I'd have a hard time keeping all this joy behind closed doors much longer.

I refused to let so many months go by until my next visit to Tri-Ess. And this time, I wanted Melissa to share in the adventure and meet the people. We rented a hotel room and got ready for the February '94 meeting together. There I set up a virtual photo studio. The desire to capture my image as a woman had been so strong that I had taught myself photography—and shot portraits of my whole family at Christmas time. The hotel room looked glamorous with a tripod-mounted camera, separate flash unit, and a white umbrella. Melissa was my photographer and turned out to have a great eye for what would look good on film.

Later, at the meeting, I learned that most crossdressers love photos and videos. "How many crossdressers does it take to screw in a light bulb?" Susie joked. "Two, one to screw it in and another to take the pictures." Yet, she didn't seem to know why we love pictures so much. Meanwhile, my girlfriend was astonished by how agreeable everyone was and how matronly they looked. She had expected flamboyant drag queens, like in the movies.

Ironically, as she accepted me more as a crossdresser, I felt increasingly restored as a man. Previously my masculine strengths had seemed an utter farce in the face of the humiliating truth. They were a big yes-but. Melissa turned them into a yes-and. *Yes*, I was rugged, handsome, and reliable, *and* I was a crossdresser. To her, I had a defect, but it wasn't the whole story. Only when I saw myself through her eyes, could I upgrade my own view of my crossdressing from invalidating defect to mere defect.

Thankfully my three-ring circus of not knowing who I was, who I wanted to be with, and what I wanted to do was resolving. I was safely out of my marriage with Betsy and feeling great about a future with Melissa. I was no longer confused about being a crossdresser, nor ashamed of it. I was getting comfortable with it and discovering the joy of dressing head to toe—hair to shoes.

In the meantime, I had been able to take a good long look at radiology and never found a part of it that satisfied me as a scientist or a doctor. In search of a new specialty, I gave up on the idea of combining the two and instead focused on my wish to be a doctor, listening to people's stories and helping them with their problems. After considering internal medicine and emergency medicine, I ended up selecting psychiatry because I knew personally the power it had to relieve misery and confusion and I was curious to learn about other people's private perils and see if I could help.

After a year and a half of long distance, Melissa and I were both keen to live together. Although she considered moving for me, I couldn't bear the thought of pulling her away from the music industry. Because I could do my training anywhere there was a teaching hospital, I decided to join her in Los Angeles. With my three rings of uncertainty resolving into action, I scaled my therapy back from four times a week on the couch to once a week in a chair. And ultimately, I expressed the depth of my gratitude to Joshua and wished him farewell.

By the beginning of May '94, I realized that I only had two months left in Chicago, so I didn't need to worry about news of my crossdressing leaking out. But on the other hand, I'd have to be extra cautious in the City of Angels. After all, I didn't want to begin my new career by being known as the Crossdressing Psychiatry Resident. So I decided to use my last four weekends in town to dress up as much as I could. I made plans and nicknamed them the Grand Slam.

Because I no longer had to crack the books at home for radiology, I had time on my hands. And because some family money had recently been passed on to me, I finally had some cash on hand. Though I had traditionally seen crossdressing as a vice, I now started to see it as an endeavor worthy of time and money and wholehearted effort. There would be no more Starve It nor Deprive It.

To hell with whatever anyone might think, my femininity was precious to me and I would feed it. No one in my life would ever be all cheery about it. No one would remind me to be diligent about it. No one would ever give me something fun to wear. No one, not my girlfriend nor mother, nor sisters nor father, would ever be thrilled if I became a great crossdresser. If I didn't take care of this part of me, no one would.

I had big plans for the first weekend of the Grand Slam. I'd get a room at the Holiday Inn Friday night and Susie from Tri-Ess would come by, then we'd go to THP together as girls. Now that I felt like more of a beauty than a beast, I was so excited that I could hardly sleep. But then, Thursday morning she paged me while I was reading CAT scans to tell me she had to cancel. Something very legitimate had come up. *How could she do this?* I caught myself thinking. *Doesn't she know what it means to me?*

But I soon reminded myself that she had already been more than kind and really wasn't responsible for the depth of my disappointment. Still, I could barely face the prospect of dressing up by myself, sneaking out of the motel, driving through traffic, and arriving at THP knowing nobody.

To soothe my nerves, I rented a car right after work—one day before I really needed it—and drove out to the suburbs. I practiced my route from the motel to the nightclub. I worried about whether people from other cars might see me at red lights. I figured as long as I wasn't too close to the car in front of me, I could always inch ahead a little to break off eye contact with anyone who might pull up alongside me. I found a few parking spots that would minimize my walk from the car door to the club door and felt much better by the time I returned to my apartment. But I was still so revved up that I couldn't settle down without a sleeping pill.

Friday evening in my motel bathroom, I prepared to shave my legs for the first time. I didn't know how I would explain bare legs later on but figured I could at least cover them up until the hair grew back. I started out with furry tree trunks, and because of all the hair, I kept jamming up razor blades and having to use new ones. Nevertheless, the whole process felt spiritual and erotic, and underneath it all, I discovered I had legs. They were long with narrow knees, shapely calves, and elegant ankles—real assets. Pulling pantyhose up my newly smooth shanks sent chills up my spine.

An hour or so later, I made it to THP, washed a drink down, and settled in next to one of the other few crossdressers. She chirped on and on about how she had saved money by making her breasts out of birdseed. The absurdity of it all helped me relax, and gradually I started to mingle. Thankfully people were friendly.

"Oh, my god, you look like Demi Moore!" boomed a cherubic brunette in her forties. "You have to meet my friends." That's how I met Josie, a waitress who was checking out THP with a man she was dating and a few friends from work.

I hung out at her table, and we had so much fun chatting that we exchanged numbers and promised to keep in touch. All the while, men would approach, offer us drinks, and ask us to dance. In a state of shock, I let Josie shrug them off for the two of us. But when a particularly stubborn one asked me to dance and refused to take no for an answer, she looked at me and said, "Don't worry. He won't bite. Why don't you go ahead? I'll watch your purse."

It was magical. It was like I was a college girl at a cocktail party—a Wellesley girl at a Harvard party. *How could this be real?* I wondered. *Who would have thought such places existed?*

Eventually Josie and her friends left, but I stayed on until closing time. As the lights switched on at two a.m., I was resting my legs on the empty seat next to me, my feet aching from so many hours in high heels. Out of nowhere, a tall man appeared and pulled up a chair. It was amazing how such things just seemed to happen that night. Flustered by being caught lounging like that, I began to excuse myself, but he winked, "Don't put those legs down on my account." He was clean-cut and handsome. Although polite, he didn't waste much time suggesting we go somewhere together, and I invited him back to my car.

There he started to kiss me and feel me up. When I felt the hard bulge in his pants, I realized that my simple fun was rapidly turning into serious infidelity. So I ended our little interlude before things went too far. Still, I knew that it wasn't fair to Melissa and that I'd have to do a lot more work on this whole *man* issue.

In the meantime, I looked forward to the second weekend of the Grand Slam. As I had become interested in psychiatry, I had become pals with Tammy, a psych resident who would let me see patients with her when she was on call for the emergency room. She was an attractive, introspective woman whose horizons had been broadened when her beloved younger brother revealed his homosexuality to her immigrant Chinese family. When I told her I was a crossdresser, she was wonderful and we made plans to dress up and go to next weekend's Tri-Ess meeting. We had fun there and visited a nearby lesbian bar afterward. Within a year, I had gone from fearing that I would never find a single accepting woman to finding two. But although Tammy seemed game and we might have made an interesting match, my heart had, for a while now, belonged to Melissa.

Weekend three of the Grand Slam, Tammy and I went to the Gay Pride parade by day. Then we freshened up back at her apartment. She changed into evening clothes, and I changed from man into woman. We snuck out of her building and headed back to Boys' Town for dinner. Because I had never done anything like that before, I chose the gayest restaurant I could find. It was a stylish little bistro just off Halstead. Yet lo and behold, who was there but Casey, my biker-chick hair stylist. With her handiwork covered up by my wig, however, she didn't seem to recognize me.

I'm not long for this town, so what the hey? I thought, as I strolled up to her table, tapped her on the shoulder, and smiled broadly. "Hi, Casey." Suddenly surprised by a crossdresser, she gave me a friendly but blank look. "Casey, it's me, Rick Novic."

"Oh, my god!" she screamed, as she got up from her chair and gave me a huge hug.

I loved it, even as I became acutely aware that we'd become the center of the whole restaurant's attention.

Tammy and I traipsed around the rest of the night exploring every gay bar and club we could find. I had never dared enter such places before. That night, we just swished around amidst the boys. I was astonished by the incredibly graphic porn on the video screens at one club and the shirtless men groping each other in its dimly lit back room. Who had ever heard of such things?

By weekend four of the Grand Slam, it was time to go back to THP. By now, I had gotten in touch with Josie and she had invited Tammy and me over to her apartment to get ready together. The three of us sipped drinks, sang along with Madonna, and tried on outfits. "You must try on this," Josie insisted, as she stormed through her closet. "And I *have* to see you in that." It was a dream come true. We arrived at the club, buzzed and smiling. We grabbed a table, and before we knew it, guys were hitting, and we were dancing. Again, I had that divine back-in-college-but-this-time-as-a-girl feeling. Although I was a good girl this time, the experience was no less intoxicating.

In the four weekends of the Grand Slam, I had taken my crossdressing one giant leap forward. What was I doing? I didn't know exactly. For once, I was just following my instincts rather than fighting them. It was like *I want to do this. So I'm doing it. Who cares why!* I tapped into a boundless energy that's hard to describe, like I had been released from prison and was finally free to do things I had dreamed of for decades. As each weekend approached, I felt the euphoric apprehension of an athlete before a big game or a young woman before prom night. Afterward, I wanted to relive it over and over again with anyone who was there. I couldn't wait to see the pictures. I wished there was video.

My Grand Slam had been so much fun that I knew I would have to keep coming back to Chicago. Melissa understood and agreed to fly back with me for Halloween. It was too bad that I had to leave town after finally learning to love it. How could my life in Los Angeles ever compare?

7

Young Again

After settling in with Melissa in L.A., I began my new career. I would be doing a three-year residency in psychiatry, with my time divided between seeing outpatients in the clinic for problems like anxiety and depression, inpatients on the psychiatric ward for suicidality and psychosis, and inpatients on the medical wards who had difficulty coping with their illnesses. Right away, I found mental health much more engaging than radiology, though I soon realized it wasn't going to have near the same camaraderie. There'd be no more Jack, Liam, and weekly volleyball with dinner and drinks to follow.

Psychiatry residents were of all different ages and nationalities, and neuroses. Everyone seemed to have their own special reason for entering the field. At least mine didn't make me difficult or mean-spirited, like some of my new colleagues. But for every snake, there was a songbird. And more importantly, I found psychiatry to be every bit as compelling up close, as it had looked from afar. My sincere interest in the field helped me to face its challenges and endure its politics.

While Melissa and I were seeing each other long distance, I could never get enough of her, so it was no surprise that I liked living with her. For a number of years now, she'd resided in a spacious 1930s townhouse in the Mid-Wilshire district with rustic-looking furniture, jute rugs, and a few too many knick-knacks for my liking—not that I cared, because day after day I delighted in her company. I could see that I was hitching myself to someone very special. Both of us eager to pitch in and make things work, we made easy roommates and settled into a cozy routine. Although I was nervous I would lose my privacy and freedom, Melissa promised she wouldn't be a live-in cop, like Betsy.

Because we lived near the hospital, I started to ride my bike to work. I finished early one day and spied a lingerie shop along my route. I bought a pretty pink negligee "for my girlfriend" and pedaled off to my new home to try it on and enjoy myself, like back in Chicago. I lay in bed, eased myself into the mood, and just as I was reaching up under my new nightie, my girlfriend burst through the door and stopped short with a jolt at the sight of me. Apparently we had both assumed we were alone in the apartment. Suddenly, with heart pounding, I was facing one of my worst nightmares. Since medical school, I had feared being caught red-handed someday and losing everything: wife, kids, savings, reputation. Of course, I had already crossdressed with Melissa, but I was still scared of how she might react to catching me like this. Perhaps part of me needed to know before putting down any lasting roots.

"Excuse me," she said politely, then nervously asked, "What are you doing?"

"Uh, just uh, enjoying my new purchase," I said mustering up some confidence. "Want to join in?"

She looked over both shoulders, as if making sure no one else in the apartment might see her agreeing to something naughty. "Sure."

Our sex life was abundant. We had sex every night except for the few nights we would come back late after going to a party or seeing a live band. We had plenty of regular sex, and I wondered whether I liked it because on some level I was imagining myself in Melissa's body and vicariously basking in her pleasure. I wasn't sure, but I developed a sexy form of narration that I would occasionally use to enhance this effect. From first kiss to final thrust, I would ask her questions like "Do you like it when a man does this?" or "How does it feel when a man does that?" I was more into it than she was, but we were committed to working everyone's favorites into the mix. She was more into candlelight, classical music, and kisses on the neck.

Occasionally I'd wear lingerie to bed, but mostly for vibrator or reversal sex. We both grew very fond of the Hitachi Magic Wand. As Rita had demonstrated back in Indiana, if a woman touched it to her clitoris, she could reach orgasm pronto. I discovered the same was true if I touched it to the head of my penis. If Melissa and I wanted to have a quickie on a weekday night, we might have "vibro" rather than regular sex. I would put on my bra and panties, and she'd usually take hers off. While she started to stimulate herself with the wand, I would straddle her and press myself against it as well, and soon we would both be on the edge of oblivion.

We even reached the final frontier, complete role reversal. The idea was that I would be the sweet yielding thing lying back in her negligee and Melissa would be the swaggering swordsman, strapping it on and giving it to me good. Not only did we do it, but we got very, very good at it. I made her a special dildo thong, and she would slip a tiny vibrator inside it next to her clitoris. Then whenever she'd grind into me, she'd feel it even more intensely than I did. Moments later, like a man, she would come before me and joke that it was time to hit the showers. But she'd keep going while I played with myself a bit and soon I'd join her in the land of bliss. She made love to me like this almost every week. I was ever thankful and hoped I'd never yearn for anything more.

One Sunday morning, she and I woke up early and went for a hike in Topanga State Park. All the way up the trail, we kept a lively conversation going. We talked about her father's prostate cancer and how we felt about our families. We compared our experiences in therapy and found room for a few good laughs along the way. A refreshing breeze hit us as we emerged from the live oaks onto the naked hilltop.

"You know, I'm really glad I moved out here to be with you."

"Really?" she said, turning to me and looking moved.

"Yeah, I wake up every morning and see your smiley freckly face and think, *Thank god I'm not back in Chicago with Betsy anymore. I'm with a really good person, in a really good place.*"

"You do?"

"I do. I . . . *love* you," I said, hesitating a little because neither of us had actually said the word before.

Sweaty jog bra be damned, Melissa moved in for a hug and a kiss, then replied, "I love you too."

After a warm embrace, I pulled back and asked, "But, why? I can drive you crazy sometimes with my CD stuff." I replied in code in case other hikers were in the vicinity.

"Yeah, you can, and your CD stuff can be a real pain sometimes, but I choose not to dwell on it, because it's only a part of who you are. Everyone's got something, and yours may be a little more taboo. But despite it all, I think you're a nice guy with a good head on your shoulders and you understand me. I can be myself with you and not feel like I'm too much. You're soothing, devoted, and honest," she cracked a little smile, "maybe even a little too honest at times."

"Okay, let's quit while I'm ahead, or you're ahead, or whatever," I blurted out, feeling reassured.

Little did I know, but by joining Melissa in L.A. in the summer of '94, I had just moved to one of the best crossdressing cities in America. In retrospect, it was a hell of a thing to leave up to chance. A lot was happening out here amidst the palm trees, strip malls, and hazy sunshine. In fact, the first organization for heterosexual crossdressers had been founded here by Charles/Virginia Prince in 1960. Although originally known as the Hose & Heels Club, it eventually turned into the alpha chapter of Tri-Ess and was joined in greater L.A. by Powder Puffs, CHIC, and Ladies' Knight Out. I honed in on CHIC and Ladies' Knight, because they seemed more like social clubs with events, rather than support groups with meetings. Melissa gave me the okay to go to one event a month. That way, it didn't take too big a bite out of our social life.

She would have preferred for me to go on my own, but I wouldn't hear of it. One reason I wanted her to go with me was to make sure she was okay with what I was up to. If it was going to be hard for her, I wanted us to have the chance to talk it over right away. But more than that, I wished to share the significant events in my life with her just like she did with me. I was willing, if not always thrilled, to participate in her events; I hoped for the same from her. I had treasured the two times we had dressed up together in Chicago and was hungry to learn more. It seemed crazy to learn from anyone but Melissa, because she was the woman I admired most, and I had the utmost respect for her style and sensibility.

Each month, we drove to a different event and it felt like our own secret adventure. Nobody knew where we were going, and we didn't know exactly what we'd find. Each outing was like a vacation to a faraway place where the rules of everyday life no longer applied. I was Alice journeying deep into Wonderland. And it was all the more meaningful and real because I shared it with Melissa. Meanwhile, my adventures without her, back in Chicago, were fading into the mist of *Did I do that or just dream it?*

She and I didn't dare get ready at our apartment. Generally, we would check into a motel near our destination and ask for a room on the first floor and in the back. So that Lissa wouldn't be recognized, I outfitted her with her own wig, and she went by the name Maggie. Nevertheless, just getting from the motel room to the car could make her very nervous, especially if we hadn't been able to park right outside our door. I wasn't so scared, because I had already been out in public a few times. But my girlfriend was still like I had been, back at Tri-Ess when I felt I'd have a heart attack if anyone saw me in the corridor. I'm not sure what she thought might happen, but her instincts told her it would be a disaster for me to be seen in a dress and for her to be seen at my side.

On one of our outings, a group of people saw us scampering across the parking lot and just seemed to ignore us. Was I passing? Perhaps I saw a double take, but no one stopped to mock us or harass us in any way.

I wonder why both Melissa and I had such fears about how strangers would react. Maybe our expectations were based on how people would have behaved back in school. Surely, I would have been stopped and taunted along with anyone who cared to associate with me. Yet so far, adult life was turning out to be a lot more polite than the mean streets of adolescence. No grown-up I knew, for instance, after noticing someone walk with a limp, would ever stop and stare, or dream of mocking that person, like they might have in high school.

Typically the crossdressing groups held their events at people's homes in the suburbs. "Apparently, whoever's hosting this party isn't too worried what the neighbors think about men dropping by in wigs and dresses," I whispered anxiously to Melissa outside an elegant front door, as we waited to be shown into our first CHIC barbeque. In a minute, our larger-than-life hostess arrived, and upon learning we were new in town, she made a point of introducing us to everyone: perhaps twenty crossdressers and about ten chatty wives—many more than I was used to in Chicago, but then L.A. was supposed to be a more progressive place. Before I knew it, I was busy learning about all the fun places to go and things to try in my glamorous new hometown, and my honey seemed like she was fending well, fast in conversation with two wives by an outdoor fireplace.

"Some of the wives are pretty pissed off," she said under her breath, as we sat together in the living room awaiting a formal presentation. "It seems they didn't find out until much later on."

Although Melissa had burst my bubble about the barbeque, I was still pleased to see that she wasn't rattled and gave her hand a little squeeze.

Our presenter that night was Espy Lopez, an accomplished engineer who was starting Classic Curves, a line of lingerie designed especially for crossdressers. She spoke about the geometry of the female form and the importance of wearing hip padding to create a realistic hourglass figure. I could readily see the utility of her product from the convincing way she put herself together. As she fielded her final question from the crowd, I hustled up to meet her and signed up for a fitting later on that week.

While Espy was joking about being a *decorated* combat veteran, Melissa tapped me on the shoulder. "I have someone I want you to meet," she said, as I turned around and beheld a lovely, laughing strawberry-blonde in a floral skirt. "Uh, *Alice*, this is Valerie." I had to look twice to see that Valerie was a crossdresser and probably someone about ten years older than me. Still, the way she sounded and moved kept tricking me into thinking of her as a woman.

"Are you sure you're really a man?" I inquired playfully.

She nodded. "I know, can you believe it?" she said with upturned hands. "And kind of a macho TV star," she added, though unwilling to give Melissa and me any details. To top it off, she introduced us to her long-time girlfriend, who seemed to be having every bit as much fun as she was. Valerie inspired me that night and showed the two of us how this crossdressing thing might work out in the long run.

Compared to the 1950s-America of my marriage with Betsy, my union with Melissa felt like Camelot, our own special kingdom, with its own special customs; or maybe more like Amsterdam, a peaceful place with unusual openness and tolerance. Although Lissa and I weren't married, we knew each other better than most married couples did. Feeling secure in my relationship with her, I allowed myself to experience more of life as a woman.

Through my new mascara'd lashes, the dull gray realities of everyday life now seemed Technicolor. I no longer needed to travel to a foreign country to experience the exotic, just seeing my own neighborhood from a female perspective was adventure enough. It was like exploring a parallel universe that had been going on around me, while year after year I'd remained oblivious.

Even a simple trip to the supermarket could be a journey of discovery. By now, I had a good grasp on cosmetics, but what were all those other things in the women's aisle? It was all so mystifying and exciting. What was a panty shield or a depilatory cream? What was the deal with all those hair colors? Why so many types of pantyhose? How did a girl ever know which to wear?

Melissa humored me with many an explanation and didn't object too much when I would try something zany, like douching, just for the sake of experiencing it. She even held forth on some of the finer points of grooming. "Women like me, or your sisters," she said, "don't go to the supermarket for our makeup; we go to department stores. And we don't buy hair color off the shelf; we get it done at the salon."

"Well, la-di-da," I replied, and we both had a good laugh. I loved all the things we could say and do together.

Yet, I couldn't help yearning for more than what was offered at the private picnics and pool parties. I suppose I wanted the things any budding young woman wants: shopping, dining, dancing, attention. For the time being, we accommodated my growing needs by taking our monthly adventures further afield. I hoped to find something like THP nearby—like in Orange County or San Diego—but not right in my own backyard. Although L.A. featured the famous Queen Mary Show Lounge, it was too close for comfort and I would be very concerned about being recognized there.

Although Melissa and I had fun foraging through a few new clubs, I wasn't finding anything that gave me that back-in-college-but-this-time-as-a-girl euphoria. So, as planned, she and I went back to THP for Halloween and had a great time with Josie and her boyfriend. I went as Little Red Riding Hood, and he went as the Big Bad Wolf. With Melissa and Josie in costume as well, we all took Olive Garden by storm. Later on, Big Bad Wolf and I won second place in the costume contest and we all did ecstasy and danced the night away.[25]

In November, Melissa and I drove down to San Diego. We dined together as girls in Hillcrest, then slinked over to the Brass Rail, a rough-and-tumble club that came close to the atmosphere I so fervently sought. Men of all kinds bought us drinks, and I soaked up every compliment.

As we started to pack up the next morning in our motel room, I turned to Lissa like a bright-eyed, bushy-tailed kid sister beaming with newfound pride. "Did you see how that Mexican man was hitting on me last night?"

"Uh yeah, how could I miss it," she said with a roll of her eyes.

"Wasn't that cool?" I persisted enthusiastically. "He was ready to take me to Tijuana with him for the weekend."

My girlfriend looked somewhat aghast.

"I'm getting pretty good at this," I said, the words escaping my mouth as I realized I'd gone too far.

"You just don't get it, do you?" she scowled. "How would you like it if I flirted with a man like that?"

"We could both flirt," I suggested.

"Well, I'm not interested," she snapped and then drew a deep breath. "Seriously, how would you like it if I let a man put his arm around me in front of you?"

Now it was my turn to catch my breath. "I guess I wouldn't want a front row seat for something like that. Sorry."

"I know you like to flirt," she said sympathetically, "but I just can't be around for it."

I didn't want to risk hurting Lissa's feelings again like that, so I decided it was time for Alice to strike out on her own. I would miss her dearly on my monthly outings, but I was now strong enough to go it alone. Meanwhile, inside, I worried whether I would ultimately want to receive more than just a man's attention. I feared the fate of restless young Guinevere, whose yearnings for the "simple joys" of maidenhood would mean the ruin of Camelot.

Up until this point, I had seen myself as an essentially normal man trying to live an essentially normal life with the woman he loved. But now Rick was falling faster and faster down the rabbit hole and watching more and more of him become Alice the further he fell. Though frightened by the process, I embraced it as much as I fought it.

I needed to know what it felt like to be a woman in every possible way. But how much further could I go without radically changing my life? What would be next? Hormones, boyfriends, electrolysis? Would I be forever restless until I finally faced the music and accepted my fate as a transsexual? What would that mean for my relationship with Melissa? How would I ever face the rigors of transitioning at the hospital?

Now that I was training in psychiatry, I looked back on my HIV crisis and began to realize why I had fallen apart so badly after experimenting with sex as a woman. Deep down, I'd liked it too much and knew I'd have to make major changes in my life if I was ever to be truly happy. Oh, just a few small things, like calling off my marriage and rethinking my lifelong self-image and hopes and dreams for the future. *Yikes,* my unconscious mind must have screamed at the time, *I'd rather obsess about the small, but terrifying, chance of getting AIDS.*

My reaction could be characterized as the homosexual panic a man might suffer after his first sexual experience with another man. In such a panic, a fellow who thinks of himself as straight may be overcome by the fear that he's gay. And often such a man will turn out to be gay, or at least bi.

Perhaps my reaction was more severe because I hadn't just been with a man; I'd enjoyed being a *woman.* So I had to deal with the additional fear that deep down I wanted to be a woman. In that way, I would more precisely characterize what I went through as transsexual panic. (Anne Vitale, Ph.D., describes such panic and more in her article on Gender Expression Deprivation Anxiety.[26]) I had come a long way since then and was now comfortable with my transgender feelings but still didn't know for sure if I was a crossdresser or a transsexual.

Hence, I thought it best to continue psychotherapy and started to look for someone to work with. Because I wasn't so desperate this time around, I had the luxury to meet with three different therapists before choosing one. Because I hoped to be a psychoanalyst someday, I made sure all three were training analysts. I asked them up front if they had any experience working with transgendered people. It turned out they had virtually none and didn't know of any of the TG organizations in town. I was surprised, but Joshua hadn't had any expertise with transgendered people either. Nonetheless, he had been immensely helpful to me.

So I decided to go ahead and choose one of the three and reenter therapy with the goal of figuring out whether I was TV or TS and how to be the best-adjusted one I could be. Although I didn't think it was fair to hire a person on the basis of his/her gender, I made an exception and chose the one woman among the three candidates specifically because she was a woman. I had never worked with a woman before and thought it might be easier to express my more feminine feelings with her. I was afraid a man might find me pitiful or creepy, whereas a woman might think, *You know, I feel like that too sometimes.* Caroline could relate to me in that way and turned out to have many other strengths beyond the simple fact of her womanhood. She encouraged me to develop my own ideas about being transgendered, and she helped me feel grounded, as my identity and needs grew increasingly unorthodox.

As I went out and met more transgendered people, I failed to see the supposed sharp line between myself as a crossdresser and other people who were transsexuals. Valerie told me about one friend of hers who had been thoroughly convinced that she was "just a crossdresser" only to decide a year later that she'd been thoroughly wrong. Although I was nothing like the classic primary, started-out-gay, transsexual, who feels like a woman trapped in the body of a man, I felt a lot in common with secondary transsexuals, especially those transitioning around my age. A secondary, or started-out-straight, transsexual is someone who has managed pretty well as a conventional man, then later on realizes that what he most deeply needs is to live as a woman.

I began to see both crossdressers and transsexuals as on a spectrum of transgender identity that goes from feeling a little bit like a woman to feeling entirely like a woman. Or perhaps the spectrum runs from men who want to be women occasionally—crossdressers—to those who want to be women all the time—transsexuals. After all, most human traits don't exist as all-or-nothing phenomena. There isn't just the—less common—blonde hair and more common brown hair; there's dirty blonde, light brown, and countless other shades. Despite information to the contrary put out by both the crossdresser and transsexual powers-that-be, I figured there just had to be shades of gray between crossdressers and started-out-straight transsexuals.

Five years prior, but unbeknownst to me, researchers had formulated the notion of "autogynephilia," which linked crossdressers and started-out-straight transsexuals as otherwise-normal men who are sexually aroused by the idea of being women (even if they claim they are not, as was shown by penile blood flow studies).[27] It is an intriguing notion. However, I would broaden it by replacing "are sexually aroused by" with "find profound satisfaction in." And I would get rid of that awful name; it's a step back. "Autogynephilia" sounds too much like pedophilia and other unsavory sexual proclivities. (For more, see the educational website maintained by transgendered physician Anne Lawrence.)[28]

Meanwhile, I felt threatened by how much I enjoyed being a woman. Could I possibly be more yin than yang? I wondered where I was on the TG spectrum and truly hoped I was more crossdresser than transsexual. After all, my personality and mannerisms were much more male than female. And being a guy had always been comfortable for me, even if being a girl was turning out to be more fun.

But would it truly be more fun, if I did it full time? Or was I just skimming the cream off it? After all, I was only living out the most appealing parts of being a woman, like shopping and socializing. Would I like fighting for respect at work? No, but ironically I had chosen one of the few prestigious professions in which it's better to be a woman; most patients prefer a female psychiatrist. Would I like being a sex object? Hell, yes. Would I like struggling to find a man who wasn't afraid of commitment? Hell, no. Would I enjoy having the kind of super-close female friends women do? Yes, very much so. But would I like being expected to honor all sorts of social obligations and be the glue that kept my family together? I didn't think so. So overall, it seemed like I was in the middle of the spectrum, pretty evenly bigendered, perhaps half-a-woman trapped in the body of a man.

Honest as my assessment was, it failed to point me down one path or another. Not locked into a standard boyfriend role with Melissa, continuing on as a man looked like a good option and seemed to offer me sufficient space for my femme self. She made it clear, though, that "If you were to ever decide that you were transsexual, then our relationship would be over. I've always dreamed of a full, happy life with a man and children. There are some compromises I'll never make." The very thought of jeopardizing her dream made me tear up instantly.

As if that weren't enough, another hardship to transitioning would be that, standing six feet tall, I'd probably get read a lot (i.e., identified as something less than a real woman), and I was only beginning to grasp how trying that could be. I may have felt 50% woman, but not woman enough to leave Lissa, transition on the job, and start to live as a transsexual. Yet I couldn't completely trust any of my conclusions, for I'd been so deeply shaken and surprised in the past. What if a man fell in love with me and offered me a whole new life?

To find my way through the forest, I maintained my faith in the notion that being a crossdresser is like being gay—or more precisely, being a *transsex*ual is like being gay and being a crossdresser is like being bi. From *Tapestry*, I learned that, just like homophobia describes prejudice against homosexual people, *transphobia* describes the even worse prejudice against transgendered people. Extrapolating from documentaries like *The Celluloid Closet*, I began to see that transphobia was pervasive. It influenced—if not shaped—the thoughts of the reporters and movie-makers who presented us to the rest of the world, the mental health professionals who studied and sought to help us, and even the lawmakers who decided whether we were worth protecting or persecuting.[29]

Oh, my god, I realized, *it's not that we're screwed up; it's just that we've been trained to think so.* As I became aware of the often-tragic consequences of homophobia and transphobia, the last vestiges of my shame and anger at my parents gave way to rage against those who have perpetuated these prejudices, including many prominent people in psychiatry. As previously mentioned, psychiatrists still list crossdressers and transsexuals in the official book of mental illnesses—and they only removed gay people from the book in 1986, though they had started the process in 1973.[30]

Instead of seeing myself as a screwed-up straight man, I began to see myself as a different kind of person altogether. Therefore, the narrow rules of masculinity, which governed how a straight man should act or even what he could or couldn't say, applied no more to me than they did to an over-the-top interior decorator. I no longer needed to suppress or second-guess the things I wanted to do. I had just as much right to my pursuit of happiness, radical though it might be, as the next guy, or gal, or whatever the hell I was. My new mindset helped me hold my head high and negotiate with Melissa for the things I needed.

That December, I implored her to at least check out the Queen Mary with me, as Rick and Melissa. We decided that, if we ran into anyone, we would just say we were checking out the drag show for a good laugh. With one quick circuit around the club, I realized that I had finally found what I'd been looking for. The QM was everything I liked about THP, and it was open nearly every night of the week. While there, I heard about yet another tranny club in town. It was called Peanuts and was supposed to be even racier. Still, I felt I couldn't risk being seen in drag at either of these places. They were just too close to where I lived and worked.

So I made another trip back to Chicago that winter. As always, Josie was incredibly accepting and so excited to see me. Even when I wasn't dressed up, I could act as feminine as I wanted. It felt so liberating, and Josie got a kick out of it, whereas Melissa had been mostly annoyed. "It's pure fun for her," she explained over the phone, "because you're not *her* boyfriend."

Josie and I raced around the northwest suburbs like Thelma and Louise. I was out in wide-open public for the first time, and things seemed to be going smoothly. Though I hoped it was because everyone thought I was a woman, the truth seemed to be that most people could tell I was a man. Nonetheless, it didn't ruin the great time we were having, gallivanting through the mall, getting our nails done, and shopping at JCPenney, where I bought a new dress to wear to THP that night. Once there, a nice man from Greece took a shine to me, and Josie egged me into asking him to join me, her, and her boyfriend, as my *date* for dinner the following night. He said yes. Thank goodness, he turned out to be such a perfect gentleman.

Although I had a wonderful weekend, I was daunted by the difficulty of having to plan a trip out of town every time I wanted to have a quality experience *en femme*. At the same time, I realized that, although I didn't look exactly like a woman, I didn't look much like my male self either. It would be very difficult for anyone to recognize me in drag, especially if I didn't come up and say hi. Even if someone did, then wouldn't that person be in the same boat, i.e., what was *he* doing in a drag bar? Having convinced myself it was safe to go out in L.A., I then made my case to Melissa, and she tentatively agreed. "Why don't you go to the Queen Mary in February, and we'll see how it goes."

Since the early days of our relationship, I had seen the stress she experienced over me being a crossdresser and had encouraged her to reach out to a friend for support. However, the first time I suggested it, she spoke up sharply with something I had previously felt myself but never put into words. "Once you tell a soul, you lose control of it forever." Only when it became clear that her boyfriend's crossdressing had gone from sexual quirk to passionate pastime, did she decide it was worth the risk.

She confided in Lucy, a long-time friend whom she had felt increasingly fond of over the past year. Rather than judging my sweetheart and urging her to dump me, Lucy promised to support her in whatever way she chose to handle the situation. "Hopefully she'll keep her mouth shut," Lissa fretted, and I assumed she would, with the possible exception of her boyfriend, Derek. Meanwhile, she and I did our best to forget our embarrassing admission so that we could continue to enjoy our time with them as a foursome, as usual.

As we moved forward in the winter of '95—as if there was really one to speak of in La La Land—our careers were going well. Melissa accepted an offer to be a VP at Arista and report to "one of the nicer guys of the music industry." I was most of the way through my first year of residency and settling in. For the first time in my career, I had been given an office. It was a ten-foot square with three white walls and a picture window overlooking a flowerbed and palm trees. I had a desk, along with a chair for me and one for my patients. That was about it except for two shelves over the desk and a file cabinet alongside it.

I loved learning the art of therapy. On my own initiative, I would videotape sessions of me with patients (with their consent) and review the tapes with Dr. Prendergast, my program director. I also savored the chance to think more about those big questions I had encountered on the misty borderlands of mental health with Dr. Posner back in Boston.

First, where is the line between diversity and disease? Unlike some of my more traditional colleagues, I haven't ended up finding anything that's particularly unconventional to be unhealthy; sometimes it is; sometimes it isn't. With experience, I learned that many things can be worth talking about in therapy, but they shouldn't be deemed pathologic unless they impair a patient's personal or professional life or directly harm others.

Second, can people change? Or is accepting your difficulties and learning to cope better the most you can realistically hope for? I learned that that depends on which particular difficulty we're talking about. If a patient struggles with clinical depression, for example, then it can usually be overcome with medication. However, if a patient toils with traits like shyness or a short temper, then there is no proven remedy. These people do best with therapy focusing on how to manage these difficulties and possibly turn them into strengths. As I see it, my job begins with knowing which treatments have been shown to work for which problems and sharing that information.

Unfortunately, like Posner back in Boston, many mental health professionals skip such a discussion and simply begin the type of treatment they're most familiar with.

Third, can you help someone else change? Could I help people overcome their difficulties? As an aspiring psychiatrist, I certainly hoped I could make a difference. And indeed I have, although no one I've seen has experienced meaningful growth or change without a high degree of motivation. Hence, the kernel of truth in the classic joke, "How many psychiatrists does it take to change a light bulb? Just one, but the light bulb has to really want to change." By taking the initiative to see a psychiatrist, a person demonstrates some motivation to work on a problem, and if that runs deep, growth can occur through better coping and change is possible by finding and implementing an effective solution.

At work, I loved the challenge of helping others evolve, while at home I was going through my own metamorphosis. Strangely enough, I was an adult man who felt increasingly like a teenage girl, one who was all too exhilarated by her new powers and prospects. I felt a little out of control until I learned that gay people often compare coming out to being a teenager all over again.[31] It seems to be a natural reaction for anyone facing a world of new possibilities. As I got to know other new girls on the scene, I realized they were going through it too. At least we could experience our growing pains together and, with any luck, have a lot of fun in the process.

Face it, I told myself. *You may be thirty-two years old as a man, but as a woman you're sixteen. Part of you is a girl interrupted. You may not have known it at the time, but she was ready for her first bra when all the other girls were ready for theirs. She wanted to go to the beach in a bikini. She envied the girls who got to cheer for your high school. She wished she could be cute and light and boy-crazy when everyone else was. She's been hidden away for so many years that she doesn't even know what she wants anymore. But she's sure eager to give it all a try.*

Most crossdressers keep that part of themselves locked away for years, perhaps forever, free only to fantasize about what might have been. I was fortunate to liberate myself while I was still somewhat young. I was determined to make up for lost time and explore all the new options available to me. I was tempted to pursue each to excess to find out how much I might enjoy. Like a teenage girl, I was immature and unsure of how to behave as a woman. I needed to develop a whole new set of social skills. Like a teenager, I reveled in my appearance, while simultaneously obsessing about my flaws. Were my arms too strong to go sleeveless? Was I too tall for high heels? Also, like a teenager, I eased my inhibitions with alcohol and celebrated my rites of passage with drugs.

Just that one peek at the Saturday-night crowd at the Queen Mary had left me amazed and intimidated by the talent of L.A.'s transsexuals, drag queens, and even crossdressers. The bar had been raised. There would be no more time to wonder *why* I wanted to do this; it was going to be hard enough to figure out *how,* how to get as good at being a girl as boys get. Though my spirit may have been sixteen, my flesh was thirty-two. Though I still looked young, I knew it couldn't last forever.

8

Arts and Crafts

The relative peace and prosperity in my life from '95 to '96 allowed me to make a thorough study of female impersonation (this chapter), while navigating the transgender night scene (next chapter). Never mind the cost in money or time, I became devoted to doing everything I could to improve how I looked and acted as a woman. To fend off my old Starve It tendencies, I would remind myself of the recurring delight I took in nearly every crossdressing purchase I'd made so far.

Melissa also helped me break away from penny pinching and be more generous to myself. One evening after work, as we were preparing dinner, I approached her with a catalog. "Which of these dresses do you think would look better on me?"

"Well, they're both very nice," she replied, looking them over. "Why don't you get both? They're not terribly expensive."

Despite such good will, I considered myself lucky to have one night out a month and didn't dare push Lissa for more. So I had to make the most of my time between outings. Almost every day, I would find a way to learn more about being a woman. At the hospital and outpatient clinic, I would study every one I came across. And at home, I'd drill on my walk, my talk, and getting my clothes just right. Cultivating my femininity even became worth some sacrifice to my appearance as a man. By now, my legs were always relatively bare from shaving each month and I began to wonder what I could do to make my face prettier and my body more slender.

I couldn't believe how much there was to looking and acting like a stylish woman. Femininity was starting to look like chemistry, a big broad field with its own substantial subdisciplines. But instead of physical chem, organic chem, and biochem, there was hair and makeup, body and fashion, and speech and mannerisms. It was a brand new world full of color, diversity, and, of course, glamor.

Like most men, I had been powerfully affected by it but oblivious to the details. I had never been a guy who cared what the starlets were wearing to the Academy Awards. And though I'd scoffed at all that feminine frippery, I had always in my own secret way adored it: the silky, smooth grip of panties on my bottom, the thrilling flutter of a hemline at my thighs.

As I learned more about women's clothes, I could hardly believe all the choices they had. The proliferation of styles, fabrics, fits, and colors blew my mind. It was like our society consisted of two types of people, the plain sex and the decorated sex, the earthworms and the butterflies. But I now sensed I was no ordinary worm; *I* was a caterpillar.

One day, while shopping at Macy's, I noticed something truly mundane and suddenly realized how big a deal women's clothing really was. While riding the elevator, it struck me that there was one floor for men and four for women. The decoration of distaff was big business! That realization dovetailed with the fact that most women I knew seemed to need about three times as much closet space as their boyfriends and husbands.

When I thought about why, I began to appreciate how much more appearance counted for women than it did for men. People really cared how a woman looked and were often tough about it. Sloppy was not seen as relaxed. Wrinkles weren't seen as distinguished. But if a gal looked good, she could have impact. Men weren't able to take their eyes off her. Women would notice her too, and they'd envy and admire her. From a visual standpoint, being a man just wasn't the same. Although I had always been considered good-looking, I never wielded that kind of wallop. In terms of who had the sex appeal, straight life was a world of haves and have-nots.

One day, I learned how it felt to be a *have*, when I went for lunch at a cruisy gay restaurant near work. The moment I entered the room, I could have sworn about ten guys looked up and checked me out before going back to their soups and salads. I'd never experienced anything like it. Later, so many people stared at me as I returned from the restroom that I figured I must have left my fly wide open. Although their attention struck me like a blast of fresh air, gay men still just weren't my scene. Fortunately, as a woman at places like THP, I had begun to feel that same sort of sex appeal.

Typically in the straight world, women are the sex objects and men are the sex hunters—women the suppliers, men the consumers. A young woman's body is a precious commodity, and to advertise it, she needs clothes that are more shape-showing and skin-baring than men's. Think of the classic man in a jacket and tie with his lovely date in her short sleeveless cocktail dress. Treasure though it may be, a woman can't put her body on display all the time. There are rules that govern how much sex appeal she can show off in different places. It goes without saying that what's okay for the beach is not okay for the nightclub and what looks great at the nightclub is not appropriate for the office. Because women want to look their best in every situation, they have an astounding array of options to draw from. (For more, see Appendix B.)

Though I'd come a long way since my clandestine trip to the Tiffany Club, there was still ever so much to learn about going from man to woman and back again. As I strove to master each step of the process, I sought professional help and scrambled to find solutions that wouldn't jeopardize my life with Lissa.

Of course, looking like a beautiful woman starts with getting your body into the right shape. And that's no easy feat for those of us who happen to be men. I couldn't just put a bra on, stuff it with socks, and suddenly be Sharon Stone. For starters, I was six feet tall and couldn't do a darn thing about it. Women *are* really much shorter than men, and by even more than you might think, because they're typically walking around with two inches of extra heel compared to most men. Statistically, the average American man is 5'9" and the average woman, 5'4".

That's five inches of difference—nearly half a foot—and I was three inches taller than the average man. Without thinking about it, I tried to make up for some of those inches by slouching a little in drag, that is, until I saw how bad it looked on someone else, and it's been tits up ever since.

Although I was always lean for a man, I was a little thick, all around for a woman. So I said farewell to weight lifting and focused exclusively on running. I also learned how to watch what I ate, like Melissa did. Within a few months, I had lost fifteen pounds and managed to keep them off. I even tried Phen-Fen for a while before it was pulled off the market for causing heart damage. All at once, it occurred to me that I had nearly fallen prey to the same insane quest for thinness as my sister Miriam, who had been anorexic for a while in college. I promised myself to be more careful in the future.

I wanted to create a body that spoke to me: soft round breasts that beckoned *Touch me,* a little waist that whispered *Throw your arms around me,* and a bubbly back side that teased *Take me from behind.* One of the nice things about dressing up as a woman was that I got to choose the size of my body parts. I found that C-cup boobs looked best in proportion to my body and that the silicone ones were the most realistic. Although expensive, they felt so real that it was practically a turn-on just to touch them, as they sat on the display counter at Jim Bridges' Boutique. Jim's was one of two tranny shops in the immediate vicinity of the Queen Mary. The other was Lydia's TV Fashions, and soon they were joined by Countessa's Closet.

From Espy and others, I learned the magic ratio for eye-catching curves. For optimal sex appeal, a woman's waist should be small and her hips no more than 40% larger. Otherwise, she might look too thick through the middle or wide through the rear. To achieve these proportions, I learned to cinch my waist in and pad my derriere and hips out, and the effect worked. I saw my shape in the mirror and set off my own sex-object radar.

The process of getting ready routinely began the night before, when I would shave my legs and soon added my armpits. Later, I tried waxing, but it gave me ingrown hairs. I loved my bare legs and was prepared to wear long pants every day as a man if I had to. But could I still wear shorts? Would anyone ask why I didn't have much hair on my legs? Some people would ask and at first I replied, "I've never been very hairy." But because that didn't really explain the stubble on my legs, I soon settled on, "I do it for bicycling," except if I was with friends who were seriously into cycling, then I did it for swimming.

Although Melissa didn't mind seeing me dressed as a woman, doing things to my body was a different story. She missed the hair on my legs. One day, she came back from a therapy session referring to my shaving as "mutilation of the body."

"My body is mine to do with as I like," I countered, then in a kinder tone offered, "Maybe you won't mind my bare but muscular legs once you get used to them."

A month later, when I asked her if women plucked their eyebrows, she tried to avoid the question. When I pushed for an answer, she got exasperated and claimed that they just had naturally thinner brows. I soon learned the truth from a female friend and defiantly began plucking.

Eventually she got okay with my plucked brows, as long as I didn't overdo it. We worked out a similar compromise when it came to me using a beard trimmer to thin the hair on my forearms. Unfortunately, there was no way to be subtle about shaving my chest to accommodate plunging necklines.

I reassured her I wouldn't do anything that would seriously harm my look as a man, and I meant it. But deep inside, I was already curious about hormones and plastic surgery. And the curiosities of today had an uncanny way of becoming the wants and needs of tomorrow.

Typically I would go out on a Friday night and try to leave work early to begin my transformation at a carefully chosen motel. At first, my beauty routine took over two hours and usually began with me in my boxer shorts shaving my face and chest. I preferred to put my makeup on before my girl clothes so that I kept cool and didn't start to sweat. I always applied concealer and foundation first, then moved on to blush and contour, and finished with eyes and lips.

Although most women think of concealer as a little something to cover the dark circles under their eyes, most of us crossdressers see it as the cornerstone of our makeup and the most important trick of the trade. At the CHIC Christmas party, Valerie had discreetly pulled me aside to let me know my beard was showing through my makeup. She explained that even the closest shave doesn't eliminate the blue-black shadow of beard roots beneath the surface. Not only that, but most conventional concealers and foundations aren't strong enough to cover it up, especially for someone like me with light skin and dark hair. That's why the average man can't jump into a dress and wig on Halloween without looking silly.

Though most crossdressers bought their makeup from places like Jim's or Lydia's, Val recommended I call the theatrical makeup shop she used for an appointment. While I made no mention of being a crossdresser over the phone, I tried to explain that privacy was essential. Nervous to start with, I got irritated when I arrived at the store and learned what my privacy would consist of. I was escorted to a beauty station that was off to the side, but still in front of the main picture window, making me clearly visible to patrons and passers-by. I struggled to control my anger, while the store manager explained that she didn't have any beauty stations in back. The only saving grace was that the shop was located far off the beaten path of anyone I knew.

Fortunately Rhonda, the blue-haired makeup artist assigned to me, looked like she had just come from working with the band KISS and couldn't have cared less about me being a crossdresser. She put me at ease with a little small talk, while she set about her craft. Her eyes popped when she saw my midnight-black five-o'clock shadow, and she reached back into her kit for an industrial-strength concealer designed to cover bruises. The thick reddish stuff worked wonders. Then like a painter, she mixed several different colors of makeup on a palette until she'd concocted a foundation to match my face. I ended up feeling so relaxed with her that day that I didn't ask too many questions a month later when she suddenly had to leave the store. She started working out of her home, and I drove there for my next makeover. When I ran out of makeup, I would call her and she would send it to me—but always late. Finally, she flaked on me the night before my first professional photo shoot. As I agonized over my face at Expressly Portraits the next day, I tried to learn a lesson from it. Just because Rhonda or someone like her might accept my lifestyle, that didn't mean I had to put up with unreliability, mediocrity, excess charges, or anything else subpar.

I needed to get more comfortable coming out to people so that, if I started to have doubts about someone I was working with, I could simply move on and find someone else without getting hurt. Within a week, I turned over a new leaf by walking right into one of the best theatrical makeup shops in L.A. and asking for the manager. I let her know I was a crossdresser and explained what I needed. She was a petite, soft-spoken Israeli named Shoshanna, who rose to prominence in the '80s on the set of *Dynasty.* Apparently moved by my earnestness, she took me on personally. Under her tutelage, I learned to apply concealer and foundation in a way that said *elegant for the evening.* I would have preferred *light and natural,* but Shoshanna explained that that just wasn't possible.

To see if I could lighten my need for makeup, I tried laser hair removal. But unfortunately, it was brand new at the time and made my face break out, while the hair grew back in a month the same as it ever was. Then one Sunday morning, Melissa and I woke up and ambled over to our twin bathroom sinks to begin the day. "What do you think about electrolysis?" I inquired, while shaving in my pajamas.

"It doesn't work," she replied, pulling her hair back to get it out of her face. "I've been doing it on my chin for years, and I still have to go back."

"Maybe so, but people in our community find ways to make it work."

"Well, with your heavy beard, it would take forever and hurt like hell. And not only that, it would look weird," she said, starting to get snippy.

I decided not to mention that friends of mine had had their whole faces numbed and been worked on for hours by two electrologists at once. And I still might have given electro a try back then if it weren't for all the time and expense and how upsetting it might be for Melissa.

Once my foundation was done and set with powder, I moved on to blush and contour. Contour powder was especially helpful in toning down the more masculine features of my face. By and large, men have jaws that are wide and angular and chins (also technically part of the jaw) that are long and square. In contrast, women have jaws that are narrow and sloping and chins that are short and pointy. When most people think of the differences between men's and women's bodies, they think *penis vs. no penis* or *breasts vs. no breasts.* But I'll tell you *jaw vs. no jaw* (strong vs. delicate jaw) is my choice for number three.

I learned to use slightly dark contour powder to soften my face by "pushing back" the corners of my chin and jaw. Because passing is more important for transsexuals, those who can afford it go for facial surgery to feminize the jaw and take care of other give-aways, like heavy brow ridges or an obvious Adam's apple. You could look at facial surgery as a sex change for your public self and genital surgery as a sex change for your private self. Often people like to take time off and do it just before transitioning on the job.

With my face painted and recontoured, I then turned to my facial features. I used shadow, liner, and mascara to make the large, expressive eyes you need if you're to go from buck to doe. And I learned to draw my lips full up and down and narrow side to side to create the naturally puckered look of a fair lass in full bloom.

Once fully made up, it was time to get dressed, which of course started with undergarments. For me, like most men, the sight of a woman in pretty lingerie was always more provocative than seeing her naked. Just like a policeman looks more imposing in his uniform, a young woman looks more majestic with the emblems of her power—a bra and matching panties. Deep down, I had always envied that power, and when I pulled up my panties and fastened my bra strap, I could feel it surge through me. And for at least the first few hundred times, I was instantly aroused.

But ultimately, as many of us know, the more time you spend in lingerie, the more you get used to it. Most of the time now, it's like *Hmm, what should I wear under this dress—or these pants? Yeah, that looks right.* Pretty lingerie can still put me in the mood for sex, but it's no longer an end in itself. So eventually, women's underwear has come to mean little more to me than it does to most women. In a way, that makes my interest in women's clothes feel more legitimate. But unlike many in the TG community, I don't believe it has to be nonsexual to be legit, and I sure miss the old roller-coaster ride.

My experience with lingerie is typical of crossdressers who dress up and go out a lot, whereas those who stay closeted may always thrill to a pair of panties. Getting the most pleasure out of what little femininity is within your reach is a process I call savoring. After all, it's the wise prisoner who learns to really, really love that little slice of the outside world he can see from his cell window. Most of the time, though, it's not so conscious a process.

After lingerie, I put on various body parts, like breast forms and hip padding. I also put away various body parts. I minimized my midsection with a corset or a more comfortable waist cincher and learned how to tuck away my private parts so I wasn't betrayed by an unsightly bulge beneath my clothes. Pantyhose helped smooth out the muscles of my legs, and on Melissa's advice, I stuck to simple nude or black. Then I was ready for a dress, or a skirt and top. Eventually I branched out into pants but always something girly, like a colorful pair of capris—preferably zipped up in back or on the side.

Month after month, I was eager to try something new, and that required shopping. Because it was so much easier by phone than in person, I continued to shop mostly from catalogs. With diligence and a tape measure, I figured out my dress size as well as my bra, panty, pantyhose, necklace, bracelet, and ring sizes. Still, I often had to order things in two different sizes so that I could try them on at home and keep the one that fit better. For a while, I made sure people thought I was ordering for Melissa. "*She'd* liked this in light blue. I think she's a size 12 or 14." Eventually I learned to relax and say, "I'd like this in light blue, sizes 12 and 14, please," realizing that the salesperson would politely assume it was for the woman in my life; no explanation was necessary.

My first time shopping as a woman had been when Josie and I had gone to the mall together in Chicago. Then, feeling sure I had been read by the lady at JCPenney, I worried that she might see me as some sort of pervert or straight man doing something he wasn't supposed to do. But regardless of what she thought, she graciously played along with the idea of me being a woman. Nonetheless, I felt compelled to give her an explanation and came up with a white lie, one that I was to use often.

I told her I worked in a drag show. Fortunately she seemed to believe me and didn't have too many questions for me. I liked this cover story, because it meant I was buying a dress for my job, not trying one on for an illicit thrill. Additionally, it meant that I was presumably gay and therefore not doing anything terribly surprising or unexpected. In fact, she was happy to help me out and show me to the ladies' dressing room. There Josie and I tried things on and asked for her advice. Another saleswoman came around to see what was going on and soon joined in the fun. I liked saying that I was a performer, not because I thought there was something wrong with being a crossdresser, but because I was afraid others might think so. I also considered saying I was a transsexual, because that also sounded less sexual and more legitimate than crossdresser.

I was meticulous about the fit of my clothes, and no purchase was final until seen by Melissa and Hagop. Hagop was a tailor who ran a modest dry-cleaning shop across the street from my supermarket. He was a short man with a heavy accent and an ebullient personality. With pulse quickened, I had introduced myself to him a couple weeks before Halloween '94. I showed him my red silk dress and asked if he could design a Red Riding Hood costume around it—for me. He got a kick out of my request and made me a beautiful red hooded cape.

Because I was worried about my secret getting out, I used my middle name, John, instead of Rick. For a while now, I'd been John with anyone I came across in the pursuit of crossdressing, and often just John (with no last name) if at all possible. If other crossdressers needed to know my male name, then too I was John. Soon I was John to a whole number of people.

The week after Halloween I returned to the dry-cleaning shop. "Hagop, you wouldn't believe how much people liked my costume."

"Great," he chuckled with a rolling r.

"Check this out," I insisted, plunking a picture down on the counter.

"John, that's amazing! Look at you and that big wolf. That's so funny."

After sharing a few laughs about the Halloween party at THP, I plucked up my courage. "Hey, do you think you might help me out with this too?" I asked, pulling a little black dress out of my laundry bag. "It's never quite fit right."

Hagop paused for a beat as dawning realization spread across his face. Then he smiled, "Well, let's have a look at it."

That was the beginning of a beautiful relationship. Month after month, Hagop helped me get each new outfit ready for its debut and I would bring it back to him the following Monday for cleaning and often mending and further alterations. He knew women's clothes like the back of his hand. He offered to design a few dresses for me and sent me off to choose fabrics. He coached me on things like combining skirts and tops, camouflaging muscle, and finding the best way to zip myself up.

His encouragement gave me the confidence to wear styles I never would've dreamed of. I showed him pictures of how I looked in each outfit with full hair and makeup and beamed with pride when I told him of the compliments I got in this dress or the drinks bought for me in that dress. The back of his shop became my home away from home, where I would relax, unwind, and sip Armenian coffee.

Once I'd wiggled into a piece of Hagop's handiwork on a Friday night, I was ready for accessories. As if I didn't feel decorated enough at this point, now came the shiny ornaments. On top of everything else, the average woman isn't ready to leave the house until she's put on her earrings, necklace, bracelets, watch, and rings, not to mention a possible anklet or toe ring. Here I exercised restraint and went mostly with silver and gold-plated jewelry. Real gems and gold were much more expensive and not worth it for going out once a month.

And, of course, I couldn't just skip out of the motel in my trusty black Oxfords. Women's footwear, I soon learned, was truly a world unto itself, with a stunning panoply of styles. Like lingerie, ladies' shoes can be powerfully provocative. I couldn't go too crazy here, though, because I was self-conscious about my height. So I stuck mainly to flats. Additionally, the only shoes available in size *thirteen* tended to be either exceedingly sensible or completely outrageous. Unless I looked extremely hard, the heels were either one inch or five.

When it came to purses, I bought a few day and evening bags that coordinated with everything. Most of the time, I just threw my wallet and keys into the smart black handbag I kept pre-packed and ready to go. Maybe if I had been a woman every day for decades—and was otherwise bored with it—then I might have gotten as excited about Prada bags and other status items as my sisters.

It was always easiest to save my wig for last. That way, I didn't have to clip my hair back while doing my makeup, or risk messing it up while pulling on a snug little top. Without a wig, I looked and felt like a man in a dress. But each time I put one on and flipped my hair back, I was all woman. That's why we crossdressers consider it our crowning glory. It became like a magic finger snap that took me back and forth between life as a man and life as a woman.

Even if I donned a wig before getting dressed, it still had the same dramatic impact. Somehow the combination of long hair and no beard says, *This is the face of a woman.* Long hair alone caused people to gape at hippies and wonder, *Is that a woman or a man?* And of course they weren't even using beard cover.

Because it's the first thing someone sees, your hairstyle is vital to the impression you make. In fact, nailing a star's hairdo is the key to impersonating a celebrity. The art of hair is extensive. Not only are there lengths and styles, but textures, colors, highlights, *and* accessories, which include scrunchies, headbands, butterfly clips, big barrettes (worn in back), smaller barrettes and clips (worn on the side), hairpins, bobby pins, and goodness knows what else. I loved learning about all these things as well as hair lore like pony tails for athletics, hair down and hemline up for dates, but hair up and hemline down for the ultimate in elegance. Who'd have thunk?

Unfortunately, even if I grew it out, I couldn't wear my own hair because I had a receding hairline, so I had to go with wigs. As I tried a few on in the back of the shop with Karen, my new Korean wig lady, I discovered that the right or wrong coif could make or break me as a woman. I couldn't just pick out any style or color, I needed ones that would complement and feminize my face. Blonde and red hair were fun to try, but they didn't seem to go with my skin. Wearing short hair, or long hair pulled back or severely layered, could be stylish, but it exposed my relatively angular face and left me looking mannish.

So I settled on a wavy one-length style in a dark chocolaty brown, my natural color, and let it cascade down to my shoulders. Still, I needed bangs and my hair tucked behind my ears to keep my face from looking too long. As I became more certain about what I liked, I invested in human hair wigs, because they had the shiny look and the slippery feel that the synthetics just couldn't simulate.

With purse in hand and hair in place, I was good to go. But then who was I? After just a few times out, I stopped feeling like Rick Novic in a dress. For a while, I felt like a male actor playing a female part. But soon I didn't feel fully that way either. I felt like I was doing something halfway between being myself and portraying a character: I was portraying the female version of myself.

So I was being myself, but in a very unfamiliar way, unfamiliar because I hadn't had the chance to grow into it and make it a part of my routine. Learning to behave in such a foreign way made me feel like an actor and gave me a profound appreciation for their craft. Like a thespian, I had to get used to turning when someone called my character's name. I felt like such a phony when I was out at a club and someone cried, "Alice, Alice," and I would ever so slowly realize, *Hey, she's talking to me.* Once, a friend actually snapped her fingers in my face and said, "Yoo hoo, Alice, don't you even know your own name?"

Also like an actor, I had to work hard to stay in character and think, *What's the right way for me to sit on a barstool?* Or like someone doing improvisational comedy, *What's something cute a girl like me might say to a kind older man?* Eventually I played the role so much that I no longer needed to think about it. I could slip in or out of it without much effort. *Alice* was the way I looked and acted in certain settings, and *Rick* was how I was in others.

To get there, I spent a lot of time learning my part. Most men have no idea what it takes to be a terrific woman. Though I studied every one I came across, I was mesmerized by Melissa. I noticed things about her even she wasn't aware of. I learned to mimic her and strove to be as animated as she was. Although at times it annoyed her, most of the time she found it harmless and funny. Alice may have owed her looks to her parents, but her charisma came from Melissa.

I had to learn how to walk and talk all over again. I discovered that talking like a woman was less a matter of raising your pitch and more a matter of *Lighten up. Brighten up. Be a little more tentative and a little more polite—if you don't mind.*

Some readers may think, *There you go again. Aren't you just generalizing about another part of female behavior?*

To which I say, *Yes, but that's precisely the point.* If you want to sound like a woman, you had better come up with the best generalizations you can and—if anything—overemphasize whatever seems most common and distinctive about female speech. (For more, see Appendix C.)

To do a convincing job of speaking the dialect, I would even change my style of conversation. I noticed how women didn't just communicate; they engaged, they entertained. They spoke a lot about people and feelings and brought up little things I wouldn't think worth mentioning. They were sweet and supportive, at least on the surface, rather than overtly competitive. I emulated them. Just like putting on my breast forms, I would put on my emotions and allow myself to be more perky, playful, sensitive, and sentimental. I'd keep my skepticism in check and remind myself that it was always prettier to be a Pollyanna than a cynic.

It was one thing to talk like a woman, but doing it right required mannerisms. Not naturally effeminate, I fought to keep my elbows in and my wrists limp. It seemed both contrary to my instincts and to years of reinforcement that screamed, *Don't do it. It's social suicide!* I faced the same hurdle when it came to tilting my head, touching my face, and clutching my pearls (touching my sternum when referring to myself).

You may think I'm describing flamboyance rather than femininity. "Maybe *some* people act this way, but not the women *I* know," a female friend once proclaimed, before I brought her attention to the fingers she had just drawn daintily up to her necklace.

"Not the women you know, eh?" I said, arching an eyebrow. No native speaker knows a language quite like somebody who has studied it as an adult. Meanwhile, I worked on other skills like moving my eyes up, down, or to the side without having to move my whole head at the same time. That way, I could master classic expressions like coyly ogling someone from the corner of my eye, seductively lowering my gaze then raising it back up, and impatiently rolling my eyes up and to the side.

Strange as it sounds, *sitting* was a real physical challenge. I noticed how women would sit with their legs together, crossed, or cutely curled under. So one evening, I decided to figure it out for myself. I flitted around our living room dressed only in a waist cincher and black knit skirt, while Melissa sat on the sofa perusing *Billboard* magazine. Settling into the chair opposite her, I first sat with my legs together. It felt a bit strange but wasn't much of a problem. I then crossed my legs at the thigh and then the ankle, while her eyes remained resolutely on her trade journal. "Uh, Liss," I said to get her attention, "does it look better if I sit this way?" I crossed my legs at the thigh. "Or this way?" I crossed them at the ankle.

"Most women sit the first way," she said, barely looking up.

"But I'm afraid if I sit this way, my thighs will look like two tree trunks on top of each other," I explained, while demonstrating.

"You know, you're kind of right," she said, begrudgingly looking over in my direction. "I guess you'll have to cross at your ankles. It's a little more demure, but it looks fine. While we're on the subject, do you have to do so much practicing when I'm around?"

"No, but it's like I'm learning tennis and you're a club pro. A little help from you goes a long, long way."

"Listen, I know you think I'm *fabulous* and all, but really you've got to cut me a few breaks."

"Okay," I conceded in response to the seriousness in her tone and headed upstairs to our bedroom. There I pushed a small couch in front of the full-length mirror and tried to lounge with my legs curled under me and slightly off to the side. I felt like I was bending myself into some pretzel of a yoga position. Nonetheless, it was such an adorable way to sit that I stretched out for months so that I could hold that pose for my next photo session.

I was so focused on honing my womanly skills that I would even practice some face touching and leg crossing at work. Thank god, I was a new resident in a big hospital where few people knew me or expected me to act straight. The anonymity was liberating.

Back home, I started to work on my walking. I struggled to sashay rather than stride. At first, I tried to walk like I always did but wiggle my butt as I went along. It was pathetic. Espy told me to keep my legs together and lead more with my pelvis than my shoulders, then my butt would wiggle along automatically. It took me months to fully understand and implement her advice.

Although my crossdressing might draw fire from Melissa, my faith in her proved difficult to shake. For a while now, I had been convinced that she was the best possible person for me. I could never do better, only equal. And even then, it would be difficult for me and whoever else to reconstruct the kind of relationship she and I already had. So I never thought of jumping ship, only working harder to stay afloat as we felt the stress and strain of my female ambitions.

Birthdays were tricky for me, because Melissa would ask what I wanted and I would try to be honest with myself and her. For my thirty-third birthday, what I wanted more than anything else was to get rid of my mannish hooked nose. For most of my life, I hadn't thought much about plastic surgery and considered it frivolous, except if you truly hated a part of your body as much as my sister Kathy had hated her nose. When we were teenagers, she'd had to cry her way through my father's conviction that plastic surgery was too risky and vain. After much hemming and hawing, her nose job went without a hitch and her self-consciousness was relieved.

Now that it looked like I would be spending a good chunk of my time in female form, I wanted to look my best too. I explained the situation to Melissa one evening, as we were taking turns warming up frozen dinners in the microwave.

"Even if it's relatively safe, I still don't want you to," she said, cracking open a window and lighting a cigarette, as she sometimes did when she felt overwhelmed. "I like your nose. I don't want you going around with a fake nose."

"Who ever gave you control over what I do with my body?" I countered. "I don't give you a hard time about your smoking. A lot of men would."

My love looked momentarily stunned by my counterattack.

"You know how long I've been dealing with this crossdressing stuff," I pleaded, "and how important it is to me to be the best crossdresser I can be. Why do you have to make it your life's ambition to keep me from that?"

"I just think you're making a mistake. Nose jobs always look so obvious."

"That's because you only notice the obvious ones."

"Just look at your sister Kathy. No one has a nose that little and perfect."

"Okay, but what about Miriam and Laura?"

"What about them?" she asked, shifting from emphatic to confused.

"They've had their noses done too," I said with a flourish, as Melissa began to see that plastic surgeons were perfectly capable of making natural-looking noses. "But, what do you *really* want, other than to block me from what I want?"

"Well," she said taking a long drag on her cigarette, "I don't really have any, uh, special requests—not like your crossdressing."

"There must be something you've always wanted." I was determined.

"I've always wanted to feel part of a couple. I'd like you to help me support that new Blue Grass band we signed. And I'd like you to fly to Maine with me for my cousin Ted's wedding."

"Your second cousin."

"Whatever, and I'd like you to do it without any grumbling."

After a moment's thought, I agreed, pleased with the notion of more participation for more freedom.

"You're such a good-looking man. Why do you have to do it?" Melissa emoted, still desperate to stave off disaster. "You'll end up looking too feminine."

"C'mon," I urged, "just taking the hook out will improve my looks either way."

"But you're the only man I'll ever have," she said with resignation, as her voice faltered and her eyes grew damp.

Moved to the edge of tears myself and sensing that she was right in a way I couldn't fully understand, I gently lifted her chin up and promised to simply ask my surgeon for a straight nose, not say that I was a crossdresser, not ask for one that would also look good when I went out as a woman.

Melissa replied with a weepy smile and a warm embrace.

Stuffed and bandaged for days after my surgery, I felt the deep satisfaction of enduring hardship in pursuit of a dream. Though bruised for a week, the fact that I would soon see my new nose gave me that same surge of optimism that I had felt with each teenage birthday. Things were only getting bigger and better, and the sky was the limit. *Better be careful,* I thought, *I could easily make a habit of this.* Finally, as my unhooked nose emerged from the swelling, I looked much the same as a man, but as a woman I wouldn't have to worry about my profile ever again.

Not long after recovering from surgery in early '96, I hoped to make my body more androgynous by taking a low dose of female hormones. Because I didn't want to give my girlfriend the chance to object this time, I snuck forward very cautiously on my own. I even had some sperm set aside at a fertility clinic because I hoped to have children some day and wanted to guard against the unlikely event that I might become infertile. Secretly, I had been on half the transsexual doses of estrogen and a testosterone blocker for two months when I came home from work one day to find her pacing in the living room. "What's the Tyler Clinic?" she asked gravely.

I felt a wave of panic and realized I'd have some explaining to do. Feeling flushed, I whipped my jacket off and threw it over the back of the couch. "How do you know about the Tyler Clinic?"

"I know I shouldn't have done it, but your credit card bill was just lying out on your desk. I'm really sorry. I shouldn't have looked. But what is it?"

"You're right. You shouldn't have looked . . . But since you have, let me tell you—"

Is it awful news? Is it going to scare me?" she asked, with her fingertips pressed anxiously up to her lips.

"No, or at least it shouldn't. I didn't want to trouble you with this. But I went on a low dose of hormones to soften my skin and round out my muscles."

"What does this mean?" she asked, as her eyes widened. "Do you want to grow breasts and be a transsexual?"

Although it was the obvious thing to ask, I felt humiliated and stung by her question. "No, that's why I'm only taking a small dose. You know I'm trying to do anything I can to improve my look as a crossdresser."

"Is that all there is to it? Because I'd rather know now. Cut my losses short, so to speak."

"I'm not planning on going TS. If I were, I would tell you."

"But how do I know you won't feel that way in the future?"

"I don't have an easy answer for you. Sometimes I worry that I'm TS, but it just doesn't feel like something I want to do."

"You may feel that way now," she asserted, "but you told me when we started that you'd never want to dress in public. It's not that I think you lied; it's just that you don't really know where this process is going."

"Fair enough. But I know a lot of what it might be like for me as a TS, and I can tell you I'm not especially tempted." Melissa was about to say something, but I held my hand out to stop her. "You're right. I can't give you a complete guarantee. But I can't guarantee that I won't die on the freeway sometime either."

"I guess that's all I can hope for—for now."

"I promise you if I ever change my mind, you'll be the first to know."

"Oh, that makes me feel better," she said with a roll of her eyes. "I guess this is what I get for being a snoop. I won't be doing it again anytime soon. I know I kind of brought this on myself, but still, it scares me."

"You know how much I would love to share everything with you," I said softly. "But for our own peace of mind, we've seen that it's better for me to handle certain things on my own."

She nodded silently and seemed relieved. Nevertheless, we continued to feel uptight around each other. For the first time since I'd come out to her back in Chicago, I worried that she might finally get fed up and leave me. I was on my best behavior for days, and things seemed to settle down.

I discreetly continued on hormones, and after a few months my sex drive waned. It's not that I minded sex; I still liked it very much. I just didn't feel like initiating it. "I don't know if you're still taking those hormones," Lissa warned, "but I miss the old lusty you. Our sex life has gone from amazing to adequate." Because her happiness was as important to me as my own, I decided to drop the hormones if my drive dipped any further.

It didn't, yet after a few more months, my nipples became tender and prominent enough to make me self-conscious when I took my shirt off at the beach. I didn't like looking weird like that. I was a lean, athletic guy who could pull off shaved legs and a hairless chest, but protuberant nipples? I didn't think so. I tried to back down slowly on my doses, but my nipples didn't return to normal until I had stopped the testosterone blocker and all but the slightest bit of estrogen.

"For once, you're taking a step back," Melissa said with a big grin, when I explained the situation to her.

"How 'bout that, eh?" I bantered back. "But thanks for backing off and letting me figure it out for myself."

By now, femininity had become my art. I wanted to see how far I'd come with it, and nothing could show progress better than pictures. In mid '95, I had gone to Expressly Portraits and was fairly pleased with the results— despite Rhonda having flaked on me. But by early '96, I wanted to rise above the level of mall photographers. Tired of sneaking around doing things on the cheap, I decided that I deserved the same nice things as any other woman of my station and insisted on the same kind of professional photographer for my next big photo session as my sister Laura had had for her wedding.

In fact, getting ready for it felt like getting ready for a wedding. I planned outfits and poses for months. I tore pages out of magazines and catalogs and did sit-ups by the score. Then I chose dresses and went to fittings with Hagop. I decided to do the shoot at home, so I had to make sure everything looked just right. More used to temperamental movie stars, Jordan, the photographer, got such a kick out of me that he asked if his girlfriend could come along. Because they and Shoshanna would be coming over, I wanted to offer refreshments and had to figure out what to serve. Finally, that morning,

I went for a manicure and made sure Melissa wasn't having second thoughts, before doing my best to relax and enjoy my big day.

Sure, it was expensive to bring Jordan and Shoshanna to our apartment, but there was simply nothing else I wanted half as much at the time. Why else was I working and earning? Like a bride on her wedding day, I loved being the focus of everyone's attention and the fact it was my turn to be queen for a day. But also like a bride, I could get hung up on wanting everything to be perfect. At those times, Melissa encouraged me to take a sip of wine and loosen up a bit.

"You don't want to look tense in your pictures," she cautioned and then stepped up and sweated the details for me. She was my second pair of eyes and had a great sense of what I would want to see in a picture and what I wouldn't. She had already taken so many of me that she knew my angles better than any photographer could and of course cared more. She knew how things like a wrinkly skirt or a stray lock of hair would drive me batty later on, so she would stop Jordan from time to time to tidy me up. I knew there wasn't a thing in it for her and loved her all the more for it.

Nervous and excited about my pictures, I couldn't wait to see them. How would I look, with my new nose, better clothes, and countless other improvements? How real and how pretty. Finally, they came back. I was overjoyed by the results. I looked at a picture like the one on the cover of this book and saw someone who was all woman, but still very much me.

I constructed a little game to see how real I looked. I mixed one of my girl pics in with some recent pictures from a family vacation. You might call it the transgender equivalent of Russian Roulette. Over Mexican food, I showed them to a guy I played beach volleyball with. As my heart rose in my throat, I tried to be nonchalant. "Those are my parents. That's my sister Laura and her husband. That's my sister Alice." Suddenly, I regretted what I had done, but the die had been cast. I quickly placed another picture on top of the stack and concluded with, "And there's my sister Kathy."

"So you have three sisters," he replied, "nice looking family." I was dying to tell him what I had gotten away with and ask for a high five. But I didn't dare, for there was no telling how he might react. Although I sensed I could keep winning this game with other friends, it was far too nerve-racking. Nonetheless, my Beautiful Woman Fantasy had come true, at least on paper.

Eventually I got a pretty good handle on why crossdressers love pictures—or at least why this one does. Many of us find that a large part of our true self has to remain hidden except when we're actually crossdressing. Looking at pictures gives us lots of little opportunities to express and appreciate our female side. If we were able to be—and to see—that side every day, then we'd probably feel much more like TSs or GGs do about photography; i.e., it's okay, but looking good and feeling good is where it's at. But because we can never get enough girl time, pictures help us stretch it out, like snapshots from an all-too-short vacation. (A few of my favorites may be found at www.aliceingenderland.com.)

With all the improvements I had made to my look as a woman, I was again eager to sally forth into public to see if I would pass. Striving to stay calm, I slid into the Glendale Galleria in a jean shirt and leggings with Valerie at my side. I wondered if we'd be seen simply as two lady friends out for an afternoon of shopping, and it sure felt like it when we were both addressed as ma'am on entering Nordstrom. Our luck continued, as we seamlessly slipped into one dressing room after another. By the time I escaped to the parking lot with my purchases, I was so pleased with myself that I didn't dissect the more subtle feedback I'd been getting all along. But after a few more trips to the mall (one of them solo), my heart sank as I began to understand it.

Most people would walk by busy with their own cares and concerns. That was passing. But often, a few heads would turn. That was looking good. But then, they might double take before going back about their business. That was being read. Occasionally someone would tug a friend's arm to signal, *Hey, look over there.* That, of course, was obvious. After being read by a few people in every crowd, I had to face facts—I did not pass.

It happened because I attracted attention, and with attention came scrutiny. I couldn't help it, and in a way, it was a compliment. If I may toot my own horn, I was a slender brunette standing six feet tall—quite a sight under any circumstance. If I had been short, round, and gray, I'm sure I could've coasted by, under everyone's radar. As it was, I caught people's eye, and then, I suppose, they noticed that something didn't look right, maybe my strong jaw or heavy makeup. And instantly they'd begin to doubt whether I was really a woman or some kind of man trying to look like one.

After some thought, I realized that passing in pictures had given me a false sense of confidence. I passed in all my pictures, because Jordan had specifically avoided shooting me from angles that brought out my masculine features. Even then, I still didn't pass in about half of his originals. But of course, I had thrown those out and forgotten about them. To pass in public, you have to look womanly from all angles.

I felt bad because most crossdressers I knew claimed that they passed. Many assured me that I would too, if I only did things right. Ultimately I learned the truth. Even if you're relaxed, casual, walking the walk, and talking the talk with a tall GG at your side, you still may not pass. Most crossdressers don't pass.

Most non-Asian transsexuals don't pass either, not without facial feminization surgery. I mean this as no slight. I think of plastic surgery as a modern-day miracle, and one that's especially important for people in our community. I am, after all, a transgendered Jewish girl with a nose job and proud of it.

Obviously some crossdressers pass, but why do so many others think they do? Maybe it's just plain more fun to think so. After all, we aren't men who fantasize about being crossdressers; we're men who fantasize about being women. It's more of a thrill to believe you're living out your dream rather than a close-but-not-quite version of it. Maybe I should have kidded myself about passing, but that's never been my style and there's so much more to be learned by staying in touch with reality.

Often crossdressers think they pass because their friends say so. At a gathering of CDs, telling someone she passes has become a way of saying, "I like you and want you to feel good about yourself." It's not a way of saying, "I'm not sure whether I'm talking to a man or a woman right now," and even less a way of saying, "Now which of these crossdressers is your husband?" Being passable has suffered the equivalent of grade inflation. *Passable* now seems to equate with *attractive and appropriate looking.*

Traditionally crossdressers have seen getting read as a disaster, and perhaps in some places it is. Yet in most of these United States, you might *feel* like you've been caught committing a crime, but you haven't—at least not since the 1960s. Maybe it's just been my luck, but I've never been harassed by hateful rednecks or overzealous security guards.

For me, getting read was like bumping up against a hard physical wall that limited how fully I might live out my fantasies. I would have loved to have been one of those rare little stealth crossdressers. I would have loved to be completely believable as a man *and* as a woman and was amazed by how close I could come. But I knew I'd never have the true experience of being a girl at a bar, on a date, or at a bridal shower. No matter how good I got, I'd always be a *crossdresser* at a bar, on a date, or even at a bridal shower. It was just too bad, but all too true.

The stakes of not passing are even higher for transsexuals. I know very few people who've gone through transition and surgery so that they could go through life known as a *transsexual.* Most TSs wish to be known simply as a woman like any other woman. It can be a crushing disappointment to find that some aspect of your anatomy or bearing betrays you and forces you to live day after day as a real curiosity item and very alternative kind of person. One *good* thing about not passing is that it forces you to grow as a person. If I had always passed with ease, I probably would've continued to think I was doing something bad but getting away with it. I wouldn't have been spurred on to get comfortable and even proud of being a crossdresser. Similarly, transsexuals who've made peace with the fact they aren't just like any other women tend to be better adjusted. A patient of mine once nailed it on the head when she smiled playfully and said, "Dr. Novic, I'm *not* like all those generic—oops, I mean genetic—girls. I'm special!"

Another good thing about not passing, at least for me, was that it freed me to wear whatever I liked. I didn't have to worry whether this skirt showed too big a thigh or this top, too wide a shoulder. I didn't have to worry about giving up the ghost; it had already been given up. But whether it came to primping or passing, the most important thing was that I never stopped looking for ways to improve my crossdressing or my attitude about it. Thus prepared, I approached each night on the town with a smile and bright sense that *Anything can happen and probably will!*

9

Into the Night

While honing my craft in the mid '90s, I was also stepping out into L.A.'s astonishing transgender night scene. I first dared to go out dressed in my new hometown when I returned to the Queen Mary in February '95. Parking directly behind the club, I was able to slip discreetly through the back door and into the soft red glow of the back bar. There John, the bartender, introduced himself, fixed me a free drink, and reached up to ring a bell. "We have a new girl here tonight," he announced. "Let's all give a great big welcome to Alice." One by one, the regulars came up and wished me well: Brenda, the tough-looking TS who watched the back door, Debbie, the GG dwarf who managed the club, and Tina, a barely readable Valley girl in sexy cut-offs. Two dowdy crossdressers and a man at the opposite end of the bar stopped their conversation and raised their glasses to me. Yet, despite another warm reception from my peers, I was still nearly as tense and tight-lipped as I'd been back in Boston.

The Queen Mary was the jewel in the crown of the Southern California transgender scene. People I knew from Chicago and, in fact, t-people from all over the world would book trips to L.A. just so they could see the club—and here it was, practically on my doorstep. It had a storied past beginning in 1962 (the year before I was born), when the building was purchased from none other than Mae West. In a recent interview, owner Robert Juleff told what it was like back then:

> It was totally different. Drag was illegal . . . In the beginning, our showgirls had to wear male attire underneath their female clothing, so when you walked in the door, you could tell right away that this was a boy in drag. Our kids wore black slacks, white shirts, ties, and boys' shoes. Then they put girls' clothes on over that. So it was quite different. But all in all, the shows were just as good then as they are now . . . It became very popular very quickly.[32]

But drag show notwithstanding, he went on to explain, "Crossdressers and drag queens didn't frequent the bar in significant numbers until the late 1970s, because, after all, they would have risked arrest and jeopardized the club's liquor license." By the '80s, it evolved into a rather rare gem, a true blue full-time transgender nightclub. Although t-girls flocked to gay bars with drag shows in every major city, only in places like L.A. and New York were there enough of us to take a place over. By the time I arrived, the QM had been tranny for over a decade.

In truth, it was like two clubs in one. The front, known as the show room, was a sit-down club with a popular drag show, with acts consisting of comedians, celebrity impersonators, and striptease artists. Eventually a couple of hunky male strippers were thrown in for an extra thrill—although all male and "female" strippers stopped tastefully at their tight little thongs. Weekend after weekend, the tables filled with tourists, gay men, and bachelorette parties.

The back belonged to us crossdressers, transsexuals, and our admirers. It had a softly lit wood-paneled barroom with Olivia prints on the wall, a small almost completely mirrored dance floor, and a fenced-in patio, which we used year round. In the early evening, it felt like an intimate place to catch up with friends, while later on it could bustle with excitement and intrigue.

Eager to find someone to pal around with, I talked with Tina for a while at the back bar. She looked soft and adorable, with red hair and freckles, and stood an enviably tiny five feet four inches. Although her arms were the slightest bit thick, she looked even more real than Valerie, so convincing that I had to ask, "Are you TV or TS?"

"TS," she said, in a way that seemed both tentative and proud, as she leaned in and, with a tug at her neckline, gave me a peek at where two unmistakable breasts disappeared into the top of her bra. After two years of hormones and electrolysis, she explained, her body had reached such a point between male and female that at times she got read as a woman even when she wasn't trying. She worked as a man designing movie posters and video boxes but needed to butch it up during the week by wearing tight T-shirts under flannel shirts and baggy pants so as not to look too voluptuous. Though she loved her work, she couldn't wait for each Friday night, when she would convert back to womanhood and stay that way until Monday morning.

We really seemed to hit it off, and she positively bubbled with all the fun things we might do together. Gleefully I realized that if she meant even half of what she said, I might have just won the lottery. Before racing off to Peanuts, she very kindly made sure I had others to talk to at the Queen Mary. As the night wore on, I was struck by the commonality I felt with most of the crossdressers and many of the transsexuals I met. They were a lot like the people at Tri-Ess, CHIC, and Ladies' Knight, except a bit younger and wilder, like me. We all seemed to share the same hopes, dreams, and concerns. Finally I felt like I fit in.

Days later, Tina followed our conversation up with a phone call, and we started getting together each month on my night out. True to her Valley girl image, she was in fact from the San Fernando Valley and, just after high school, had discovered the joy of going out to clubs in feline form. Having done it off and on for ten years, she knew the scene well and enjoyed taking new girls under her wing.

I slowly came around to tell her my male name and the fact I was a psychiatry resident. Still, I went by John rather than Rick and left my last name out of it, as a safeguard against gossip—or even blackmail. Perhaps that was a bit paranoid, but I preferred to err on the safe side. Having been around crossdressers for years, my tiny new friend understood that we could be touchy like that and let me spill things at my own pace. Though publicly she would say she was a preop transsexual, privately she confided that she wasn't sure what she was. She mostly dated men but still seemed interested in women and pined for her ex, a lovely MTF who lived much as she did. Although I came to realize that she once had a rougher side, she now came off as chatty and insecure in an endearing way.

She was amused by how I had to plan things nearly a month in advance but humored me nonetheless. Generally we'd meet at the Queen Mary at seven or so, go out for dinner, then head back to the QM for cocktails followed by Peanuts for dancing. We'd go for "breakfast" when it closed, and I might not get to bed until four.

Although I had dined in drag a few times out of town, Tina started me out at gay restaurants in town, knowing they would be easier. Everyone's favorite was the Venture Inn, just down the street from the Queen Mary. Straight people rarely strayed in, and the staff *expected* to see a few trannies every Friday and Saturday night.

From there, she encouraged me to try the kind of mainstream restaurants I would ordinarily prefer. The first time we were about to give it a try, though, I started to freak out as I thought about how utterly improper and outrageous it was for a man like me to flounce right into a restaurant full of normal people—possibly even a few I knew—in a *dress*. Tina noticed the quiver in my voice and insisted that I have a good stiff drink at the QM before stepping out into the fray. We could take her car over to Teru Sushi, a tony Japanese restaurant down the street. There, I should just do my best to relax and follow her lead.

I've been to a straight place before, I reminded myself, as we drove down Ventura Blvd. *It'll be fine.* I smiled as I thought of how Melissa and I had hooked up with Josie and her boyfriend and made Olive Garden feel like our own private Halloween party. Even one dinner companion had proved enough support for me at gay restaurants, provided she wasn't as anxious as I was. Melissa had been great, but she was always a little nervous about the two of us being recognized. Tina was even better, though at times, she was concerned that my getting read would end up getting her read as well. Still, I couldn't imagine myself ever feeling confident enough to swish right up to a maitre d' with a nervous newbie like me in tow.

Tina did just that when we arrived at Teru Sushi, and as the hostess walked us through the thick of the teeming restaurant, a samurai chef greeted us with a booming blast of Japanese. In shock, I watched as my teeny pal turned and looked him straight in the eye. "And the same right back to you!" she replied, in a cheerful voice that made me think of Little Orphan Annie standing up to Daddy Warbucks. Bit by bit, I was beginning to understand that most people don't know what to think when they see a crossdresser. They'll take their cue from you. If you send signals that say, *This is fun and normal for me,* they'll tend to think the same.

For now though, I felt my gait stiffen as we continued on through a gauntlet of tables on our way to the backyard Zen garden. My gaze remained resolutely focused on where I was going. If people were aghast and staring, I would just as soon not know.

Easing into my seat, I started to take off my little black cardigan, when I noticed a man at a nearby table of four gazing at my emerging arm. Realizing his faux pas, he hastily looked away. Nevertheless, I put my sweater back on and felt a wave of self-consciousness that spread to other aspects of my appearance. Was my short fuchsia dress riding too high up my leg as I sat? Horrified, I placed my napkin down over my hemline and hoped it didn't look too bizarre.

"Can I get you guys something to drink?" the waiter asked, and we ordered Kirin Lights. I was miffed that he had referred to us as "you guys," but Tina told me not to be ridiculous.

"How is Melissa handling your crossdressing and all?" she inquired, after our drinks arrived and we ordered an assortment of sushi.

I made relatively short work of her question, preferring not to linger there too long on a party night. "What exactly were you hired to do at the Dressed To Thrill Banquet?" I asked, switching the subject as our spicy tuna arrived.

As Tina entertained me with her adventures as fetish model and under-the-tablecloth leg massager, I found myself all too soon with an empty glass and a full bladder pressing up against a tight corset. I tried to ignore it, but it soon became painful. I wasn't going to make it through dinner without going to the bathroom. Anxiously I asked if she would go to the ladies' room with me.

"We can't just abandon our table," she explained. "Go ahead."

"You know, I read somewhere that legally you're supposed to ask the manager first before using the ladies' room."

"Oh, you're such a geek sometimes, Alice. Just do your thing. It'll be fine." Rising from my chair, I felt the duct tape that was pulling the skin on my chest into the appearance of cleavage and told myself, *For all anyone knows, I'm a transsexual, just like Tina. L.A.'s a big city. People here know transsexuals go about their lives just like everybody else. I'm sure that's how I come off.*

Fortunately there was no line to get stuck in outside the ladies' room, nor was there anyone in it, as I swiftly settled into one of the two stalls. For some reason afterward, I couldn't resist fixing my lipstick in the mirror by the sink.

Just then, a gorgeous young girl came through the door and began fussing with her hair alongside me. While I did my best to lose myself in the lines of my lipstick, she turned to me with a knowing smile and said, "You look great."

"You too," I replied, in a tone that I hoped didn't betray too much boyish zeal, as I threw my lipstick into my purse and hustled out of the danger zone.

Just like that first night at Teru Sushi, people were generally polite at the fancier restaurants Tina and I chose. Not that we were snobs, but beskirted and bejeweled as we were, we didn't exactly feel like McDonalds. So we rarely ran into mean-spirited teenagers or young children with anxious, overprotective parents.

Besides, women's lib had proclaimed for years that it was all right for a woman to do anything men did. So I reasoned it was okay for me to do something women did—get dolled up and dine out.[33] Thus, I justified my right to dine anywhere in a dress on the basis of men's lib, or simply *What's fair for the goose is fair for the gander.*

But as time went on, I began to doubt how much of a gander I really was. Increasingly, I felt like I was half woman and therefore had the same right to go out and look pretty as any other woman—whether men shared that right or not.

"Did you know that I'm half woman," I announced one night, while *mi amiga* and I were sipping Margaritas at a gourmet Mexican restaurant. "What the hell are you talking about?" she replied.

Giggling, I pulled a family picture from my purse and proclaimed, "See, one of my parents was actually a woman."

From dinner it was off to the Queen Mary and Peanuts, where Tina would introduce me to all the cool people she knew. Although I stood eight inches taller, I was thrilled to be her "little" sister. And though she hesitated to corrupt me, I pleaded for more. So she included me in fetish balls and kinky after-hours parties. Once, we stopped by to see a hooker pal of hers on our way to Peanuts, and her wayward friend wished us off with, "Have a good time and don't do anything—without getting paid for it."

I couldn't believe what I had just heard but nervously kept my mouth shut so no one could see how much of a square I was. *Toto, I've a feeling we're not in Tri-Ess anymore.*

From the moment I first peered inside, Peanuts struck me as foreign, glamorous, and frightening. After all, Tina had said that, just the prior week, a screaming fight had erupted, with one girl ripping the other's wig off and both being unceremoniously escorted out the door. It was a club of velvet curtains, cast-iron fixtures, flickering shadows, and mysteries I wouldn't fathom for years.

It took place every Monday and Friday night at Club 7969 on West Hollywood's notorious Santa Monica Strip. There a tightly-quartered island bar overlooked a large dance floor surrounded by cocktail tables, while a smaller adjoining room contained a back bar, pool table, and cozy banquettes. By the stroke of midnight, both rooms filled with sexy-looking queens and their ravenous admirers.

Who are these people? I thought as I gazed out on the crowd for the first time. Very few of the girls were American. Most were slightly built youngsters from Latin America and Southeast Asia, and the air was full of Spanish and an exotic language I later learned was Tagalog, the native tongue of the Philippines. They all looked so believable that, once, when I dared bring a radiologist friend along, she got impatient. "So where are the crossdressers?" she asked.

"No, Nicole," I answered, trying not to laugh, "the question is *Where are the real girls?* You're the only one I see in this entire room." Basically, the Peanuts girls looked so good that you could only tell they were TGs by their confident swagger and unabashed exhibitionism. If I hadn't been involved with Melissa, I might have been curious to date one of these beauties as Rick.

I found them so intriguing, and none that I saw seemed to be the foreign equivalent of a crossdresser like me—assuming such people existed in other cultures. (Years later, I learned that they do exist in Latin cultures, but they're usually family men so deeply closeted that they'd never venture out into a public place like Club 7969, at least not in female form.)[34] The ladies I spoke to at Peanuts referred to themselves as gay, but they weren't at all like the headpiece-and-tail feathers drag queens I had seen on TV coverage of Gay Pride parades. With boobs and butts jiggling, I figured they were transsexuals—which made me think, *Are most of them pre-op or post-op?*

"In here," a buzz-cut Chicano man in oversized clothes explained, "it's the best of both worlds!" and referred to the girls as "she-males." They, however, called themselves *reinas*.

"Who are these girls and why are there so many of them?" I asked Tina. Although she was friendly with a lot of them, she couldn't tell me, because she was really much tighter with the other white chicks. I asked a few some questions in English and even rudimentary Spanish but was frustrated by loud music and tough-girl attitudes. I tried to make friends but ran into flakiness and a real language barrier.

Nevertheless, my curiosity was piqued. Eventually, after a heart-to-heart with a Spanish-and-gay psychologist colleague, I gathered that effeminacy, sexual passivity, and drag have long been traditional for a certain portion of gay men in Latin culture. "*Reina* means drag queen," he said, "but more of a Latin-style drag queen." (For more, see Appendix D.)

A lot of the Peanuts girls were prostitutes, and they could get quite aggressive. Just once, I went to the club as a man, and it wasn't ten minutes until a dusky brunette with barely covered implants came up, grabbed my crotch, and said, "You like?"

Often the pros resented the competition that could come from an amateur like me giving away a freebie. And the word was that some of the more desperate ones didn't have any qualms about stealing, even from each other. I found out firsthand when my purse was snatched off a nearby table once while I was dancing. I found it later, devoid of cash under some wet paper towels in the ladies' room trash. Thank goodness, my car keys were still there.

Still, I was curious about these girls and finally connected with one named Juanita, who—unlike the others—was affable and approachable. Often after finishing up late at the hospital, I would drive over to the corner of Santa Monica and La Brea and shoot the breeze with her as she worked.

At twelve thirty, the Peanuts dance floor would clear and a racy drag show would begin. The five showgirls would then take turns offering inspired impersonations of Madonna, Whitney Houston, and more, while stripping down as far as pasties and G-strings. Tipping, there, had evolved to a fine art. As a friend performed, the pros would take turns sashaying out onto the dance floor to pass her a bill in a tantalizing moment of girl-on-girl action. It was like a paid ad for the tipper. Often a man might wait for a favorite performer to take the floor and then emerge from the crowd, pull a wad out of his pocket, and shower her with dollar after dollar. After the show, the dance floor would pack until two, when the lights flicked on.

Rubbing their eyes, people would stagger out to their cars and caravan down the boulevard to one of the strangest sights I've ever seen. By day, it was a diner called the Yukon Mining Company in a very nondescript strip mall. But by midnight, it would come alive, and by two a.m. on a Friday or Monday, it would absolutely hop, as everyone from Peanuts came over to grab a table for "breakfast" or to turn tricks in the big empty parking lot. Out of nowhere, a parade of cars driven by lone Latin men would turn into the lot. One by one, they would cruise by, exchanging stares with every girl they passed. Feeling a bite on the line, a gal might slink up to the window, haggle a bit, and jump in.

According to Juanita (and a colleague of mine who interviewed a number of these ladies), most of the men were interested in blowjobs, but surprisingly, more wanted to give than receive. A John could satisfy such a craving for about fifty dollars without leaving the comfort of his own car. He and his new feline friend just had to find a quiet residential street or back alley. I couldn't understand why such macho men would want to give oral sex, but I was to learn more later on. Sometimes a man might insist on intercourse (generally as the insertive partner), and that was about a hundred dollars plus the price of a cheap motel room—if he didn't care to take the apple of his eye home with him.

The drive-through marketplace would be in full swing by two thirty, when an ocean fog would roll in and limit visibility, making everything all the more surreal. I loved watching the scene unfold over scrambled eggs and fresh cut fruit. If Tina and I stayed long enough, we'd see some of the same girls who'd been squired off earlier now dropped off to rejoin the action.

Once in a while, police cars would drive through to break it all up. Once, unfortunately, I saw a girl forced to lie face down on the pavement, while the cops put cuffs on her. Around then, famous—and married—comedian Eddie Murphy faced a scandal when he was arrested for picking up a Yukon girl. Not caught in *flagrante delicto,* he was able to tell police, and later the press, that he thought she was just a hitchhiker. And thus, he emerged relatively unscathed. Good for him. Rumor had it he'd always been respectful—and generous.

I was scared, but also a little thrilled, by the idea of being mistaken for a prostitute. Unless I kept my eyes on the asphalt, I'd get propositions just walking from my car to the restaurant and back. And it wasn't over when I got back on the road. Once, I stopped at a nearby red light and a black Cadillac pulled alongside me. When the swarthy-looking man inside motioned me to roll down my window, Gidget here thought he might be asking for directions.

"Where are you going?" he asked in a thick Middle-Eastern accent.

"Home," I chirped, realizing that *Back to my motel room* might not be the wisest thing to say.

"Can I go with you?"

"Sor-ry," I singsonged, as I rolled my window back up.

Although the Yukon and Peanuts were quite spectacular, the Queen Mary was where I finally began to let my guard down and evolved from being uptight to its polar opposite. I became as soulful and forthcoming there as I might have been at a support group. At the time, people seemed to appreciate it, but in retrospect, it must have been a little much for a nightclub.

In the process, I learned that some of the girls coupled up and "played" with each other. I toyed with the idea, but as I began to feel more confident in myself as a woman, I lost interest and feared competition in bed. I imagined a strange sort of wrestling match with me and another girl scrambling to be the one who got pinned. Or maybe each of us would take turns biting the bullet and being the man while the other got to be the woman of the hour. By the same token, flirting with other crossdressers was fun but often left me feeling confused about the role I was playing. On the other hand, when a man came up and offered me a drink, he let me know exactly what I was. For all practical purposes, I was a woman.

And there were plenty of men in the L.A. tranny clubs, in nearly the same one-to-one ratio you'd expect at a straight club. I was going to get to be a college girl at a cocktail party again and again! Although on some level I knew not to look these gift horses in the mouth, I couldn't keep from asking them questions. It wasn't too hard to learn that almost all of them came from the straight world, and some even admitted to being married. Many seemed elusive, while still others were quite palpably apprehensive. "I'm afraid of being seen in a gay bar by one of the gay guys from work," a loquacious gray-hair explained. "So I'm always ready to give the classic alibi: I'm just here to see the drag show."

Most of the guys were emphatic about being straight as opposed to gay, and that was true enough in that they were attracted to regular women and not to regular men. But would the average straight man be interested in a transgendered woman? Eventually, one by one, I asked three really cool straight friends. Each said no, and I believed them, because these were guys who had already shared other secrets with me. The best any of them could offer was "I suppose if I fell in love with a woman and then found out she used to be a man, I could maybe get okay with it."

So in reality, the men in the clubs were neither gay nor straight nor bi in the conventional sense. They were a breed unto themselves. We called them admirers or tranny chasers, because they liked looking at us and getting us drunk—and chasing us around the bar and dance floor, the parking lot and boulevard. And god bless them for it. I loved getting hit on so much that I once stopped and lingered with a man who was buttering me up as I waited in line outside the L.A. Fetish Ball, until Tina pulled me aside curtly. "He's not waiting to get in, you fool," she barked under her breath. "He's a homeless man roaming the street!"

The L.A. Fetish Ball was an annual event that usually took place each summer on several floors of a classic old hotel decorated to look like something out of a Batman movie. There was a choice of bars and eerily lit dance floors as well as a bizarre theater in which people would be tied and whipped and have various body parts pierced, all before an adoring audience. To keep out looky-loos, no one was allowed in without a costume or a very stiff cover charge. Although mixed, the event was more straight than tranny or gay, so it wasn't as explicitly sexual as I had imagined.

Nonetheless, the women there looked rather sexy in their skimpy leather and rattling chains. I had a little red vinyl motorcycle jacket and miniskirt on and was doing my best to compete. And though I may not have made much of a splash, at least I was seen as more genuine. One true believer pointed out an all too perfect looking girl to me and muttered, "It's as if S&M meant nothing more than *Stand and model.*" Personally, I didn't know if deep down I was one of the truly kinky, or just one of the girls trying to look her naughty best.

As we fluttered about town, Tina kept her eye out for a new beau. But unlike other TSs, she was okay with the idea of a boyfriend who was a crossdresser. She seemed to know something they didn't. Although we never talked about it, I even got the sense that she might have been interested in me if I weren't already in love with Melissa.

In the fall of '95, she met a guy named J.T., a husky fellow who loved club hopping and could fill a night with lively banter—and whose sarcasm was hilarious as long as it wasn't directed at you. He was also a crossdresser but seemed happy to go to the transgender clubs as a man or a woman. Either way, he was known as J.T. I was first introduced to him at Peanuts alongside an interesting Gothic-looking genetic woman. I later learned that they used to be a couple until he came out to her and she decided that they would be better off as friends. I always tried to glean as much as I could from the lives and loves of other CDs and share it with Melissa. And this time, it turned out to be a good thing I did.

Tina totally clicked with J.T., and for a while, I hung out as Alice with the two of them and a fun-loving 6'5" bearded crossdresser named Giganta. Also trying to include them in my male life, Liss and I met them after work one day for dinner, with Tina in female and J.T. in male form. Despite Melissa screwing up and calling me Rick—instead of John—a couple times, we all had a great time. Heartened by the chance to integrate the two halves of my life, I invited them to join us and my four best straight friends for my upcoming birthday dinner. Although Tina passed well, I didn't care too much if anyone read her, because I liked being known as a guy who had friends from all walks of life. Even if one of my friends suspected I too might be transgendered, it would be okay, because I now sensed that I would want to come out to them eventually.

In the meantime, Tina had perfected her Marilyn Monroe impersonation and was scheduled to perform on amateur night, Sunday at the Queen Mary. Wanting to show my support, I decided to pop out there for a little while in male mode. Thinking it would be harmless enough, I asked Melissa if she'd join me. We arrived just in time and found seats in the front row so that Tina could see us.

Then Butch—the crusty old drag queen MC—started the show by strutting out to work the crowd. Suddenly, we were sitting ducks. She came up and asked Melissa, "So who's this handsome fella you're here with?"

"My boyfriend."

"Was it his idea to come see the show?"

"Yes."

"Then, honey, are you sure he wants a girlfriend and not a boyfriend? Better hold on tight in this place, sweetheart." A drumbeat sounded backstage, and Butch moved on to her next victim, while the audience roared. Melissa didn't seem her usual sparkling self for the rest of the show, which concluded with a blonde-coiffed Tina emerging from a giant cake looking remarkably like Ms. Monroe. Although she lip-synched a rousing rendition of "Happy Birthday, Mr. President," I couldn't enjoy it because I was too busy worrying about Melissa.

Afterward, we congratulated Tina and joined her, J.T., and Giganta for a drink at the back bar. There J.T. joked, "I guess word of Alice's wild nights got back to Butch."

And Tina laughed, "Yeah, she sure put you on the hot seat, John." Then Giganta joined in with a big long rolling laugh.

I winced, as I saw my girlfriend looking troubled and confused. Everyone was having a grand old time at our expense. "Yeah, real funny, ha, ha, ha," I said facetiously but was unwilling to show them how badly that had hurt. After making a little small talk, I explained that Melissa and I had to be up early next morning, and we headed out to the car.

"Rick, do they all know something I don't?" she asked, somewhat surprised by my hasty retreat.

"No," I said while feeling guilty for every man I had slow danced with over the past year—not to mention the one I'd made out with back in Chicago. Biting my tongue, I explained that I was just upset at myself for putting her in the line of fire at the drag show and furious with my friends for laughing at us rather than being grateful we came. Melissa understood and added that J.T.

was probably jealous of my relationship with her. Nevertheless, we decided it would be a lot easier for both of us if I kept my TG life separate from her and my regular life.

After cooling off for a few days, I took the easy way out when it came to Tina. I called her home number when I knew she was at work and left a message on her machine explaining that Melissa and I had decided to go skiing for the weekend rather than having a birthday dinner. I didn't bother to work through what had happened between us, because I sensed we were drifting apart anyway as she became more involved with J.T. I ran into her surprisingly little after that, though we've always been pleased to see each other and have the chance to catch up.

I struggled to find a new gal pal and had to get comfortable going to clubs by myself and trusting that I would know enough people to fit in and have fun. Why so hard to find a new bosom bud? I think it was because most crossdressers were married and secretive, and thus nervous to share phone numbers (cell phones and email were only just catching on) and hesitant to commit to plans. Pre-op TSs tended to be single, but so many were unreliable or only interested in hanging out with each other.

"C'mon Jerry, it's your turn for a throw-in. Throw it with two hands over your head like I showed you at home." I could hardly believe it, but here I was at ten a.m. Saturday morning on a soccer field, after a late night alone at Peanuts, warming up eight highly distractible five-year-olds in shiny red shirts and baggy black shorts. Jerry looked up at me, awestruck and immobilized. He had a rock-em-sock-em-robot head and a freckled face that somehow conjured up Melissa for me. Her recently divorced sister Jeanie had just moved to town with him in tow. I plunked a knee down on the wet grass behind him and guided his hands back into the ready position. "Okay now, Jer, you can do this. Jackson, Cole, give him someone to pass to. That's what you're supposed to do in a game."

Anxious about her son's loose muscles and delayed milestones, Jeanie had asked if I could take him to his soccer games. One of the other "dads" was coaching, and before I knew it I was helping him out. Impressed with my know-how, he was happy for me to fill in for him when he was out of town and declared me official assistant coach. Shifting gears so fast from peppy party girl to seasoned soccer vet seemed bizarre, but somehow worked just fine for me.

Meanwhile, Melissa and her sister were on the sideline preparing orange slices and water bottles for the kids. "Hey Champ," she announced, ambling over to me with a whistle in hand. "The other team's all here. Don't forget you're referee-ing today," she reminded me with a heartwarming smile, as she placed the whistle around my neck. I had volunteered to ref whenever we needed one, because it kept me in the action and gave me a chance to render more real-time assistance to the little fella.

So far, she and I were managing to keep our relationship together despite continued tension over my transgenderism. How on earth did we do it? For starters, we communicated well. We talked all the time and functioned well as a team. And although our relationship had been built on sharing, we had also begun to understand the areas that might be better kept private. I realized that I needed to focus on Rick when I was with her, and although I was disappointed for Alice, I knew that this was what Melissa needed and what we needed as a couple. It seemed a small enough price to pay.

At the same time, she herself brought a lot to the table. She was a sophisticated and capable woman who had already made a satisfying life for herself by the time I arrived. She had a great career, wonderful family, and loyal group of friends. She knew who she was and liked it. She didn't need to be the wife of Mr. Perfect to feel good about herself—although, she said, that would have been nice.

Because she was often tired at the end of the week, but energized on Saturday, we scheduled most of my girl nights for Friday. But unfortunately, by the end of '95, one night a month no longer felt like enough. Each time I went out, I felt like I had to live a lifetime in a night. With trepidation, I asked her if I could have two Fridays a month. And rather than clobbering me as I feared, she said yes provided I could be occasionally bumped to Saturday if we had important Friday plans. When I let her know how much that meant to me, she explained, "Giving you another night isn't such a big deal. I'm just so relieved I don't have to go with you anymore."

Often Lissa would use one of those Friday nights to check out up-and-coming performers for work. Initially it was hard for her when people asked where I was. She would say I was "on call at the hospital" but felt irritated at having to lie like that. She had never before had to do such a thing. I felt bad but didn't know what else to do, so we consulted a couples therapist.

Although Rebecca didn't have any experience with crossdressers, she came highly recommended and seemed reasonably open-minded. She looked sturdy and sensible, like a California version of Barbara Bush, and worked out of the den of her elegant home, often with one of her dogs at her feet. As Melissa explained the burden of keeping my secret, Rebecca—it turned out—had very strong feelings on the subject. "You've been lucky to live so long without having to keep a secret," she piped up, in a voice clear and confident.

"Really?" Melissa remarked, somewhat surprised.

"My husband and I had to keep one for years. I had lymphoma at the time I was applying to psychiatry residencies. I had to keep it hidden so I could find a position in town and stay here with him and the kids."

My girlfriend was now doubly surprised, because she and I weren't used to therapists who volunteered such personal information. Nonetheless, we both really appreciated it, and Melissa felt much better about having to say I was on call.

Several months later, I still felt the need to crossdress more yet didn't want to infringe further on my time with her. So I suggested taking a weekday night in addition to my two Fridays a month. Melissa felt it would be relatively harmless and gave her okay. Because my best weeknight option was Peanuts from eleven p.m. to two a.m. Monday night, I had to adapt. I learned to get half my sleep from five to nine p.m., then wake up and go to the club, and then get the rest of my zzz's from three to seven a.m.

Whereas crossdressing had been the main challenge of my life, Melissa's bane continued to be anxiety. She worried too much about everything. Surprisingly though, when it came to my more feminine impulses, I never experienced her concerns as unfounded or unreasonable. In fact, they were very much in line with a study of seventy crossdressers' wives I read about at the time.[35]

She worried that I might be gay but unable to face it. "Perhaps you're rushing deeper and deeper into your relationship with me," she would fret, "so you don't have to face your true desires. Then maybe years later, you'll wake up and realize that you have to leave me and our kids to be with a man."

"I'm not gay," I would reassure her. "I'm not even attracted to men. I like women and especially you." Once, when she responded with a particularly quizzical look, I explained, "Yes, I am in a way bi. But if I wanted to be gay, I would face it, break up with you, and find a man. I'm not interested in that now or ever." Happy for the opportunity to speak frankly, I continued, "Being a man with a man is a perfectly fine thing; it just isn't my thing. The only way I'd want to live with a man is if I was a woman."

Which brings me to Melissa's second major worry: what if I were really transsexual and unable to face *that*. As previously mentioned, I worried about it too. Although I didn't *want* to transition and be TS, I had to admit I'd already eaten many of my words, like "It's just a sexual thing" and "I'd never want to dress in public." Ultimately, like the chance of a fatal accident on the freeway, it was a risk we both had to live with.

Lissa's third major concern was that she might be judged harshly. If anyone found out about me, they might think she was a fool, without really knowing us and how happy we were together. She was almost as embarrassed to be the girlfriend of a crossdresser, as I was when I first realized I was one. It was stigma by association. Now she had her own secret identity that she had to manage. I understood and hence rarely came out to anyone without discussing it with her first.

Often I would check in with her from my motel room Friday before beginning my makeup. And sometimes she'd seize the opportunity to barrage me with all her worries. Many times she'd ask questions she had asked before, and not even so long before. Most of the time, I was patient, but sometimes I'd get sweaty and annoyed. Then I might feel like she was trying to control me and sabotage my mood. Once off the phone, I'd feel rebellious and all the more determined to cut loose.

We accepted these conflicts as part of a real working relationship and did our best to figure things out as they came up. Ultimately we developed a system that allowed me to go out and make friends as Alice, while keeping it all at a respectful distance from her. I would spend my three nights a month at a favorite motel near Peanuts and carry a cell phone in my purse. And I promised to drop everything and come home immediately if she needed me. When Melissa wasn't seeing a band for work on one of my girl Fridays, she found that they were good for seeing movies with friends. She loved movies and welcomed the chance to see the ones I wasn't interested in.

Since I had moved in with her, we had had two separate phone lines. Naturally I gave my crossdressing friends my number so they'd either reach me directly or my private voicemail. Then I would talk with them from behind the closed door of my little den. By now, I knew to be discreet and Melissa knew well not to snoop, so she had no interest in listening in. I got even more discreet when I finally joined the computer age and started to use email often instead of the telephone.

By the winter of '96, I couldn't believe how much farther I had fallen down the rabbit hole. Rick Novic was now a man with an androgynous nose, a weight-watcher's body, and estrogen in his veins. In fact, I no longer thought of myself as a man, but more as a *person,* or man-woman. And I had to admit it was a lot easier to get fired up for my adventures as Alice than my conventional life as Rick. By now, I had a social life with many friends who knew me only as Alice. Not only had I learned to turn to that name as a woman, I sometimes turned to it by mistake as a man.

Why did I like crossdressing so much, and what exactly did I like about it? On the most basic level, I savored the clothes, body modifications, and situations—like slow dancing with a tall man—that made me feel most like a woman. I loved being a woman whenever I went out and couldn't stop worrying that I might want to do it full time.

Just like Melissa loved the disco music of her teenage years, I fell in love with the pulsing electronic dance music of my first nights on the town. Originally it was called techno, and then later on it became known as house. It was like an electronic disco with the bass and drums pumping out twice as many beats (about 140 a minute), making an energetic pump-tee-pump rather than simple pump-pump rhythm. Catchy synthesizer licks would declare the melody. And above it all, a diva would wail about dancing, love, and the night, pausing just long enough for her male counterpart to rap in and tell us about his hard driving passion. Each new song was a delicious variation on the theme and seemed to emerge mysteriously from the one before.

It was a sound that beckoned a girl to dance. And I sure couldn't— not that I let that stop me. I would jump onto the dance floor and flail my arms around in poor imitation of a pop star. Eventually I realized how silly that looked next to the graceful girls at a place like Peanuts. But because TG nightlife revolved around such clubs, I figured I had better learn to love dancing, and look half decent doing it.

Like many crossdressers, I had the disadvantage of growing up straight, white, and male. Talk about having three strikes against you. In high school, I had put up with a little dancing because Fiona liked it. In college, I had gone to the big Boston clubs a few times in search of wine, women, and song. Yet far too frequently, when I'd ask a girl to dance, she'd simply squeak, "No thanks, I'm dancing with my girl friends." That made absolutely no sense to me. Nonetheless, I'd fade back into the woodwork, with all the other lone wolves. It all seemed to be about girls cheerily putting themselves on display and guys looking on, full of hormones and frustration. I needed that like a hole in the head.

But now was my chance to prance rather than prowl. I took on dancing with the same ironically-rather-masculine meticulousness I had applied to other facets of the feminine mystique. I watched women and tried to analyze what they were doing step by step. But all too often, there were too many body parts moving too fast to follow.

Fortunately Melissa was a good dancer. So I asked her to show me what she did. She felt silly dancing at home but humored me. Nonetheless, it was hard for her to teach me something she had done naturally for years. She would say "Try to copy me," and "Just relax and move to the music," which sounded like good advice, except as soon as I relaxed, I would lose the beat and revert to a manly rocking of my shoulders and shuffling of my feet.

Realizing it was going to be a long time until I could disco down with the divas, I committed my daily jogging time to dancing and approached it in stages. First, I had to learn to find the beat and move to it. To break it down to basics, sometimes I'd simply bop to the beat of a metronome. Then I'd play dance mixes I had bought from the DJ at Peanuts and count the beats out loud.

Next, I had to learn to sway my hips and dangle my arms gracefully. I'd sashay and twirl and follow every motion in the mirror. Then, when I thought I was getting somewhere, I'd put on a waist cincher and heels and start all over again. Finally, I had to lose the look of forced concentration on my face and learn to dance with a serene smile—in public.

And not just in public, but next to pretty little Latin and Filipino girls who seemed like they came out of the womb waltzing. How could I boogie down on the same floor without looking mannish and clunky? Often I would try too hard and soon feel warm under my wig. Then I would downshift into a slow, sensual mode, by ignoring every other beat. Taking the pace down from 140 to 70 beats per minute helped me keep cool. But just as I was getting into a groove, the DJ might segue into a snappy *cumbia*, forcing me to speed up and match a completely foreign 100 beats per minute.

The first time this happened, I caught two queens in strappy spandex looking at me and snickering. "You, really good dancer," giggled the bustier of the two, in what I later learned was a heavy Venezuelan accent. Wishful thinking led me to believe she might be paying me a compliment, but when I came to my senses and realized she was making fun of me, I felt my face go red. I retreated to the bar as soon as I could without making it look too obvious.

Most of us older white girls were in the same boat. Even transsexual tennis pro Renee Richards, in her day, found it surprisingly difficult to *mover la colita*.[36] Once, at Peanuts, when I was trying to be friendly to a particularly clumsy new girl, she started to ape all my moves. And before I knew it, I had become part of a pair of six-foot crossdressers putting on a pathetic game of Simon Says for the amusement of the entire crowd. Although she didn't mean to humiliate me, I was furious and felt like giving up. Meanwhile, the svelte young queens continued to glide effortlessly through the night, every weekend more impressive and intimidating. It was like the rich getting richer and the poor remaining dirt poor.

I had to break the cycle. I didn't care if I looked a bit foolish for a while. Gradually, I got better and convinced myself I was a decent dancer, long before I really was. But at least that way, I was able to stand tall, have fun, and get the experience I needed. I always enjoyed dancing in the mirror at a club and learned to turn my back to the crowd and warm up that way, before facing them with confidence.

Ultimately I discovered there's no better come-hither than smiling pretty on the dance floor. And as my dancing improved, men started to come up and offer their appreciation. Once, as I walked off the hardwood at Peanuts, a tall, thin man stepped in front of me. He had honey-colored hair and a look of mischief on his face. "Don't stop," he commanded.

"Huh," I reacted.

"Please," he implored, as he reached into his jacket and pulled out a fifty-dollar bill for me.

"Okay!" I replied, as he took my hand and led me back onto the dance floor. I was tickled pink, but a little nervous about what he might expect for his money. Fortunately he required no more than a little companionship and conversation. It turned out that he was an Emmy Award winning writer, but that night, he made me feel like *I'd* just won an Emmy.

For my first couple years in Cali, I wondered where the classic American drag queens were. In retrospect, I would count many of the Queen Mary showgirls as DQs, but I didn't get to know any of them for years. When Trilogy opened in '96, I had my first chance to mix with American-style queens. It was a restaurant where all the waitresses were friendly drag queens who took turns dancing, lip-synching, and occasionally even *singing* for the crowd. Their poise impressed me no end, especially when I learned that they all reported for the dinner shift as men and left as men. Although about half of the troupe worked by day as professional dancers and makeup artists, none had the advantage of hormones, implants, and full-time femaleness. All of a sudden, I felt like the glove had been thrown down. I wanted to be the first straight (well, at least for the most part) guy to do *girl* as good as the gays.

Still, I kept this inner nonsense in check, hung out at Trilogy as often as I could, and made friends with all the waitresses, a couple of whom even went on to join the show at the QM. Again, curiosity struck. Who *were* these unusual men-women? And how different from me? Why were they so fabulous, while most of my peers were so plain?

With all but a notepad in hand, Lois Lane here pieced together that drag queens really were quite different from crossdressers. Unlike us, they considered themselves gay men like any other gay men except that they had discovered that they were good at drag and enjoyed doing it. Hence, the name *drag queen,* as in *queen* (a term gay people use to refer to any gay man) who likes drag—as opposed to, say, *leather queen* (gay man who likes leather) or *rice queen* (gay man who likes Asian men). Another big difference was that most drag queens *never* felt terribly excited by women, nor aroused by women's clothing. (For more, see Appendix E.)

It was incredible how rare a sight drag queens were among American gay men. I thought I might run into a few more as I explored the big dance clubs in the heart of West Hollywood. And once in a blue moon, I did, but most of the time, all I'd see was a poster or leaflet announcing drag shows at midnight on this night or that. Yet these places were impressive in their own right. They were magnificent multifloored structures throbbing with the best music and the most happening DJs in town. Stylish men, looking fresh from the gym, hob-knobbed around in their tight clothes. Although hot and bothered by each other, they weren't the slightest bit interested in a woman, or anyone who looked like one. Whenever I went to such places in drag, I was treated with kindness and curiosity, but never with flirtation or desire.

There was really no better showcase of gay talent and flare than Halloween. This was (and still is) the traditional time for every gay man in L.A. to camp it up in a ball gown or something else equally outrageous. Santa Monica Boulevard closes to traffic, and the sidewalks fill with onlookers. Thousands of people in spectacular costumes congregate in the street and parade up and down the strip. Many work in the movie industry and are highly skilled in areas like makeup, wardrobe, and set design. The costumes are elaborate, and so are the props. Some people dress up as couples or groups. Some even dress up their dogs.

The first time I joined the parade, I made the most of my extra muscle and strode the strip as Wonder Woman, swinging her golden lasso. I rubbed shoulders with a lovely Pocahontas embedded in her own styrofoam canoe; an uncanny Bill Clinton chasing a chubby Monica Lewinsky in her black beret and stained blue dress; even a crew of vintage stewardesses in matching uniforms from the 1960s. Not wanting Melissa to miss out, we went the following year as Xena the Warrior Princess and her beloved companion Gabrielle. We posed for pictures and hammed it up for video. The crowd cheered, and we felt like stars.

I wondered where all this enthusiasm for drag went each year after Halloween until I discovered Drag Strip 66. It was a once a month event hosted by an out-of-the-way gay club called Rodolfo's. Each time, there was a new theme like Women in the Military or Chicks from Outer Space. So each month, people were challenged to come up with fresh ideas. I loved the creativity and color of Drag Strip but could never feel at home there the way I did at the Queen Mary or even Peanuts. The feeling there was *We're gay men on a wild, fun art project*—which was well and good, but it wasn't me. I preferred places where the vibe was *We're expressing the woman inside and want to be around men who care.*

As I got better at being a woman, I was more consistently approached by men and became a genuine sex object. Often my big African-American friend Darius would greet me at the Queen Mary by looking me up and down and shaking his head. "Damn, Alice, you don't give a man a chance!" Often we would speak for a little while, then he would fix me in his gaze and proclaim, "I swear, I can't just stand here and talk to you without wanting to kiss you. Can I kiss you?"

At first, I was dumbstruck by the notion of being as thoroughly kissable as a soft, sweet woman or a precious little child. After a moment, I'd manage something like "Oh, Darius, don't be silly" or "I bet you say that to all the girls." But later, as I got more comfortable with my sex appeal, I let myself enjoy it by wagging my finger and saying, "Okay, but just one—and on the cheek."

I had never really understood why so many women would complain, "We're not just sex objects." It made me feel like shaking one and shouting, "Well, at least you get to be a sex object!" I had always thought I'd love it, and now I knew I did. I think most young girls take it for granted. But ask a woman who has recently put on weight, and she'll tell you that the only thing worse than being a sex object . . . is *not* being one. Such a woman would know how I had felt year after year. Hearing girls grumble about being sex objects had been as hateful as hearing someone complain about being rich. Sure, there are complications, like people pursuing you for your money, but oh, to have such problems.

Now that I was a sex object, I was blessed with one such problem. Even if I didn't look for trouble, it came looking for me. I couldn't put off the man issue any longer. For a couple of years, I had focused on simply being a woman, rather than being a woman with a man. But now, some Steve or Tom was offering me the chance every time I went out, and it was getting harder to resist. I let a guy take me to my car one night when I had to park a few blocks away from Peanuts, and I could hardly believe how much I liked walking with him and even holding hands. There was no more denying it. When it came to men, I wanted to do all the things a woman did—and allow all the things a woman allowed.

It's hard to say whether I was unusual in this way. Three large studies, involving over a hundred participants each, have shown 28-48% of crossdressers have had sexual experiences with men.[37] However, we don't know how many would like to but can't for lack of opportunity or respect for their wedding vows. Perhaps the best way to gauge it would be to find out how many fantasize about being women submitting to men.

Deep down, I'd always been electrified by the idea. But what had seemed an impossible fantasy was, by the spring of '96, a near weekly possibility. The desire I once saw as demonic possession, I now saw as part of my true self. Still, my desire was problematic, and I puzzled over it with Caroline as we sat face to face across a small table with two cups of coffee amidst the pastel colors and discreet floral arrangements of her office. She was about fifty years old, elegant, and soft-spoken.

"So far," I explained, "I've refrained from extracurricular activities since moving in with Melissa because I don't want to mess things up between us. But *can* I swear off men forever?"

"I don't know. Can you?"

"I suppose so." I brought my coffee cup up to my lips and drew a sip. "But I don't want a life based on neglecting my most basic needs. I want a rich, full life with room for my needs as a man *and* as a woman. I want a life with Melissa and occasional sex with a man." I looked to my therapist for a response but saw only riveted attention. "I know how outrageous that must sound. Do you think I'm being selfish, crazy, or irresponsible?"

She thought for a moment. "No, but that might depend on how you go about it."

"I don't want to sneak around and be unfaithful. That's not who I am. That's not how I want to treat Melissa."

"Being faithful," she explained, "is not fundamentally about living by the conventional rules of marriage, but living up to the agreements you make with each other."

"But would Melissa ever agree to an open relationship? I can't imagine even asking her for such a thing."

"But this is important to you, isn't it?"

I sighed and took another sip of coffee. "You know, there's really nothing else I want more. No fancy car or big house, no single thing I can think of would mean as much as this little bit of freedom. It would allow me to look forward to marriage and children without feeling like something was missing."

Later that week, I was on call at the hospital, and Melissa came to join me for dinner at a nearby deli restaurant adorned with huge autographed movie posters. We sat in a booth, and paradoxically the noise of the busy restaurant gave us the privacy we needed. I explained that I had been looking back on my engagement to Betsy and realized I had panicked so severely because I was signing up for a marriage that would forever outlaw some of my most basic needs. At the time, I hadn't known about the woman inside me and what she might want in life, but my body had known and had hit an alarm consisting of sweats and chills and obsessive fear of HIV.

"You're quite a case," Melissa teased.

"Anyway, I want to make sure nothing like that ever happens again."

"What are you saying?" she replied anxiously.

"I'm saying that there will always be a part of me that wants to be a woman with a man."

My love's eyes widened as she sucked in a breath.

"I don't want to be tempted to do something that would be considered a crime worthy of tearing up everything we have together, not to mention the kids we hope to have."

"So," she said with a furrowed brow.

I looked around to make sure no one was listening. "What if we were each allowed to have a discreet sexual relationship on the side?" My hair stood on end as I waited for her reaction.

"Isn't that what all men want, and all women should refuse?" she protested, but at least she remained at the table and didn't lose her cool.

"Believe me. If I was simply a man and not part woman," I said slowly and effortfully, "I would *never* want to burden you with a request like this. I would be meticulous about safe sex," I hastened to add.

"I should think so," she gasped. "But how do I know you won't leave me for a man? I don't understand how you could have sex with someone without the risk of falling in love and wanting to be together."

"I know that for you sex and love are practically the same thing, but for me they can be different."

"Um hmm," she replied with some skepticism.

"Like I've always said, the only way I'd ever want to be in a full-time relationship with a man is if I were on my way to being a full-time woman, which I'm not." Though she was still tense, I could tell she was listening. "I assure you, in my heart nothing has changed. I want to be with you more than anybody else, male or female, and always will."

"As far as you can tell."

"As far as I can tell."

"If I'm to agree to anything like this, then I'd feel better if we were married."

For a while now, we had looked forward to spending our lives together and having a family. Melissa had always wanted to do it as a married couple, but I had wanted to do it without getting married. Friends and colleagues now thought of me as an alternative kind of guy and suspected I was bi. I liked it that way and didn't want to give them a reason to see me as a regular straight man with a wedding band and all the expectations that came with it. "Okay," I conceded, "maybe it would be better if we were married."

"I think I can live with this, but I'm really not thrilled about it."

"I know. I know," I echoed, feeling bad for her. For a moment, neither of us knew what to say. "Of course, you could have someone on the side too," I offered.

"I am not interested in that kind of thing," she enunciated. "I'm either happy with you or seriously looking for someone else. So if I ever have an affair, it will be a sign of serious trouble."

"Well, you know I want you to be happy more than anyone else in the world. So please let me know how we can keep our relationship happy and strong."

"I will," she said firmly. "And I expect you to do the same."

We both felt exhausted by our negotiation and didn't touch the subject for about a week. Then one night over dinner at our kitchen counter, I tried an indirect approach. I brought up the shy aerospace executive I had been working with and the fact that, over the years, he had seen a number of Korean masseuses for more than just simple massages. Though his wife would have no doubt disapproved, he had otherwise been a good husband and father for over thirty years. The unspoken moral of my story was *See, you can be a good family man without being absolutely exclusive.*

Reading right between the lines, Melissa spoke up. "Hey, don't bring this stuff up through the back door. I only agreed to the *possibility* you might do something like that, but I hope you never will. And I would never want to hear about it."

I understood, so through the front door we formalized a don't-ask-don't-tell policy in which I agreed not to tell too much about my life as Alice and she agreed not to ask. She preferred to trust me with the black box of my girl nights rather than having to think too much about its potentially painful contents.

Her other stipulation was that I not discuss our arrangement with any of our friends. She feared that people might judge her as foolish and our marriage-to-be as a sham. We both knew it wasn't but still didn't want the hassle of extra scrutiny. I personally didn't want to tell people about it because I didn't want to sound like a philanderer. My intention was always to be bimonogamous. I was just a simple man-woman hoping to share *his* life with one woman and *her* life with one man.

Our final agreement was that I could look for a boyfriend as long as I upheld *safety, priority,* and *discretion.* Safety meant I must be ever diligent about safe sex. Priority meant Melissa must always come first. And discretion meant I must keep it all to myself and my transgendered friends. I thoroughly appreciated the freedom she allowed me and was determined to live up to her trust.

With my needs as a woman secure, I was able to focus on being a better man for Melissa. I stopped practicing my femininity around the apartment and renewed my focus on her and the things we needed to be content as a couple. We continued to treasure our time together and support each other's endeavors. She was really enjoying her new position at Arista and helping them branch out into folk music. I was finishing my second year of residency, and psychiatry was rewarding me with fascinating windows on the world, like what it's like to be a young female chef with a controlling mother or a recently retired attorney now questioning his lifelong marriage (or, of course, a shy aerospace exec with a penchant for Korean massage).

I told Melissa that I wanted to surprise her with a ring and a proposal, but first I needed to know her size and taste. With her effervescent approval, I went shopping and bided my time, just as I had done with Betsy. But this time, I hoped to be more romantic and much more at peace.

One Saturday night that May, I told her we were going to a residency potluck dinner but that she should dress up a little "because our hostess is Filipino and kind of formal." We then got in the car and approached the freeway.

"Rick, you better get in the left lane soon or you'll miss the entrance," she exclaimed.

I just stayed in the right lane and broke into a smile from ear to ear. When I got on the 10 bearing west instead of east, she knew we were heading for the Surf Club, that special restaurant where we liked to celebrate our most significant occasions.

"Oh, my god. Oh, my god!" she burst out with glee, sensing what was about to happen.

Once there, I left the car with the valet and took her by the hand. We walked over to a table at the piano bar overlooking the beach. Once I caught the pianist's eye, he segued into one of our favorite songs, "The Power of Two" by the Indigo Girls. As Lissa shed tears of joy, I presented her with a ring I knew she'd like. "Will you marry me?" I asked on bended knee.

"Yes," she said resoundingly and then sniffled, "I can't believe I'm crying. I thought they only did that in the movies."

We kissed and, before we knew it, a bottle of champagne appeared. I wish I could claim that too as part of my plan, but it actually came from some nice people sitting at the next table. After we toasted each other, she reached into her purse for her cell phone, "Do you mind if we quickly share the good news with our folks?"

"Why not!"

Thus, we were engaged. This time around, I felt much different than I'd felt a mere six years before. To be honest, I was a little sad that I would never get to be a bride and that I was further renouncing my own chance to be a woman some day. But I felt thankful to have someone like Melissa in my life and pleased to be planning a future together.

Although I was calm, she had her own jitters, which came out a couple months later at an upscale Italian restaurant. "Sweetie," she began, "I have something I want to talk about."

"Okay."

"Would you be able to stop crossdressing if I asked you to?"

Her question startled me. Maybe she had had a change of heart and might still leave me over my crossdressing and the hardships that came with it? Although anxious and alarmed, I figured the time had come to stand up straight and be strong. "I think I'd be able to, but I wouldn't want to—not for any long stretch of time. That's just the way it is. I'll be absolutely heartbroken if you can't live with this. But if that's the case, I'll have to leave and live on my own again."

"Well, that's pretty much what I figured. I just wanted to be sure of it. It's not the crossdressing *per se* that bothers me; it's whether it might keep you from being outgoing and enthusiastic in the rest of your life—you know, the one you share with me."

"You know, you're right. It's easy for me to feel alienated from people who don't know about my transgendered side. It's something I need to work on." As Melissa started to smile and tear, I reached across the table, held her hand, and welled up a bit myself.

In September '96, we had a small but majestic outdoor wedding at my uncle's house in Telluride. We wrote parts of our ceremony, and it felt very true to who we were and what we believed in. Although I'd have rather worn the wedding dress than the tuxedo, I was pleased as punch for Melissa, and we had a great weekend with all our friends and family. We planned a safari to Africa for our honeymoon but scheduled it several months later so that we could relax after the wedding and have a whole new adventure to look forward to.

My favorite moment was one not caught on video. It wasn't even part of our wedding day, but part of the night before. At our rehearsal dinner, I rose from my seat and took advantage of the opportunity to speak informally to the people we cared about the most. Although my exact words escape me, I remember feeling like I was absolutely glowing, as I spoke of my appreciation and affection for Melissa. When I wrapped it all up into a toast, the smiles that had spread through the crowd erupted into cheers, hoots, and applause. Minutes later, she took the floor and glowed back with the same tenderness and warmth. In that moment, I felt like all the important people in our lives were looking at us and blessing us with the thought that these are two people who *really* know each other and love each other and are excited to spend their lives together.

10

A Fresh Perspective

If the misery of our poor be caused not by the laws of nature, but by [the prejudices of] our institutions, great is our sin.

-Charles Darwin,
The Voyage of the Beagle

My third and final year of psychiatric training had started a few months before my wedding, and I continued to enjoy my patients and the chance to learn about their lives. I felt they were trusting me with something precious and real, something rarely heard even by their closest friends or family. In addition to the therapy I provided, I also learned how to help people with psychiatric medication and was impressed by the difference it could make.

Yet my own feelings would often color the way I viewed a patient and his/her issues. This became undeniably clear when I volunteered to work with Pilar, a transsexual woman who had transitioned twenty years ago but was now having problems with her boyfriend. I felt all too interested in her situation and life. Was I somehow flawed as a psychiatrist for her and others? I really needed to talk it over with one of my supervisors, but to do so, I would have to reveal that I was a crossdresser.

George Prendergast was a heavy-set man in his early fifties, devoted to the residents training in psychiatry with him. He was informal in his clothes and manner, and remarkably understanding of human foibles. One day in seminar, he presented a hypothetical case to a group of us. "What if you're called to the emergency room to evaluate a college professor who's been in a minor car accident? He's not injured, but you find bruises on his body that, he says, come from kinky sex with men. What do you do?"

My fellow residents—a number of whom were from the former Soviet Union—suggested doing everything from committing him to the inpatient ward to notifying the university of his proclivities.

Dr. Prendergast reigned in his trainees and advised us to simply inquire whether the prof was troubled by his sexual activities, and if not, "then by all means respect his privacy and let him get back to his life." These instructions helped convince me of Dr. P's tolerance for diversity and the value he placed on privacy. Although warm and down-to-earth, he was an extremely private man, who never spoke about his personal life and deftly deflected all questions about it. Rumor had it that he was gay, but handling it in the most traditional, quiet way.

However, just days before I planned to come out to him, he said something troublingly transphobic in seminar. He described how the husband of one of his patients had gone "so far off the deep end that he picked up a *transsexual*," the implication being that no one in their right mind would ever do such a thing. His comment bothered me until I stepped back and realized that we all grow up in a society with certain built-in prejudices. We buy them without ever thinking about it, unless an event comes along that makes us check our assumptions.

I hoped to provide such a consciousness-raising experience for George, as I entered his office for weekly one-on-one supervision. It was a white box like mine, but it was a little bigger and contained a couch, which I sat on. Although I was distracted by children playing in the courtyard outside his picture window, I did my best to concentrate on the matter at hand.

"George, there's something that affects my work with patients that I need to share with you."

"Sure, what is it?"

"It's of a very sensitive nature, so I really need you to keep it confidential."

"Okay," he replied with a slight frown.

"I'm a crossdresser."

His jaw dropped a little, and he continued to look concerned. "Is it something you need help with?"

"Well, not really, I'm pretty okay with it by now. It's something I've batted around in therapy for six years and done pretty regularly since I was back in Chicago."

He exhaled, relaxed, and smiled wide. "I *never* would have imagined."

"That's the way it often is with our people."

"I've always appreciated your open-mindedness but never would have imagined this is where it came from. I'm curious to learn more."

"Well, I'm happy to talk about it with the few people I can."

"I'm pleased you've come to me and happy to help you look at how it influences your work. I also want you to know I have enormous respect for you and what you've had to deal with."

I was thrilled with Dr. P's response and expected him to reciprocate by coming out to me. When he failed to, I couldn't help but feel a little disappointed. But after a moment's reflection, I realized that I had come to him for support, which he had kindly given. But just because I had chosen to make my business his business, that didn't mean he had to do the same.

As I met with him week after week, my doubts about myself as a psychiatrist began to dissolve. In addition to my fascination with Pilar, I was also curious about many of the women and gay men I worked with, and George helped me see that it wasn't simple prurience, but profound empathy that I felt. In this way, I tapped into a genuine and lasting interest in a great many of my patients, but still, I was self-conscious about it.

"So you show a little extra enthusiasm. It might just be the most healing thing you provide for someone," he offered from his years of experience. Working with gay patients in particular opened new horizons for me. I was impressed by how similar their struggles were to ours in the transgender community. Although I wasn't the same as a gay, lesbian, or regular bi person, I had come to see them all as members of my extended family and thus became an advocate for the rainbow of diversity rather than the uniform gray of assimilation.

I disapproved of the people who said, "Yes, I'm a crossdresser. But other than this one small flaw, I'm a normal straight man with the same views as everyone else." My mentality was *Yes, I'm a crossdresser. And because of that difference, I'm accepting of all people who are harmlessly different.*

I was disgusted by the approach mental health professionals traditionally took toward sexual minorities. I wanted no more of their narrow-mindedness. I could think of only one place to go to find a better way . . . the Center, the Gay and Lesbian Center.

I started making phone calls and soon had a meeting with some sympathetic people up there. Although I didn't come out to them, they liked me and we worked out a proposal. Dr. Prendergast, who had increasingly become my mentor, obtained official approval for me to do a three-month elective, as a psychotherapist and psychopharmacologist there. Things worked out so well that I stayed on after my elective and worked part time at the Center until the end of the academic year.

There, I became especially close to Tim Hsu. He was a relatively big, soft teddy bear of a Chinese-American man. He and I led a therapy group for people who were in too much turmoil to wait the week or two it took to be assigned an individual therapist. We really clicked. Although I was a psychiatrist in training and he was a psychologist, we were both passionate about mental health and deeply moved by the plight of gay people. Coming from different backgrounds, we found each other's styles stimulating and fresh.

Like two priests, we listened as people told heart-wrenching tales. We typically worked with four or five people in a strange cube of a room with carpeted benches along the walls and no windows. One young black man told us how his devout Baptist family had thrown him out for being gay. He wept on the porch as the front door was shut to him on Christmas day. I choked up, while my comrade lightly touched his arm, looked up at his anguished face, and assured him, "You've done very well just to survive and make it here to the Center. We're here to make things better." Though never a religious man, I felt the work we were doing was sacred and experienced a welling of spirituality that hearkened back to my own darkest days.

I wanted to know Tim better and was delighted to discover the feeling was mutual, so we started to go for dinner together after work each week. Soon I came out to him as a crossdresser—and a bisexual. He had never met a crossdresser before and was very curious about me, and because he was my first gay friend since Liam, I had lots of questions for him too. I included him in my birthday dinner that year, and he included me as either Rick or Alice in some of the fun things he did with his friends, like an Academy Awards party and ballroom dancing lessons.

One night, over Thai food, I explained my arrangement with Melissa and decided to take a risk. "You know, maybe it's crazy for me to look for a good solid man out in the tranny clubs. What would you think about adding a sexual side to our friendship?"

"I'm touched," he said, composing himself. "But I really need a full-time boyfriend. Maybe I'm just old-fashioned," he added with a giggle, "but when I start loving someone, it's all or nothing. And it's really nothing against Alice, but I'd be much more excited about Rick."

"Unfortunately, Rick's already taken."

An awkward moment ensued as we realized we desired each other in ways that just weren't compatible. I felt a bit rejected and imagined that he did too, but we continued on as friends just the same. We had so much to share with each other, whether or not there was any potential for romance.

Getting to know Tim prompted me to think about gender in new ways. Although he had no desire to dress up and get into the female role like I did, in many ways he was much more feminine, as in the natural inflexion of his voice and the expressive way he gestured with his hands. *Wow, this is getting confusing*, I mused. *What are the different ways a person can be manlike or womanlike?*

I knew in the back of my mind that this was a politically incorrect question to think about, but I didn't care. I needed to explore it to figure out who I was—especially since I had decided I was not "a normal straight man except for this one small flaw." I read as much as I could and learned more about things like intersex conditions and psychological tests like the Bem Sex Role Inventory and the Combined Gender Identity and Transsexuality

Inventory. As before, I asked people questions, listened closely, and *watched* closely. In so doing, I noticed four different ways in which a person can be manlike or womanlike.

First, there's the matter of body. Were you born with a *male* or *female* body? With the exception of a few intersex conditions, the gender of your chromosomes (XY for male, XX for female) determines the gender of your body. (Perhaps undiscovered intersex conditions are responsible for variations in the following other areas.)

Second, there's the matter of gender identity. Do you feel like a man or a woman inside? And the matter of desired gender role. Would you want to live as a man or a woman? As I see it, a man who wants to live as a woman (at least part of the time) is *transgendered*. A man who wants to live as a man all the time is *regular*.

Third, comes the thorny matter of personality, mannerisms, and interests. Although some of you might not like it, I'd say if you're strong, sensible, and goal-oriented (like me), then you have a *masculine* personality. If you're sweet, sensitive, and relationship-oriented (like Tim), then you have a *feminine* personality.

I don't think I've met anyone with a masculine personality who didn't also have masculine mannerisms, like looking out the middle of your eye, holding your head level, and speaking in a relative monotone. Similarly, feminine personality seems to come with feminine mannerisms, like looking out the corner of your eye, tilting your head, and speaking with an expressive lilt. Tim did all these things as well as touching his face and "clutching his pearls" (his words, though I have since made them part of my working vocabulary). Typically someone with a masculine personality will have professional interests like a business or technical career and personal interests that tend toward athletics; whereas someone with a feminine personality will have professional interests like a people- or child-oriented career and personal interests that tend toward aesthetics.

Fourth and finally, is the matter of sexual orientation. Are you attracted to women or to men? It can be illuminating to see orientation as a fourth way in which a person can be manlike or womanlike. In that regard, a *straight* man may be said to have the standard male orientation and a *gay* man, the standard female orientation.

So all in all, I count four basic ways in which a person can be either manlike or womanlike. You can be all man, MMMM, like Bruce Willis in the movies, a straight masculine (regular) male. You can be all woman, FFFF, like Julia Roberts, a straight feminine (regular) female. Or you can be in between in many different ways.

Many gay men, like Tim, are MMFF—gay feminine (regular) males, and even more remember being effeminate as children.[38] I don't know why being attracted to men is so often connected with having a feminine personality, but according to one prominent researcher in the field, "To say that femininity and homosexuality are closely bound may be politically incorrect, but it is factually correct, and it's been known for a long time."[39] That's why a guy like Mike back in Boston might identify with Bette Davis or Judy Garland and refer to a friend as *she*. It's also why Tim was able to throw on a dress on Halloween and be incredibly believable as a woman. And why it's not unusual to see a muscled-up gay man open his mouth to bubble something about the lovely décor.

Most crossdressers are MFMM—straight masculine transgendered males. That's why people like me have to learn femininity as a second language. That's also why it's not uncommon to see a pretty, perfumed crossdresser open her mouth to bark something about power tools. Perhaps it would be more accurate to say most crossdressers are MfMM, where the small f indicates that you feel only partially like a woman inside.

In my opinion, started-out-straight transsexuals differ only by feeling more fully like women inside. So they would be MFMM. In contrast, started-out-gay transsexuals have a lot more in common with feminine gay men. They would be MFFF. I've heard from a number of started-out-straight TSs that masculine personality traits and attraction to women gave them a false sense of normality and kept them from figuring out who they were until their thirties or forties as opposed to started-out-gay TSs, who were forced to confront their differences in their teens or twenties.

You may bristle at my violations of feminist party line, as well as my departures from gay, transsexual, and even crossdresser party lines. But then, I had fallen down a rabbit hole and had to find my way in a shocking new world. I had to come up with the most accurate map I could, whether it was pleasing to me or not, whether it was pleasing to others or not. (Later, I learned that the system I came up with was surprisingly consistent with the Periodic Table of Gender Transpositions by Pillard and Weinrich.)[40]

"You were so charming with everyone from work," Melissa remarked, as we waited for our car outside the House of Blues, after a No Doubt concert.

"I'm happy to be there for you," I replied.

"Did you get a chance to call my mom today?" she asked. Now that her father had passed away, her mom had become involved with someone new. But unfortunately her new beau had just been diagnosed with a heart condition, and she was worried that he might have sunk into a depression over the news.

After explaining the meat of our conversation to Melissa and letting her know what I thought should be done, I took a step back to say, "You know your mom is just the coolest. She's like this genteel Jackie O. type who knows how to cut right through the fluff and get down to it when she needs to. If I weren't already with you, I would totally marry your mother."

"Ugh, that's gross."

"Okay, but she is totally my kind of person. She and Dale can come out and stay with us whenever they want, for as long as they want."

"That would mean a lot to me," my wife said. "Do you mean it?"

"I mean it," I replied, genuinely pleased to have stumbled onto something significant I could offer her, especially now.

I had never allowed myself to feel the full force of my womanly sexuality until it was legalized by Melissa. But now, with our understanding in place, my mind was racing through a powder keg of new possibilities. Though I wouldn't be fooling anybody, I puzzled over how far I could undress without losing my feminine mystique. *I* thought I looked pretty cute in my black bra, panties, waist cincher, and thigh-highs, and I sure hoped there would be a special man who might agree. But whatever was to happen, my bra would have to stay on and my wig too. As always, the message had to be clear: *Think of me as a woman.*

And as such, I figured, I'd best learn to give half decent head, so I stopped by Juanita's street corner to ask for her advice. "All lips and no teeth," she replied in her thick Salvadoran accent, "and breathe through your nose." Though she couldn't be as clear about how to keep anal intercourse from getting painful and messy, I soon found a couple of helpful books and learned to always douche beforehand and practice at home with a butt plug.[41]

Thus prepared and ever mindful of my pledge to safety, priority, and discretion, I allowed myself to have some of the sexual experiences I craved and hopefully settle into something steady. Naively I figured if it was easy to get picked up, it would be easy to find a boyfriend. Yet I soon learned, to my great dismay, that I might have to kiss many a frog before finding my prince.

Brian was the third in a series of men I hooked up with, and my experience with him began rather typically. He was a big shaggy-haired guy in a flannel shirt who approached me with a beery smile between songs on the dance floor at the Queen Mary.

"Ya know, you're beautiful."

"Thanks," I replied, sizing him up. He looked unkempt and a bit overweight—not an especially handsome man. But he wasn't ugly, and I wasn't sure I found any man truly fetching. Besides, he must have been a barrel-chested 6'2", and I felt womanly in comparison.

He bought me a drink, and we talked for a while at the bar. I learned he was a divorced longshoreman from San Pedro, while I let him know I was a married person hoping for a special man on the side. With glee in his eye, he slung an arm around me. "So where do you go after this?" he said, gesturing at the lively bar scene with his other beefy paw.

"Just back to my motel."

"Can I come with you?"

"Not if you're just looking for a one-night stand," I chided.

"Are you kidding?" he smirked. "I'd want to be with you again and again and again." His eyes drifted down to the hemline of my little olive-green lace dress.

"What do you like to do?" I asked.

"The usual things," he said with a shrug. "How 'bout you?"

"I like doing the things a woman does."

"All the things?"

"Yes, and *only* those things."

In the transgender world, you never know what someone wants sexually, and you can't assume every man wants to be a man. I learned very fast to make sure it was *You Tarzan, Me Jane* before going anywhere. That was especially important, because once the action began, I liked to dance my part in the classic waltz of heterosexuality: He leads, she follows, and their union is all the tighter and more exquisite if she resists a little with each step.

After finishing our drinks, we got in our cars, and he trailed me to La Serenata Motor Inn. It was a quirky hodge-podge of two buildings and a restaurant surrounding a swimming pool that I had grown fond of as my home away from home. Though in need of renovation, it was air-conditioned and well cared for.

Brian followed me through my motel-room door, and before I could reach the light switch, he backed me up against the wall and kissed me full on the mouth.

Startled, I returned his kiss, but braced my—relatively—delicate fingers against his chest and pushed him back a bit. "Easy, tiger."

He stood there outlined by the city-light streaming in through the yellowed lace curtains. He said nothing, but pressed his lips back on mine and assaulted my mouth with his tongue. What was that acrid taste, cigarettes?

Yuck, I don't know if I'm attracted to him, said a voice in my head. *Maybe I just put up with men because they're the ultimate props in my pretend-I'm-a-girl game?*

But he's not a bad guy, another voice answered, *and he's dying to give you what you want.*

As he kissed me again, I grabbed his stubbly face in my hands and felt all sorts of juices flow inside me. Without thinking, I straightened my posture, lifting my pert breasts up under his nose. He started to feel me up, fondling the soft silicone on my chest with first one hand and then the other, while I grew weak in the knees.

Before I knew what was happening, my barroom Brando nudged me over to the bed and onto my back, making me feel spacey like in a dentist's chair. As he climbed on top of me, his body—like all male bodies—felt as cuddly as a stack of two-by-fours, but by now I was a little more used to it. As he touched me and adored me, my body slowly melted into my own womanly mold of Jell-O.

I averted my eyes from his bulging belly, as he took his shirt off and lowered himself back onto me. But once he started to dry-hump me, I didn't want him to stop. I had to fight my own instincts, as well as his, in order to shrug him off. "You've got to let me go to the ladies' room," I cried.

There I exchanged my dress for a black peignoir and stockings and attended to my "feminine hygiene." Then I checked my makeup in the mirror and returned to find Brian lying naked on his back with his . . . loading crane at the ready. I lay next to him and expected him to start kissing me again but he was on to bigger and better things. That's how these men were. Long kisses and tender hugs were just too intimate for them—and admittedly still awkward for me. And all too often, their hands would wander south, while my breasts still yearned for more.

I felt his fingers glide slowly up my silky legs, and, as he approached the hem of my negligee, I rolled onto my tummy and arched up a bit. His hands slid under my nightie and groped my little round pantied behind. Then by the time he pressed a finger on my "pussy," I thought I was going to die with anticipation and delight.

All too soon, he swung me onto my back and pulled my panties down. With a look of determination and fear, he put my "clit" in his mouth.

I felt an uncomfortable raking and whispered, "Don't use your teeth," to no avail. I put up with it for a little while, before pushing him away. "Here let me show you," I said, dropping to my knees, by the side of the bed. Ever aware that my health as well as Melissa's was at stake, I pulled a condom on him.

Silently I prayed he would stay hard enough to penetrate me, *unlike* the last guy I'd been with, when I'd been shocked to discover that my experience with Mike long ago had not been such an aberration. Maybe it was because the guy had been older and nervous—or maybe because he'd been drinking? But at this time in my life, I was no longer desperate to make things happen. It was strictly *No condom, no sex.*

Quickly I grabbed some lube and massaged Brian up and down the length of his shaft and started to suck him, and again massaged him and sucked him. With his penis rock hard and his groans escalating, I worried for the first time about the opposite problem. Might he shoot his load in my hand or my mouth and leave me unsatisfied?

"Would you like to fuck me?" I asked as I lay back on the bed.

As if he wasn't used to anyone talking during sex, he grinned awkwardly and stationed himself between my legs. And, as I pulled them up and back a bit, he began to enter me.

"Oh, slowly, gently," I admonished. "I'm just a girl." I closed my eyes and went into a state of deep relaxation, as my sphincter steadily yielded to his trespassing tumescence. Soon I found myself moaning with each thrust, as if part of a womanly reflex deep in my brain.

"Ooh, faster, harder," I urged him, hoping he wasn't like that guy from a couple months ago who couldn't come with a condom on. I had felt so disappointed even though he did reach around and bring me off. It was like we had tried to have sex but failed. Afterward, I had found ways of asking Caroline, Nicole, and even Melissa if sex felt incomplete when a man couldn't come, and they agreed. On some level, we all expected it to revolve around a woman's beauty and a man's pleasure; her body and his orgasm; in fact, his orgasm in her body. Maybe we're built to think that way for the purpose of reproduction.

"Faster, harder," I repeated.

Stoked to see me begging for more, Brian picked up steam like a locomotive. And all at once, every urgent thump of his hard groin against my soft, elevated bottom told me: *You're a woman. You're a woman. You're a woman!* Then with a loud grunt, he collapsed on top of me, and I felt like I'd just received his old-fashioned seal of approval, dripped on with hot wax and punched in with a signet ring.

Restless and aroused, I soon pushed his big, moist body off me. He relaxed on his back but seemed to look away as I reached for the lube and started to stroke my clit with my right hand. As soon as I fingered my freshly fucked pussy with my left, I shook and spurted into a nearby tissue. As I came down from orgasm, I had to admit I had gotten a little gooey and probably hadn't looked as feminine as I had hoped.

I expected that big Bri would be itching to go by now, but he surprised me. Although half asleep on his back, he encouraged me to rest my head on his hairy chest.

For a moment, as I lay next to him on my right side, I didn't know *what* to do with my right arm. It was pinned under my side. I tried pushing it forward, but then it lay awkwardly like an obstacle between me and him.

When I lifted my body up and moved my arm back behind me, I felt oddly contorted but thought I'd seen Melissa wriggle into a position like that before, and it allowed me to settle in smoothly along the length of his body.

We couldn't have drifted off for more than twenty minutes, when my hand found its way down to his groin. I could barely believe it, but the old sea dog was hard all over again.

"Oh my!" I exclaimed.

He looked at me like a little boy, at first self-conscious, then proud.

"Do you want to do it all over again?" I asked.

"At your cervix," he laughed, as his rough fingers traced their way back up my black stockings . . .

Afterward, I lounged dreamily in my negligee, feeling like *I* needed a cigarette—even though I didn't smoke. Brian chatted amiably while putting on his clothes. I ambled out of bed when he seemed ready to leave.

"You're incredible," he proclaimed by the door.

"No, *you* are," I chimed back, now at his side.

"Let's get together next weekend. Here's my phone number." He passed me a piece of paper, as he kissed me goodbye.

Twice, I thought. *Twice!*

I smiled for days knowing I could satisfy a man as well as any woman out there. Cheerily I called him up. The phone rang once, twice, then "the number you have dialed has been disconnected or is no longer in service." Although I had never heard of such a thing before, I soon realized Brian had given me a fake number and figured "Brian" wasn't his real name either. It was all so demoralizing and creepy.

Many of the men I met were fun but frustrating like that, and often I learned as much from their actions as their words. What they wanted was sex *tonight,* not tomorrow, not next Friday after dinner and a movie. Why did it have to be right now? Why no interest in courting or follow-up? Initially, I figured that was just how men were, at least in nightclubs.

Later, I learned that, whether they admit it or not, many—if not most—of our admirers are married. They may only get a few nights a year away from their wives, so they're eager to take full advantage of each opportunity and careful to cover their tracks afterward. Such a man might be very disturbed by cheating on his wife and even more deeply conflicted about doing it "with a man." The stakes are extremely high. A fellow could face utter humiliation and even lose his family over something like that. But his desire is equally powerful and can be released by liquor. Once unleashed, it can be a hungry hound on the loose, doing much its master may regret in the morning.

Even if such a man has no immediate regrets, he may find it easier to cope with isolated encounters in the nightclub netherworld rather than the undeniable reality of an ongoing affair. Maintaining contact the morning after might break his compartmentalization and become more trouble than it's worth. Yet despite it all, there were always a few girls who found boyfriends and ways to make it work.

With more experience, I developed a better sense of what I was looking for. Even though I knew I couldn't afford to be picky, it helped to spell out my preferences so that if I ever met my prince, I'd at least know him when I saw him. Number one, I would really love to find a guy I could see whenever I went out. I knew that that might be impossible for a married man or an out-of-towner, but I would need to see him at least once a month.

To minimize my risk of sexually transmitted diseases, I preferred to see just one fella rather than date a few. I also wanted to find someone I could get comfortable with and who might start to give a darn about me. Then I could devote myself to him and never have to think about another man. And ideally he wouldn't want to be with any other trans woman. It would be okay if he was married; I was too after all. It would also be okay if he was single and kept dating genetic girls, so long as he still had time for me.

My second priority was more superficial. I wanted a man who was well built and tall. He didn't have to be great looking, and I didn't care about race. Nevertheless, I felt a bit shallow until I realized my preference for taller men was something else I shared with real women. Even my own sister Laura once said, "I like my men to be about six inches taller so I feel like the woman." I couldn't have agreed more.

But alas, a six-foot girl, like me, couldn't insist on a 6'6" man. They just don't make that many. But at least I could find one taller than me. Otherwise, whenever I stood next to him or danced with him, I'd start feeling like a man despite all the hair, makeup, and effort on my part. On the other hand, when some tower of power pulled me in close and made me look up to meet his eyes—well, then.

My third preference was much along the same lines. I wanted a lover who was masculine and would treat me like a woman in the bedroom and out. I didn't want to be thought of as a man in drag. Ideally I'd find a fella who'd tell me time after time I was pretty and make me feel like his own precious little piece of property.

Even if I found a man who fulfilled my first three wishes, I wouldn't be happy unless he fulfilled me sexually, and I had learned that only about half were up to the task. Fortunately it was only a year until Viagra came out, and though it carried no guarantee, it could be a sex saver. I always kept a few in my purse.

My fifth and final wish was for a guy who was good-natured and reliable. I just couldn't see a relationship working without these qualities. How can you have a discreet affair without trusting each other? How can you have an ongoing affair without the ability to make plans and stick to them?

A handful of men would take a shine to me each time I went out, and I figured out a new way to handle it. First I would joke around and dance with a guy and see what he was interested in. Generally one, sometimes two, and often none seemed to offer what I was looking for. By now I was mostly going to the Queen Mary and if I really liked a guy there, I might ask him to take me for a stroll outside the club. Fortunately it was a quiet residential neighborhood with little risk of trans bashing, and a simple black shawl blunted the nighttime chill, no matter the month. I soon, however, ran into a thicket of technical difficulties.

If a man wrapped his arm around my shoulders while we were walking, I couldn't just respond with an arm around his shoulders like two rugby players entering a scrum. Was I supposed to delicately lace my arm around his waist? It proved difficult. Could I simply lean in a little bit, but otherwise just keep walking with his arm around me? It felt bizarre. Did women ever do that? I soon noticed that they did. Still, I could never do it without feeling at least a little bit rude for not reciprocating.

For that matter, was there a right way to hold a man's hand? It turned out there was. Generally a woman likes to interlock fingers with a man, with her hand in back and his in front. But that was awkward if a fella was shorter than me. Moreover, what was this notion of *taking a man's arm*? And who initiated it? I guess I was on a crash course through finishing school. Though seemingly mundane, mastering these skills was surprisingly satisfying.

On getting me back to my car, a gentleman could have a goodnight kiss and a phone number. By now, I had learned that, if I put out too soon, he might lose interest. But I soon discovered that if I insisted on a date first, he might also back off, especially because the idea of taking a girl like me to dinner could be terrifying to a local guy. Though confident and pretty, I still didn't pass. So any man opposite me in a restaurant would look totally gay, and—unlike me with my coiffure and cosmetics—he wouldn't have any sort of disguise.

I reassured my admirers that I knew of some great gay restaurants where they would be unlikely to run into anyone they knew. Still, only about ten percent would ever call to ask me out. What's a t-girl to do? Nonetheless, ten percent was better than zero, and my prissiness gave me a way to choose who was worth putting out for.

Meanwhile, I continued to work a day a week at the Center. Firmly convinced that being transgendered was like being gay, I soaked up everything I could about being a well-adjusted gay person because therein lay the path to being a better-adjusted trans person. And people at the Center knew a lot about it, they lived it and taught it. Here, I learned how gays and lesbians go through an adjustment process that begins with emptiness and confusion, passes through shame, and goes on to comfort and pride. And here, I learned pride.

Gay thought and the acceptance it had won was decades ahead of anything in our transgender world. Their battle for basic human rights began in the 1950s with Harry Hay and his Mattachine Society, who declared gay people to be a minority worth as much respect as any other minority. "You see, darling," he explained later, "they all thought we were just straight people behaving badly. It wasn't about who we were."

From the African-American civil rights movement of the '60s, gay leaders learned not to apologize for being different, nor play it down. They learned not to let anyone step on them, whether that *anyone* was a family member, a so-called expert, or a government. And on June 28th, 1969, they proved it. Shortly after midnight, police from the Public Morals Section of the New York City Police Department showed up to shut down a popular gay bar known as the Stonewall Inn and arrest its employees. This time, however, nerves already frayed by the death that day of their icon Judy Garland, the patrons fought back. They were spearheaded by a number of drag queens and joined by the entire neighborhood. They put quite a scare in the police that night and sparked a gay rights movement that soon took hold across the country.

In the spirit of that movement, I learned how to maintain my pride in the face of pervasive prejudice that came even from people who considered themselves friends of the transgender community. In the fall of '96, J.J. Allen released *The Man in the Red Velvet Dress: Inside the World of Crossdressing,* and it received two pieces of TV news coverage.[42] The first featured a friend of mine courageously chatting with a reporter while getting dolled up to go out. The follow-up featured Richard Docter, a leading psychologist I knew, who focused on the powerful allure of crossdressing and the danger of "getting hooked."

Rather dismayed, I called him up. "Dick, you're hurting us. You're making us sound like drug addicts." He didn't understand, so I explained, "'Getting hooked' is the language of addiction. You might see crossdressing as a habit, but you *know* it's an innocent one. So you should never equate it with addiction."

In hashing things out with him, I developed the Self-Respecting Gay Man Rule. It's a simple test to decide whether a comment is transphobic or not. It goes like this. Substitute the word homosexuality for crossdressing. If you come up with something that a self-respecting gay man would object to, then you have something a self-respecting transgendered person should object to as well.

"Just imagine if you had talked about the danger of getting hooked on homosexuality," I implored. "You'd be suggesting that it was like an addiction and offending every gay man in town." He told me he had never thought of it that way. I told him it was about time he did. Granted, some things that are offensive may also be true, but the burden of proof lies squarely on the offender.

Truly rejecting the idea of homosexuality or transgenderism as a disease means there's no urgent need to discover a cause or a cure. Mid-twentieth-century playwright Jean Genet said it well, "I ascertain that I am homosexual. Okay, that's no cause for alarm. How and why are idle questions. It's a little like wanting to know why my eyes are green." Like Genet, I became less interested in why I was transgendered and more concerned with the hows and whys of the prejudice against it.

When it came to these matters, plus sex in general, my work at the Center was about to alter my world-view as much as my first Harvard physics class. Back then, when I told my professor that I was amazed at how mathematically difficult it was to understand the world, he gave me a fatherly glance and replied, "What's more amazing is that we human animals can understand it at all." I had *never* thought of it that way, but as I mulled it over, I realized he was right.

Growing up when I did, I had learned that the only okay sex was simple, pure intercourse between a man and woman who loved each other. Later, I learned that a few other things, like oral sex or monogamous homosexuality, might also be all right. My colleagues at the Center saw these attitudes as part of the *sex-negative* tradition of Judeo-Christian culture. They didn't believe there was only one kind of okay sex with a few possible add-ons.

"We're sex-positive," Dave, the director of mental health services, explained to me in supervision. "We believe *every* kind of sex is okay with only a few exceptions." It didn't matter whether or not two people loved each other or what gender they were, nor even whether there were three or four of them all playing together at once. Whatever people could agree to was A-okay. Judgment was reserved for things that were harmful, like rape or lying about your HIV status.

As I read up on the origins of homophobia and transphobia, I realized that my views had been shaped by prejudices that permeate our society, prejudices based on biblical morality and a bias against anything that *seems* unnatural. (For more, see Appendix F.) Although I never stopped believing in the fundamental soundness of the Ten Commandments and the simple joy of doing what comes naturally, I came to see that Dave might be radical, but he was right. Harmful vs. not harmful was a much better way to judge human behavior than natural vs. unnatural or in- vs. out-of-line with religious tradition. My perspective shifted.

People have been hurt by homophobia and transphobia in a variety of ways, from being beat up to losing their jobs to being put out on the street by their own families. One of the more insidious effects—and one that I knew all too well—is the self-hatred known as internalized homophobia or transphobia. Most of us grow up with this, and it's very difficult to shake. It's a voice that says, *I'm seriously screwed-up, so I should be ashamed of my feelings and never express them in action or word.* And telling yourself to neglect half the things you might enjoy, of course, can be a serious impediment to your pursuit of happiness.

One of the best remedies for homophobia and transphobia, I learned, is to come out and put a human face on the words *gay, lesbian, crossdresser,* and *transsexual.*[43] That way people can know us for the human beings we are rather than the demons we're made out to be. Unlike racial minorities, being gay or transgendered is defined by how we feel, and feelings aren't something people can see from the outside. Ironically, they're also something people often can't see, or refuse to see, within themselves. So there are many choices to make about when to acknowledge who we are and reveal it to the people in our lives.

These choices make up the coming out process. As I mentioned before, it starts by admitting to yourself that you're gay or trans, and then sharing your secret with your partner, peers, friends, family, and coworkers—usually in that order. My colleagues at the Center believed that coming out was vital for personal growth and gay visibility. Nonetheless, they cautioned that each person should do it at his/her own pace and up to a point that made sense in the context of his/her life.

I was inspired by the coming out process and how it might apply to me as a crossdresser. Of course, I had already come out to myself in the aftermath of my crisis and had revealed myself to "partners" twice, hesitantly to Betsy and then more confidently to Melissa. I had come out to my peers when I went to the Tiffany Club, dressed up, and chose a name; and then in a more lasting way when I began attending Tri-Ess in Chicago. But like most crossdressers, that's where my coming out process stopped (except for the confidences I shared with George Prendergast, Tim Hsu, and Nicole Adjani).

It was now October 1996, and although I'd been going through some of the most exciting years of my life, I felt like I couldn't share any of it with my friends. When Melissa and I got together with them, everyone could be spontaneous and talk about their lives except me. I felt alienated and unable to enjoy the kind of connection that comes with being free-flowing and genuine. I hoped to warm things up by coming out.

"Um, sweetie," Melissa said, as we were both washing up before bed one night, "I know it's important for you to come out to some of our friends, but I don't want it to dominate all future conversations."

"Okay," I replied, as I finished flossing my teeth.

"You have to realize that it's hard for me to be seen as the wife of a crossdresser. People don't understand it. You'd feel the same way too, if you were me."

"I understand, but I don't know what we can do about it," I said, at a loss.

"And I don't want my friends bringing it up with me afterward and asking me why I put up with you."

"So, should we just forget it?" I asked in frustration.

"No, but we have to be very careful about it."

We decided to start with our best friends, Derek and Lucy, and see how it went. The very next day, Lucy happened to call Melissa to see if we wanted to go out for dinner with them. "Why don't you guys come over here instead?" my wife suggested with trepidation.

When Derek and Lucy arrived, I sat down with them in the living room, while Melissa put the finishing touches on dinner. They were a funny combination. He was tall, thin, and fashionable. She was short, pretty, and soulful. Meeting their eyes, I felt an adrenaline rush that was two parts excitement and one part anxiety. Having poured a glass of wine for everyone, I now took a big gulp of mine.

"I'd like to tell you guys something about me, because I think you're great, and I'd like to feel more relaxed and open around you."

"Okay," Derek said expectantly.

"Lucy, you probably already know, but . . . I'm a crossdresser."

"You're kidding?" Derek asked emphatically.

"No, I'm the real thing." Too nervous to wait for their response, I rushed on. "Just so you don't think I look like some kind of frumpy Mrs. Doubtfire, I wanted to show you some pictures, if you don't mind?"

"No, no," Lucy allowed.

With that, I pulled my photo album out from underneath some magazines on the coffee table and opened it to one of my favorites.

"Wow, look at that!" Derek exclaimed.

"Rick, I would've never known it was you," Lucy declared. "Do you do your own makeup?"

"Yes, but some of these pictures are from a professional photo shoot. And I hired a professional makeup lady for it."

"You look just like one of the secretaries at UCLA," Derek said with a wry smile. "I would have never known you were a man."

"That's because I'm careful not to pose next to anyone small," I replied as I slowly flipped pages.

"Well, *she's* little," said Lucy. "Who's that?"

"Take a closer look," I teased, enjoying myself immensely. "Oh, my god, it's Melissa in a wig," said Lucy.

"Lissa, you're kind of hot with straight hair," Derek called out.

"Oh, isn't that silly?" Melissa replied on her way from the kitchen to the living room. She sipped some wine and joined us for the rest of the pictures.

"Um, other than posing for pictures, what do you actually do when you dress up?" Lucy inquired.

"Sometimes I go to dinner, but most of the time I go out dancing with friends."

"Where?"

"We have our own special clubs."

"Gay clubs?"

"No, they're really places for crossdressers and transsexuals and the men who like us."

"Men?" Lucy puzzled. "You're not into them, are you?"

"Well, I've been known to flirt and dance a little . . ." I caught a fretful look from Melissa. "But no, not really."

"Hey, you guys, dinner's ready," she chose now to announce, and ultimately our conversation drifted off to other topics. Afterward, we walked Derek and Lucy to their car and exchanged hugs.

"Rick, I'm really glad you felt comfortable sharing that with us," Lucy offered.

"You sure are a man of many talents," Derek said with a grin, as we all chuckled and waved goodbye.

I came out to two other couples we were friendly with, and on the whole, people were very accepting and touched to be let in on my secret. We felt all the closer for it, and a couple folks even reciprocated with secrets of their own. I felt freer to speak my mind and soon preferred my new inner circle to my other friends. I once even dressed up and took Melissa, Derek, Lucy, and two other good friends out to dine and dance among the drag queens at Trilogy and Drag Strip. Some liked it more than others, but everyone was a great sport.

As long as I limited my TG talk to colorful sidebars, my friends found it fresh and fun. But I learned the hard way from my old pal Nicole that *accepting* had its limits. In addition to being a radiologist, she was a slim, stylish divorcee who shared a lot of her single life with me, while I shared a lot of my tranny life with her. I thought it was great fun for both of us. However, once, when we were seated around a big restaurant table with some of my closest friends and I brought up something about gender, she rolled her eyes and bemoaned, "Here we go again with *Rick's World.*"

I felt humiliated and stewed with resentment. Only later did I see her point. My friends simply didn't share my interest in the transgender world. Although they didn't have anything against it, to them it was like hearing someone talk too much about their passion for stamp collecting. Nonetheless, I was wounded by how publicly Nicole chose to deliver her message and felt she should be thankful she fit so neatly into the regular, straight world and never had to concern herself with Rick's World or anything like it.

Although it had its limits, coming out to friends was a terrific thing for me. Since then, I couldn't imagine feeling close to anyone without putting my crossdressing on the table at some point. And fortunately it didn't turn out to be too awkward for Melissa; her friends never brought my crossdressing up with her, and she rarely mentioned it with them.

For a long time, relations with my sisters were based on mutual goodwill but no special fondness. I was never just itching to talk to or spend time with Kathy, Miriam, or Laura. But, encouraged by how things went with my friends, I hoped that I might restore my enthusiasm by coming out to them.

I started with Miriam. She was a pediatrician and among my three sisters the most tolerant of the complexities of life. I grabbed her between events at a cousin's wedding and brought her back to my hotel room. Melissa was out catching up with a friend at the time. Tallish and elegant with straight dark hair in a neat chin-length bob, she settled into a chair, while I sat at the foot of the bed, opposite her.

"Mir, there's something about me I want you to know because I think you're great, and I want to feel more relaxed and open around you." I used almost the same words I had used with my friends; it soothed my nerves and seemed like the best way to start.

"Oh, boy," she said with a nervous laugh.

"Well, I guess it is kind of a doozy . . . I'm a crossdresser."

"What does *that* mean?" she asked with her eyes narrowing.

"It means I like to dress up as a woman and go out for dinner and dancing."

"In public?"

"In public. I'm really pretty good at it by now," I answered with no small amount of pride.

"Isn't it a sexual thing?" she asked, having been to medical school just like me.

"It used to be. But now it's more about perfecting my craft and going out and having fun."

She looked at me, bewildered. "When did it start?"

"Well, some things happened just before Betsy and I got married that flipped me out and made me think I might be a crossdresser. They bothered her a lot too." I deliberately kept things vague but was willing to say a lot more depending on the reaction I got.

My sister gave me a pained look, like she was imagining what it would be like if her boyfriend was a crossdresser. "Did it play a role in your divorce?"

"No, at least not a primary role. I kept it under wraps when I was with Betsy. I left her mostly because we couldn't talk about, or handle, *anything*."

"Is Melissa okay with it?"

"Well, it's not her favorite thing about me, but she's used to it. And I let her know about it right up front."

"I'm glad you two are handling it well. It must be hard at times. I want you to know you both have my complete support."

"I appreciate that, but it's also *fun.*" I asserted, now all the more eager to show her I was no furry freak sneaking around in Melissa's underwear. "Let me show you some pictures."

"Okay," she said tentatively.

Sensing her reluctance, I hastily flipped through my photo album and stopped at one of my best pictures. "So what do you think?" I asked, hoping for my most fashionable sister's approval.

The words stuck in her throat as she shifted uneasily in her seat.

"Do I look pretty?" I tried to help her by being more specific.

"You look . . . fine," she stammered in an attempt to please me and end the picture show.

After that, I began to see it might not be that much fun to share this part of my life with Miriam, but I was to try once more. While on the phone with her a few weeks later, I couldn't resist telling her how thrilled I was to finally find a pair of ladies' boots in my size. Suddenly her conversation turned to one-word answers, and she changed the subject as soon as humanly possible.

After my sister Laura reacted more or less like Miriam, I never got around to coming out to Kathy. I rarely had the chance to see her in person, and it just didn't seem to be worth it when I did. Soon Miriam and Laura lapsed into a tense don't-ask-don't-tell policy. They never asked about my crossdressing, and if I ever brought it up, they got uncomfortable.

I came out to my parents for an altogether different purpose, an important piece of unfinished business. In the aftermath of my crisis, I had unfairly blamed them for causing me "sexual baggage that's too horrible to mention." So now, upon returning home for Christmas, I approached them each one on one. I let them know I was a crossdresser and apologized for blaming them. There was no good reason to think they were responsible. My mother handled it the way she handles most difficult news: She swallowed hard at my revelation, accepted my apology, then swept it all under the rug. I was disappointed to see the door again shut to further discussion, but at least her affection for me never wavered. My father, however, seemed more interested in talking.

"Besides," I explained to him over lunch at a Greek restaurant, "I've come to see it's not such a bad thing after all; in fact, it's kind of fun."

"Fun?" he gasped. "We're just glad you're happy and think you're really lucky to be married to someone like Melissa."

While we were on the subject, I seized the opportunity to ask a question I might never be able to ask again. "Dad, I don't mean to pry, but do you think there's any chance I might have inherited this?"

"What do you mean?" He seemed puzzled.

"Could *you* be a crossdresser?"

"How would I know?" Now he seemed even more puzzled, but at least not appalled.

"Well you'd know, if you like dressing up in women's clothing."

"No," he said in a way that was so simple and straightforward that it might have seemed blunt to someone who didn't know him.

Although it felt awkward as hell to be having this discussion, I was, nonetheless, going to be thorough about it. "You might also know if you're turned on by the mere thought of putting on women's clothes or being a woman."

He gave me a funny smirk and a shake of his head. "You didn't get this from my side of the family," he chuckled, and I soon joined in. Though he took all this pretty seriously, I was relieved to see he could have a sense of humor about it. As our smiles abated, he inquired, "Are you bisexual?"

His words took me by surprise. I had decided I would come out to my parents as a crossdresser, but not as a bisexual. I didn't want them to wonder if I was fooling around outside my marriage and didn't care to tell them about my arrangement with Melissa. But apparently my physician-father had seen the probable connection between my being a crossdresser and my prior panic about AIDS and didn't hesitate to speak up to confirm his hunch.

"Yes, basically. I've experimented a bit. It kind of comes with the territory," I replied, after a moment's thought. I was a proud member of the Los Angeles Gay and Lesbian Center. There was no way I was going to deny my bisexuality nor be ashamed of it, but I played it down and focused on filling my father in on past events rather than present concerns.

Despite the unusual frankness he and I enjoyed on this occasion, we soon lapsed into the same don't-ask-don't-tell policy I had with my sisters. Yet to my surprise a couple years later, he came around and was curious to know how my crossdressing had started and how it had affected my life. Since then, he has even sent me some transgender news clippings from the *New York Times* and *Buffalo News*.

On the whole, the coming out process went okay with my family—not as well as it had with my friends. In retrospect, I realized my being a crossdresser had more meaning for them. I wasn't just anybody—I was the big brother they had been proud of or the son they had lost sleep over. Coming out may have jeopardized their pride and reawakened their anxieties. On top of that, none of them had ever had a taste for the more complicated facets of life, whereas I had specifically chosen friends who did. For some time now, whenever I had met a potential pal, I'd thought, *Is this the kind of person who would like me if they really knew me?* and then acted accordingly.

After Tim Hsu, I came out to other colleagues at the Gay and Lesbian Center and had similarly positive experiences. So I decided that I would come out to gay and lesbian colleagues as I prepared for private practice. Because even they could have prejudices about crossdressers, I would usually start by admitting that I was bisexual. If they were accepting (and there was no guarantee, because many wrote bisexuals off as gay men in denial) and our professional relationship was going well, then I'd reveal the fact that I was a crossdresser.

The first person I came out to in this way was Berk Stevens, who had been chief resident when I began my training. As we sat down for lunch, I was nervous, but when I confided I was bi, he smiled warmly. When I revealed I was also a crossdresser, he couldn't wait to learn more. And when I went to shake his hand and thank him, he hugged me like a long-lost cousin. And I—having come a long way by now—hugged him right back. He and George and my colleagues at the Center were instrumental in helping me get my practice started.

Because I had discreetly let people at the hospital and in the t-community know that I was interested in transgendered patients, by the time I finished residency and established a practice in the summer of '97, I was spending a significant chunk of my time working with other crossdressers and transsexuals. I discovered, however, that most TGs didn't share my love of therapy, so I continued to seek out patients of all kinds.

Most crossdressers seemed into it only as long as I held out the chance of a cure—which I could not in good faith do. And most transsexuals saw it as an expensive obstacle on the way to hormones and surgery. So I never required them to see me any longer than was necessary to make sure they were making an informed decision. Yet, it's been a privilege to work with those transgendered people who *have* embraced therapy and the opportunity to learn more about themselves, for each one is a kindred spirit.

My TG patients ranged from men turned on by lingerie to transsexual women who had been living quietly in the straight world for years. About half of these folks knew me as Alice before seeing me in the office, so of course, I was out and proud in my work with them. For those who didn't already know, I was cautious and came out only if it seemed helpful for them to know they were being cared for by one of their own.

I continued to come out to patients, colleagues, and friends on a one-by-one basis but stopped far shy of being openly transgendered. I had personal and professional reasons for not wanting to be generally known as a crossdresser. From a professional standpoint, I didn't want to seem peculiar to my straight colleagues, and I felt that most of my patients already had enough things to worry about. And from a personal standpoint, I didn't want to cause Melissa—and any kids we might have—any undue embarrassment or harassment.

11

Single Trans Female

In February '97, Melissa and I took time from work for our honeymoon to Tanzania. Taking full advantage of a one-night layover in Amsterdam, we visited a marijuana café, a sex show, and the Anne Frank House. *Talk about the land of the free and the home of the brave,* I thought, *and the coolest wife on the planet.*

When we arrived in Africa, we suddenly found ourselves to be the youngest couple on our safari by at least fifteen years. Though older, the others were healthy and fun and didn't hold us back a bit. In fact, the eldest two were as inspiring to us as the wild animals we saw. I loved sharing the diversity and drama of life on the Serengeti with Melissa. It was an experience I'll always cherish.

It made me long for the early days, when she would journey with me into Genderland, planning special getaways together and laughing over the pictures when we got back. Since then, I'd felt like Lewis without Clark. For a time, Tina had been a terrific pal and Tim an excellent confidant. But Tina was gone, and much as I liked Tim, we were ultimately from different worlds. I swear there were times when I didn't know which I needed more, a boyfriend or a *girl friend.*

Thankfully I ran into Sonia that spring at the Queen Mary and liked her from the moment I met her. She was a Mexican-American crossdresser with ebony-brown ringlets and an ever so earnest look on her face. We soon began talking on the phone and meeting each other for dinner before the QM, and I was thrilled to find such an intriguing new chum. She had served in the navy and was now a respected officer in the Los Angeles Port Police. As a man, she was well built and medium height, which, she explained, made her a little sturdier than she'd like to be as a woman.

She lived with her wife, Risa, and son. Risa, however, could barely handle the idea of her husband crossdressing in public, and unfortunately for her, it didn't take much crossdressing to convince Sonia that she was transsexual and needed to transition as soon as possible. Nevertheless, she wished to stay with her wife as a married couple, or at least as friends and co-parents. Understandably, Risa was horrified, and not so understandably, she tormented Sonia until she finally moved out that summer.

I felt for her and had the utmost respect for who Sonia was and what she was trying to do. She was my first close friend to go through transition, and I was as fascinated with her as a newlywed would be with her pregnant big sister, while she appreciated that I was a psychiatrist and looked to me for information and support.

Through it all, she had a somewhat masculine personality and seemed generally similar to me, except that she may have received a stronger dose of whatever it was we were both born with. And though she didn't pass perfectly, she was only 5'9" and attracted less attention than I did. Maybe feeling a little more like a woman on the inside and looking a little more like one on the outside were enough to push her over the edge from TV to TS.

I knew she was doing the right thing, not because she was a poster-child transsexual, but because she fully and deeply wanted to live as a woman. Though I knew she was a pretty typical started-out-straight transsexual, I bit my tongue because *she* felt she was a late-blooming version of the classic "woman trapped in the body of a man."

She hung out less and less with crossdressers, because she needed more experience in the straight world and didn't want to jeopardize her chance of blending in. She also needed to focus on the challenges of going full time with other pre-ops who were going through the same thing. I was one of the few crossdressers she stayed close to—although we shifted more into being telephone friends.

She saved up money and vacation time and shopped around for ways to make her transition smoother. After a year of hormones, plus face and breast surgery, her body began to round out convincingly. She looked pretty in a soft, buxom way. Although she stuck by her transsexual friends, she complained how some would insidiously compete over who was more of a real woman. Meanwhile, she had chromosome studies done and hoped they would distinguish her from the pack by demonstrating an intersex condition. When she never mentioned the results to me, I inquired about them over the phone.

"Oh, they were negative," she said, sounding real low-key, though I knew she had to be crushed.

"You're probably intersexed," I replied, "but in a way that isn't detectable by today's technology."

She took solace in my reassurance but ultimately went on to see herself as neither transsexual nor intersex, but simply a woman born with a birth defect that had finally been corrected. Maybe she was right? Maybe she was wrong? But more importantly, she found the self-image she needed for the hardships ahead. She reminded me of the old-time crossdressers I had met who had insisted they were just normal straight men who happened to like the "luxurious look and feel of women's clothes." Perhaps they too were just trying to find the self-image they needed for the challenges in their lives.

With a deep sense of *that could be me*, I watched as Sonia transitioned on the job. It soon proved to be a real nightmare. The other policemen and women on her patrol boat refused to accept her as female and never gave her a moment's peace. She needed to go to their commanding officer to keep them in line and simultaneously sought legal advice. Finally, worn out by the daily harassment, she asked to be transferred to a desk job.

Eventually, by being her quiet, competent self at work every day, she won the respect of her coworkers—the respect she had deserved all along. In a similar way, she continued to be a devoted parent to her son, and her now ex-wife finally gave up her bitterness. Though post-op life wasn't everything she expected, Sonia passed increasingly well and ended up happier than she had ever been. The last time we spoke, she had become involved in Hawaiian dancing and been embraced by the women of her troupe. And she wholeheartedly embraced them back, just like others I knew who had found homes among Wiccans, women's studies scholars, and open-minded Episcopalians.

Though she ultimately left the transgender community behind, Sonia had been wonderful in reaching out to other girls going full time and serving as a de facto den mother. She'd been great at getting people started on the Internet and helping them access the resources they needed. To help me find a Friday-night boyfriend in '97, she put up a website for me, which explained I was a "fun-loving bisexual transvestite looking for a special man for friendship and sex in Los Angeles" and featured four of my professional pictures.

I listed my site in a few transgender directories, and the first day it hit the Internet, my phone nearly rang off the hook. It was a real thrill, but I learned fast to leave my email address instead of my phone number. Thank goodness, I wasn't sharing a line with Melissa.

Because AOL didn't have a special place for transgender personals, I ran a regular ad titled "T-Girl Seeks Man for Affair" along with one of my best pictures and text that clearly explained I was a transvestite and offered a link to my website. Not knowing when it would be posted, I simply entered it and forgot about it. Imagine my surprise later that week when I checked my email and found fifty letters, all having arrived in the last twenty-four hours. The flood continued for days until I had received about two hundred love notes in two weeks.

As I sifted through them all, I began to realize that most of the guys had just looked at my picture and seen a pretty girl looking for an affair. They hadn't bothered to read the rest of my ad. *Wow*, I thought, *if I were a real girl who wanted a little passion with no strings, I could start a riot—or perhaps a business.* Most of the two hundred vanished when I asked them to make sure they had really read about me and get back to me if still interested. A few somehow felt like they had been duped and got offended. Although I felt that was unfair, I pulled my ad from AOL.

I kept it to the usual transgender places and generated a steady flow of two responses a week, week after week, month after month. That was still a lot of people to deal with. In paring down my pool of admirers, I discovered three types to avoid.

First were the *sisters*. A lot of the men answering my ad let me know that they were also crossdressers. I gave a polite "no thanks" to anyone eager to get together as girls and did my best not to hold it against anyone wanting to step up and be a man for me.

Next were the *beastly boys,* you know, those one-handed typists who IM you and begin the conversation with "What are you wearing?" or the men who want to rendezvous right now or next Tuesday at twelve at the Travelodge. "Don't bother me," I told them. "There's a whole industry set up to serve your needs." And eventually I just turned instant messaging off and ignored all uncouth email.

The trickiest people to deal with were the *lonely hearts.* These were men from all over the country—and world—who longed for romantic correspondence with a transgendered woman. They would be content to go back and forth with emails for months. Some might like to be pen pals or even telephone pals forever, while avoiding any definite plans to get together.

After wasting an embarrassing amount of time talking to a man from Vancouver, I decided that I would no longer correspond with anyone without him first showing up somewhere and meeting me. If that ruled out most out-of-towners, then so be it. "What do you think?" I asked my new friend Lilly over the phone.

"That's fine," she said, "but what will you do if a guy doesn't show up? I've already had several men no-show or cancel at the last minute with the lamest excuses."

We bounced ideas around and came up with the show-up-at-the-club-and-find-me policy. I would simply let guys know when I'd be at the Queen Mary and invite them to come by and introduce themselves. If they had trouble finding me, they could ask Lori, behind the bar, for help. Then, if we had any chemistry, we could make further plans. That way, I didn't really care if a guy showed up or not, because I'd be out kicking up my heels anyway.

Often no one would show up, or so it seemed. Or I might find out later that a guy showed up and got intimidated by seeing me talk with another man. Or maybe a guy might think I didn't measure up to my pictures and not bother to introduce himself—I had heard of that happening to other girls. Because of all the no-shows and because I wasn't promising the whole night to anyone, I might double or triple book. It really was never a problem, except for one night when *three* men showed up to meet me. Ah, the simple joys of maidenhood.

I don't know exactly when I met Lilly. She just seemed to be a crossdresser in her late 40s who showed up everywhere I did and loved to dance as every bit as much. Stylish and petite in a way I envied, she had her own head of long, shiny blonde hair, which she wore instead of a wig, often rolling it up in a French twist. That plus the remainder of her English accent gave her an air of sophistication.

Over the fall of '97, as Sonia and I discovered we had less and less in common, Lilly and I found we had more and more. It didn't take much for us to go from acquaintances to friends to best girl friends. Originally from London, she had moved to L.A. to work with an American accounting firm. After nearly killing herself in a drunk driving accident sixteen years ago, she turned to Alcoholics Anonymous for help. She participated wholeheartedly and eventually became a sponsor. Soon she and her wife, who had also come over from England, had their first and only child. Unfortunately her wife had her own troubles, and they divorced three years later. Lilly, or rather Larry, retained primary custody of their daughter, who by now was twelve.

Recently Lilly had started to explore crossdressing and had stopped dating women for the time being. She stored her clothes and changed at a locker room rented out by Lydia's TV Fashions. Although traditionally diffident and reserved, she was impressed by my worldliness and daring. In many ways, I became her big sister the way Tina had been mine. I helped her overcome her fears and break out into the world of straight restaurants, shopping malls, and going wherever you please—daylight be darned. I also did a little too good a job of describing the pleasures of being a woman with a man. She tried it, liked it, and soon started joking about how I unwittingly corrupted her.

Nevertheless, our relationship was very much a two-way street. We would spend hours talking about transgender people and things. As a single father and AA member, Lilly had learned a lot about life and had interesting ideas about TG issues. Additionally, because she went out more than I did, she was closer to the other girls in the community and helped me feel connected. She knew a lot about how they all lived and what they needed. She hoped to start a business someday that would fulfill some of those needs.

In the meantime, as Melissa's husband, I'd made efforts to embrace more of her family and found remarkable acceptance among them when I looked for it. Like a tree pushing its roots into the ground, I felt more deeply involved and in love with her with each passing year. With Liss as my soul mate and Lilly as best t-friend, my life was coming together beautifully, yet I still strove for that final piece of the puzzle.

Though single, Lilly, like me, hoped for a part-time boyfriend so as not to disrupt her conventional life at home with her daughter. Like me, she wanted an affair that would be both erotic and enduring, but her wish list was a little different. We both wanted to be taken out and then *taken* in. But I could live without being taken out, and she could live without being taken in.

Despite our differences, we felt that deep down we were the same. We both loved being women in costume and part, body and *role*. I loved expressing myself as a woman and being accepted as one, whether by a man or a woman or another transgendered person, whether in person or over the phone or even just over the Internet.

In fact, sometimes I feel the only thing truly womanly about me is that I love being one so much. Maybe that makes me an autogynephilic male rather than a partial female? I suppose it's possible, and I have nothing against liking things for sexual reasons. But for a long time now, I've preferred to see myself as a man-and-woman, and I suspect my brain never fully masculinized in some key area that renders satisfaction for the playing out of one's gender role. Like a little girl who likes running around in her mom's pearls, my brain leaves me feeling quite pleased by anything that says, *Right now, I'm being a woman.*

Being a woman socially was great fun. I loved chatting on the phone with Sonia and Lilly and giving them great big welcomes whenever I saw them. We would hug and kiss and fuss over each other and what we were all wearing. I liked being able to make dinner plans with them and not have to worry if that somehow made us gay. As women, we had a license to get excited about things and be emotional. We could delight in the smallest details of life or talk about feeling scared or insecure. Later, like girls, we would look out for each other at the QM and never leave without saying goodbye.

Meanwhile, I continued to put myself out there, hoping to win the heart of Mr. Right. Though I might've wished for more, I was asked out every two months or so over the years of '97 and '98. It was intoxicating. Sometimes I'd put my perfume on and practically pinch myself. *I'm going on a date tonight— and I'm the girl!*

My best dates were with Marvin, or as he preferred, Marv, a distinguished chemical engineer from Houston. Bald and by no means tall, I never would have noticed him among the men at the Queen Mary the night he approached me with sweat on his brow and a twinkle in his eye. Some guys did the charm thing and some didn't. Marv, I soon realized, had made it a fine art. Not only did he make me feel like a woman, but the only one in the world it seemed as far as he was concerned.

Before I knew it, he had me laughing and smiling, as he explained he was a happily married grandfather of three who would love to take me out whenever he was in L.A. on business. Though I could see right through his courtly ways, I said yes. Who wouldn't want to be queen for a night?

True to his word, he would email me a couple times a year to let me know when he'd be in town and ask me where I'd like to go. "*Anywhere,*" he wrote, "gay, straight, private, public. It doesn't matter." Usually he'd pick me up at La Serenata, and we'd go to dinner and then see a movie or meander through an outdoor marketplace, like the Third Street Promenade or Universal City Walk. One rare weekend with Melissa out of town and Marv in town, I seized the opportunity to do something I wasn't supposed to do; I asked him to pick me up at home, just like a real girl.

As I finished fussing with my hair, the buzzer rang for me to let him into our apartment building. After a knock on the door, I opened it and there he was, squinty-eyed and smiling, with a bouquet of flowers. I was surprised and touched. No one had ever done that for me. He gave me a discreet peck on the lips, and I encouraged him to relax as I fixed a couple drinks for us.

After showing him around a little, we were ready to go. Although I had come out to the cool couple who lived on one side of us, I'd been squabbling with the cantankerous old woman on the other side—*wouldn't she love to have this to use against me.* So I was careful to move quickly and quietly down the corridor trusting that Marv would do the same.

He followed my lead, but as he opened the front door of the building for me, I thought I heard the click of a door opening down the hallway behind me. *Don't look! Just keep walking,* I told myself, as a jolt of adrenaline shot through me. Fortunately, his car was just out front. There, he helped me settle into the passenger seat, snuck a peak at my legs, and whisked me off to safety.

Soon we arrived at Pedals Cafe on Santa Monica Beach. I paused at the heavy glass front door, and right on cue, he pulled it open and ushered me in. Once we were seated, he told me about the project he was consulting on in L.A., and I was pleased to remember enough pre-med chemistry to follow along.

Wrapping it up, he toasted me and peppered me with questions about my life, at one point inquiring about my prior experiences with men. I must have responded then with a level of detail beyond what he had expected, for he suddenly stopped and scolded me. "You can't just talk like that. You're a *beautiful* woman. You don't know what that does to a man."

By now tipsy, I looked at him with a confused grin, as I began to put myself in his shoes.

But before I could say anything, he leaned up close. "It's practically foreplay," he explained beneath his breath.

After dinner, we strolled hand in hand along the bicycle path by the beach. The first few people we came across seemed to look us over a little too long and forced me to think about how I stood 6'2" in my strappy sandals next to my date, who stood 5'10" in his loafers. He seemed a little tense too, so I decided we needed some distraction. "You said you knew Michelle Winters. I thought she's been strictly Mike for the last few years?"

"Well, I may be from Texas, but I'm hardly new to the scene here," he asserted, as he loosened his grip on my hand. "We used to date. I'd even come up and spend weekends with her on the beach. She was awesome—" Seeming to catch himself, he turned to me. "But really *nothing* like you."

"Oh, Marv, that's really not necessary," I lied, as I gave him a little elbow in the ribs. We soon lost ourselves in our commonality and repartee, as we made our way past the other strolling couples. After a while, we stopped to look out at the ocean.

"Hey, let's go out and see the waves!" I bubbled. Leaving the path, we sauntered through a good fifty yards of sand. When we were close enough to hear the crash of the surf, I kicked off my sandals and skipped along the water's edge, my long hair blowing in the breeze. Thank goodness, I'd left the pantyhose behind that night. I felt a bit silly but figured, what the hey. It was completely dark except for a little moonlight shining down on the breaking waves. Mr. Smooth jogged to keep up with me, then laughed, and put his arms around me. Without saying another word, he put his mouth on mine and kissed me, while my delicate hippie dress fluttered at my knees.

"Should we go back to your place?" he suggested. Although I liked the idea of being made love to in my own bed just like any other woman, it felt like too much of an invasion of my life with Melissa. Instead, we headed off to the bar atop the Radisson and later to his room, where the romance continued.

After everything was said *and done,* I was so tired that I considered sleeping over—although I had never done that with a man before. I didn't mind the idea of sleeping in breast forms and a wig; I was more concerned about what I would look like in the morning. The last thing I needed was to wake up next to Marv with a stubbly mustache. He understood, and was gentleman enough to drive me back home in the middle of the night. Though sweet, his visits were all too few and far between, and I never knew when I'd see him again.

Months later, another memorable dating moment occurred, after dinner at Spazio with Jeff, a mountain of a man and former defensive tackle for the Washington Redskins. I took his arm as we made our way back to his car. Before opening the door for me, he paused to give me a kiss.

I accepted it full on the mouth, then pulled away a little and gazed up at him. "Just how big and strong are you?" I cooed, stroking his massive biceps.

"Would you care for a demonstration?" he grinned confidently.

"Sure."

He gently slid his hands down my arms and stopped under my elbows. Then before I knew it, he curled his huge arms, and I was airborne with my feet dangling two feet above the sidewalk on Ventura Blvd. My football hero wasn't even breathing hard, but he was sure making my heart go pitter-patter.

One Friday night in November '98, I arrived at the Queen Mary an hour late and frustrated from a traffic jam in Laurel Canyon. Still stressed out despite a quick drink, I worried about how my arms looked in my new sleeveless dress, as I hurried onto the dance floor. Just then, Darius cut me off and looked me over from head to toe. "Damn it, girl, *look* at you." I loved the way this big black former bus driver had always felt like my one-man welcoming committee.

"Do you like my new dress, Darius?"

"Fuck yeah!" he positively roared.

Knowing he was a good dancer, I asked him to join me, and before long, the music turned slow. Without missing a beat, he pulled me in close, and with his hefty right hand pressed firmly into the small of my back, he let me know who was in charge. His skin was clammy and his Hawaiian shirt damp. Instinctively I began to breathe through my mouth, before chiding myself, *C'mon now. He's a man. You're the one who has to be daisy fresh.*

Oblivious to the thoughts in my pretty head, he held me tight and didn't care if I noticed his . . . enthusiasm.

Hmm, I'll have to tell Hagop his handiwork got a rave review, I laughed to myself, as I started to relax. "Either that's a banana in your pocket, or you're awfully happy to see me," I whispered in his ear, as his face formed into a smile.

Between songs, he asked if I might like a little company later on. And when I explained the Date Me First Rule, he countered that he couldn't take me out in public because he was married. Meanwhile, a faster song started up, and he grabbed my hands to swing dance. He pushed me out, pulled me back in, and twirled me—occasionally stopping me halfway through, with his body pressed up against me from behind, both of us facing the mirror.

"Damn, you're pretty!" he swore as the song faded out and he led me over to the bar for a drink. By the time I washed down another one of my signature vodka-and-diet-cokes, I was ready to make this man an exception.

Back at La Serenata I sat in bed, sore but satisfied. As Darius emerged from the bathroom freshly dressed and scrubbed, I clamored for a kiss goodbye.

"Hey, hey, I just finished showering your perfume off," he said, warding me off with his arm. "You don't want to get me in trouble do you?" I had *never* thought of that before.

Though he could never commit to a plan, Friday after Friday he showed up at the Queen Mary and found me. Though frustrating, he was the steadiest man I had ever known, and I was always thrilled to feel him tapping me on the shoulder—and to watch his white van match my every move in the rearview mirror. We went on like that for about two months before he stopped seeking me out and disappeared from the club for a while. When he reemerged, he fell straightaway for a nice transsexual girl I knew—we all knew each other. Somehow he was able to go on dates with her. Still, he stuck by his wife, so she ultimately left him to look for a full-time boyfriend. Somehow, through it all, we managed to stay easy and comfortable with each other around the club.

Getting to experience compliments, flowers, and flirty dancing firsthand made me realize just how great these things can make you feel. Maybe I had lost track of the little things I used to do for Lissa, I thought, or maybe I'd never been so good at them in the first place. So from then on, I decided, I would compliment her regularly and surprise her with flowers whenever she least expected it.

Out of curiosity, I liked to politely ask many of the men who wandered my way, "What makes you interested in a girl like me?" Most of what I heard boiled down to "I'm turned on by women who've just got that little something extra." That seemed to make sense and worked just fine for me.

But one night when I was horsing around with Darius at the back bar, he volunteered, "I'm *not* a crossdresser, but I tried it once at home. I was one big fat mama." Then with a chortle, he changed the subject to his recent efforts to trim down and stay healthy.

Marv too, I learned, had tried it, but he stopped because he felt he looked too old. Nonetheless, he explained, he was still very excited by the whole idea and "Treating someone young and pretty like a total woman from first cocktail to farewell kiss is the next best thing to being there."

With my illusions shattered, I now saw little difference between my all-man admirers and the ones at the bar dying to try on my stockings, give oral sex, and get fucked—like I was when I met Prima back in Chicago. It all began to make sense: *Deep inside every chaser beats the heart of a tranny.*

Increasingly, I assumed it of every man I met, and it explained a lot of the odd questions they would ask, like "How can you *walk* in those shoes?" It seemed an accurate assumption, but at the same time, a truth not worth dwelling on. If someday my prince would come, I wouldn't want to think too much about him somehow also being a princess.

Not long after figuring this out, a nice-looking man in a jacket and tie approached me at the Queen Mary. "So you're a shrink," he said with a New York accent. "Tell me something about this crazy place."

"I could tell you why you're here—and why you *think* you're here."

"Hmm, really?" he said baffled, but intrigued.

"Really," I replied confidently, with a little look out of the corner of my eye.

"Okay, why?"

"You're *not* ready to hear it."

"Smart girl, eh?"

"Yes, and a thirsty one," I sighed, looking lonely and glancing over at the bar.

Although I had a lot of fun with admirers in my mid-thirties, my dates were far too few and not leading to any sort of steady boyfriend. Some of the men I dated seemed to satisfy their curiosity, then disappear. Others would show up at the club next week only to leave with someone else, evidently interested in a little piece of anyone they found appealing. Still others, like Marv, were only in town for a little while and might not contact me again until the same time next year.

"Remember that guy from San Diego who was supposed to take me to Rive Gauche last night?" I was calling to complain to Lilly, one Saturday morning from the privacy of my den. "He called yesterday to tell me a friend of his was in the hospital, so he had to cancel."

"Yeah, right," she said sarcastically.

"Maybe guys are worried about me getting read?" I wondered. "What's it like for a cute little thing like you? You pass pretty well."

"Yeah, as long as I keep my mouth shut."

"Even still," I replied, hoping I hadn't hurt her feelings.

Lilly admitted that though she'd had better luck with dinner dates, she hadn't found anyone to see on a regular basis either. When I asked her about a couple of very passable pre-ops we knew, she said that they got asked out a lot, sometimes by guys who knew and sometimes by guys who didn't.

"Damn, it would be great to pass," I vented, though I knew it wouldn't be all fun and games to go out with a guy who assumed I was a real girl.

"Christy's even got a boyfriend these days."

"You know, I'm so tired of waiting for a date so I can have sex and waiting for a boyfriend so I can have a sex life."

"You have sex with Melissa, don't you?"

"Yeah, but I'm talking about sex as a woman. I feel like I'm a fresh spring flower, spreading my petals and ready to be plucked. And it better happen soon, or I'll die on the vine."

"Then go do something about it." Lilly could be real direct at times, even blunt. "Pick someone up if you feel like it."

"But I'd feel like it every weekend. That could mean a man a week," I thought out loud, before explaining that even one a month sounded risky in terms of the STDs that you couldn't entirely prevent with condoms.[44] Besides, by now I had been looking for Mr. Right for three years. People had seen me flirting with countless men and probably thought I was a slut, for they didn't know how few I had actually slept with. I hated being seen that way, because I'd never been a philanderer by nature. I was really just a healthy young woman with needs trying to find someone decent and dependable—and the guys weren't cooperating.

"Personally, Alice," Lilly broke in, "I don't think the other girls at the club give a damn who you're with. Just the same, why don't you lighten up for a while? Forget about sex and boyfriends, but know that whenever you meet someone who seems especially fun—and safe—you're free to go for it."

"That sounds good, but I don't entirely trust myself to operate like that. How about if I report everything to you and you tell me if I'm getting out of line?"

"Okay, I guess you can think of me as a sort of sponsor," she said with a chuckle.

She's right, I thought as I put down the receiver. I'd been getting frustrated and no longer having a good time. I might never find a boyfriend, so I had better learn to have fun along the way. Tranny nightlife seemed to revolve around casual sex and colorful experimentation. Maybe I'd been looking for an apple in a rain forest of tropical fruit? Why fight it? Why not live off the land, rather than resent it.

No one seemed to live off the land better than April. She was a perky Korean-American crossdresser with a small but scrappy frame and barbed wire tatts around her arms. We'd been acquaintances for a while, so she wasn't surprised when I asked for her number but was overjoyed when I called. She explained that though she had lots of girl friends in the clubs, she didn't have anyone she could talk to during the week.

Again doing my best Lois Lane, I couldn't help but ask about her tattoos. They, she said, like the slight limp to her walk, were souvenirs from her days as an Airborne Ranger. She had enlisted just after graduating from high school and had served for several years before deciding she'd like to settle down and live near her family. So she left the army but continued on for a while in the reserves. In the meantime, she discovered that her personality made her a natural in sales and began work as a sales rep for a large maker of kitchen appliances.

Because her office was much closer to the clubs than her home, she used to get changed and do her makeup in the parking lot behind the Queen Mary. She got so good at it that, in the cramped confines of her car, she could transform herself in about a third the time it would take me back at my spacious room at La Serenata.

Although she was younger and wilder than Lilly, she was oddly inhibited in some ways. I never could interest her in dining out before dancing. Yet once she arrived at the Queen Mary and tossed down a drink, no one was more upbeat and fun. Traditionally she had dated genetic girls and still had her eye out for one. Although we rarely saw single women around the club, if anyone was going to find a fun-loving GG at the QM, it would be April.

Over the previous couple years, she had also discovered the thrill of sex with men. She and Lilly and I decided we really liked both men and women. We had to admit sex with men was great—maybe better than sex with women—but relationships with women were more satisfying and much easier to find. How could you choose? Who would want to?

Like myself, she continued to be boyish in certain ways but somehow knew how to make her assertiveness look peppy and her tattoos look *bad girl*. I really fed off her energy at the bar and occasionally off her cocaine in the ladies' room. We loved whooping it up on a Friday night and groggily rehashing our adventures over the phone Saturday afternoon. Like me, she couldn't understand why she never heard from men afterward even if they seemed to have an amazing time.

"Fuck 'em!" she bristled. "I don't even give 'em my number no more. All I know is, when I come to the club, they want me. And they'll follow me all over town and do whatever I say." She had long since learned to accept each man for what he was and to grab each night by the balls. Meanwhile, I decided I'd had it with being a frustrated nice girl. If TG nightlife was a jungle, then I was going to swing through the trees like April, never out of control, but unabashedly Jane, Jane of the Jungle.

I arrived at the QM early one evening in a plaid skirt and preppy headband—just like the girls I had pined for back at Nichols. I pulled a stool over to the jukebox and started entering my choices. An older man approached me, dressed in leather and looking dusty, like he had just come off a motorcycle. His name was Chuck, and it turned out that he *had* just gotten off a motorcycle. It also turned out that he had gone to Catholic school, and through his slurred words, he let me know how pleased he was to see a young lady in a pleated skirt.

Unsure of whether he was complimenting me or not, I thanked him anyway and turned back to the jukebox. Dusty, scrawny, and drunk just wasn't my type.

Chuck, nonetheless, kept talking. He told me how cute I looked and asked what I did for a living.

Feeling sassy I told him I was a *professional*—just to see where he would go with it.

He smiled wide, showed me two *hundred-dollar* bills, and slid them up my silky leg. By the time they disappeared under the hem of my skirt, they felt like they'd built up an electric charge. "There, that should serve as a retainer. I'd like to talk to you later," he said, as he swaggered off to the show room.

I was stunned. I couldn't believe what I had gotten myself into, but I was feeling too exhilarated to do anything but play along. Finishing with the jukebox, I drifted over to the bar. My benefactor soon reappeared and pounced on the stool next to me.

"What about you? What do you do?" I asked, as we waited for our drinks.

"I'm Chuck Delaney," he boasted, hoping for a flash of recognition, "national moto-cross champion '78 and '80."

"I'm sorry," I said, "but you could be the *most* famous motorcycle racer in the world, and I still wouldn't know who you were . . . but then you probably haven't heard of any of the more successful tranny call girls in town."

He laughed hard, spraying a bit of his beer. Then I laughed along with him, and we kept up a good chatter. With each passing minute, he slipped bill after bill under my skirt, while I stole furtive glances around the club to try to ward off trouble. Behind the bar, Lori looked oblivious and would probably be cool even if she wasn't. But the bouncers at the QM could be real pricks, and the last thing I needed was to be 86'd from the only tranny bar in town (or at least that's the way I had begun to think of it).

When Chuck, at last, excused himself to go to the men's room, I hastily gathered up all the cash and stuffed it into my purse before any could fall to the floor. What kind of weird twilight zone had I stumbled into? Before this went too far, I'd have to find out what he wanted of me.

"I want to go down on you," he explained, a bit embarrassed, when he returned.

What the heck, I thought, as I walked and he staggered out to the parking lot. "Um, let's take my car back to your hotel. You can pick up your motorcycle in the morning."

Frankly, I was a little scared to go up to his room, because he was so drunk. And although I felt reassured by his smaller stature, I tucked some pepper spray into my purse just to be safe. Upstairs, though, the hundreds kept flowing as smoothly as they had downstairs and I gave him the experience he craved.

Finally, with my biker bud cleaning up in the bathroom, I had the chance to count all my cash. I had earned $1200. I gave him a fond farewell but no email or phone number, in case he woke up next morning with an angry case of buyer's remorse.

I was dying to tell somebody about my adventure, and Sonia seemed to be perfect. As a trans woman, she enjoyed the story of hundred-dollar bills floating up my skirt. As a policewoman and friend, she taught me how to avoid getting busted if I ever tried it again. "It's really as simple as asking, 'Are you a cop?'" she explained, "and insisting on an answer. Undercover cops don't have the authority to lie for the purpose of a prostitution bust."

True to my word, I called Lilly later that day to report in. "Hey, how are you?" I began.

"Fine," she replied, "I heard you had quite a night last night."

"News travels fast, eh?"

"Was I not supposed to know?"

"Of course not. I just didn't think Sonia would reach you before I did."

"So anyway, tell me what happened," she said, cutting to the chase. While listening to my story, she seemed to vacillate between envious and alarmed. "I think what you did was wrong," she pronounced like a judge. "It's not that you turned a trick; it's that you put yourself in a risky situation with a guy who was drunk and potentially dangerous. You don't know the shit alcoholics pull. It wasn't smart, and it's not part of your deal with Melissa."

I considered arguing back but knew in my heart she was right. So I bit my tongue and thanked her for speaking up. Hanging up the phone, I thought, *I might not live by conventions, but I must live by my agreements.* I had promised Melissa I'd keep it safe. But safe sex was not enough; I had to be more cautious about who I had it with.

In the meantime, I had so much cash on hand that I didn't know *what* to do with it. I figured if I deposited it in the bank, it would look like income from my practice and I'd have to pay taxes on it. So—perhaps to assuage my guilt—I ended up buying the wicker-and-wood chairs from Pottery Barn that my wife and I had been eying for our kitchen counter.

Pretending to be a prostitute had been such a thrill, though, that I kept my eye out for the right chance to fulfill other fantasies. One spring night, Darius snatched me away from a conversation with April to slow dance with him. How could I say no? I often did the same to him.

"Alice, you sure are one fine woman!" he declared, while guiding me along the dance floor and tightening his grip. The familiar feel of his arm around my waist re-awakened my affection.

"*You*, you should talk. You're practically the king of the Queen Mary," I replied, thinking of his lusty charm and all my friends who had surrendered to it.

"So what are your plans for later on tonight?" he inquired—more interested than usual—as he gave me a twirl and then pulled me back in.

"They could include you if you'd like to help me live out a fantasy."

"Like what?" he asked, as his eyes lit up.

"I'd like," I whispered in his ear, "to be tied down to the corners of my bed and thoroughly ravished."

"You mean something like this," he whispered back as he clasped my wrists in his big hands and held them together behind my back, locking me in close to him.

"Ah hah," I affirmed, breathlessly aware of his belt-buckle pressing up against my waist.

"You got a room over at Serenata?"

"Ah hah."

Strange as it may sound, throughout my most wanton days as a woman, I was still living and working all but three nights a month as a rather ordinary man. The other twenty-eight nights, Melissa and I did the normal things that youngish couples without kids do: relaxing quietly at home; barbequing with friends; going to movie openings and concerts (her choices) and obscure ethnic restaurants and Laker games (my choices). Although I was busy networking, giving talks around town, and taking on new patients for my psychiatry practice, she persuaded me to take one last big trip before settling down to have kids. We decided on a week in Paris.

As we sampled the Salad Nicoise at a cafe on the Champs Elysees, I caught her staring at my face. "What are you doing?" I asked.

"You know, I can still see the bruises under your eyes," she replied.

I had ended up taking a week and a half off from work and used the first few days to get my nose job revised. As time went on, I had regretted that I hadn't specifically asked my surgeon to make my nose more androgynous. So I had recently gone back to him, explained I was a crossdresser, and arranged for him to go back in and narrow the tip.

"Don't the bruises make me look rugged?" I joked.

"Yeah," she kidded back, "in exactly the same way under both eyes." After a sip of coffee, she continued, "I love seeing you read three travel books at once and get all worked up about the French Revolution."

"Thanks. I love hearing you speak French. And thanks for insisting we come here."

"You know, you would be the greatest guy if you weren't so obsessed with crossdressing," she said with a playful smile.

"Oh, I suppose I'd get stuck on something else, whether it was mountain climbing or yacht racing," I teased back.

"That would be good!" she replied, making big eyes and nodding her head in exaggerated eagerness.

"Oh, you know what I would want to do? I'd like to fly small planes," I said, as I returned to my salad.

"No way," she insisted. "I won't let you, and you're certainly not getting me on one with you."

Oh, my god, I'm already flying with her on board. I swallowed hard, as I thought of my recent sex-capades. *God damn it. I'd be so much better off with a steady boyfriend. I've got to be careful. Whatever I do, I've got to be so careful.* Then I packed my anguish back in its box. I could work on it later with Caroline, but for now nothing was going to get in the way of the great time I was having with Melissa.

Back home in the jungle, things were growing ever wilder. Lilly and April were now coming up with their own sexy ideas and translating them into reality. Lilly, of all people, went to the Power Exchange, a very special trans-inclusive sex club in San Francisco. She hooked up with a guy and had sex in front of a crowd of onlookers—then she relaxed for a while, found someone else, and did it again!

At the Queen Mary, a vacationing firefighter from Atlanta wanted to go to bed with April. "Sure," she said, "as long as Alice can come along—with her video camera." No idea was a bad idea. I fantasized about two men taking turns at me and kept my eye out for just the right opportunity.

Things could get pretty fast in our transgender world. It wasn't like the straight world, where the girls kept the speed limit down to 60 mph. In our world, the girls were all raised as boys. We weren't trained to be prim and say things like "We're not ready," or even "But I hardly know you." Nonetheless, we still had a speed limit because we aspired to be ladylike and were often on hormones, which nipped our sex drives. It was just that ours was set to something like 90 instead of 60.

Even so, it was tame compared to the gay world, where the "girls" weren't just raised as boys; they were boys. So, few people were interested in slowing things down, and many were looking to push the pedal to the metal and go for it. In the gay scene, there were no speed limits. You could drive over 200 if you could handle it.

In the summer of '99, Chuck contacted me by email. He had found my website and discovered I wasn't really a call girl, but he wanted to see me again just the same. Still leery of him, I tried to set him up with April. "But," he wrote, "I've been thinking about you for the last six months. I don't want to be with anyone else."

Sensing my fear, he explained a few things about himself. Yes, he had been a terrible drunk last winter, but he was now sober and with "the program." Indeed, he was a famous motorcycle racer and now owned a very successful motorcycle dealership. On top of everything else, he was a married man from Palm Springs who liked to rummage through his wife's clothes when she was away. And rather than feeling angry at me for not being a real prostitute, he appreciated me all the more. He wanted to "bring me out of retirement." He made me an offer.

I had mixed feelings about tricking again, so I emailed him back with a counteroffer that I figured would price me out of reach.

"Two thousand dollars?" he replied. "How 'bout next weekend."

I gulped and made arrangements. Although still not attracted to Chuck, I was beginning to like him as a person and didn't mind putting out for him. After all, he was handing me the biggest trick I had ever heard of. And after the deed was done, I went about life each day with a little extra spring in my step because of it. Nonetheless, I would have given up all my adventures to have a good steady man in my life, because Melissa's egg timer was ticking and my life was about to get even more complicated.

12

A Full Life

Although I had never been able to completely rule out going full time as a woman, with more knowledge of what it was like for people like Sonia, it became less and less appealing in comparison with the remarkable life I led with Melissa. So by the time I was thirty-six and she was thirty-seven, I was reasonably sure there would be no more major changes. Having also reached a relatively comfortable place in her life, she and I decided we were ready for children. Kids had always been one of the things I wanted most in life. Discovering that I was a crossdresser had threatened my chances but never changed the way I felt.

To make room, we bought a house by the beach in early '99. Though we had a lot of fun making renovations, I was surprised to see that my femininity didn't extend nearly as far as Lissa's when it came to nesting. I just couldn't share the utter delight she took in choosing paint colors and setting up a proper kitchen. So, how many womanly interests did I really share?

Though I've rarely been keen on things like decorating and cooking in male mode, in female mode I've rejoiced in those activities that feel the most feminine and transformative. I can imagine transitioning, getting married, and subsequently discovering those delights as the woman of the house. Maybe it would be like when I was a med student attached to an intern who had to sew up lacerations in the emergency room. As the student observing the slow painstaking process, it was deadly dull. But later, as the intern myself, with needle in hand and responsibility on my shoulders, it was riveting.

So under the right circumstances, I might very well take to many typically female things and see them as my responsibility and privilege. Yet, I wonder how long my Martha Stewart phase might last as I felt more accepted. Then I might moderate my homemaking—and wardrobe too and stick to black slacks or cute jeans most days like everyone else.

After stopping my tiny estrogen dose and just a month of trying, I got Melissa pregnant and that November took her to the hospital for a C-section.

As the obstetrician cut into her belly, I shuddered as I realized how alone I would feel in the world without her. Then, as he pulled our little baby out into the open air, I felt like I had completed a vital mission in life, before reminding myself that, no, I had just begun one.

We were thrilled to welcome our daughter Hanna into the world. I was very excited and spent a lot of time with her—by male standards. Yet feeling much more like a proud father than a new mother, I returned to work after just one week, focused and ever more determined to keep bringing home the bacon. I looked forward to seeing her each day and holding her close but was content to see her primarily on evenings and weekends. Though I loved taking her for a brisk walk each morning and even changing her diapers, I could never sit for more than half an hour with her at the park without getting restless. I imagine if I had been her mom instead of her dad, I would have been more into it, but still, I don't think I would have made a good stay-at-home mom.

"Who's my little girl? Who's my little mittles girl? Little mittle mittles girl . . ." I heard Melissa sing one day, as I came home through the French doors into our family room and was met by the hearty smell of fresh-cooked turkey loaf and the sight of her on the couch with Hanna at her breast. Gazing at them together before giving each a kiss, I began to see the advantages of traditional life and didn't know who I envied more, my wife or the baby she so focused on.

Yet after inquiring as to my day, she bit her lip and told me she was thinking about getting back to work sooner than she had expected. "Mark called," she explained, "and said he might have some stuff for me to do the week after next."

"Okay," I said, slowly digesting the fact that our cozy new routine might soon be a thing of the past.

"There are whole parts of me that I don't want to lose," she continued.

"I understand."

"And Araceli said she could watch Hanna while we finish finding a nanny."

"I guess that'd be okay," I replied. After all, I knew how important music was to Melissa, and she was only speeding up a timetable we had already discussed.

She smiled for a moment, then held our baby extra tight and frowned. "But what if I don't like it? What if I wanna come home?" she said, clearly torn by her tough choice.

"That'd be fine too," I said, trying to help her find balance the way she'd helped me. "I can cover us. Just take your time and figure it out as you go along."

She seemed relieved and rested her head on Hanna's. After a total of two months off, she went back to work part time, and we arranged for Araceli, our cleaning lady, to baby-sit on Saturdays so that we could have a regular date night.

As Melissa grew more confident at home with the baby, she allowed me to go from three nights a month to four; Alice could have Fridays on a regular basis. Although always available by cell phone, I never liked the idea of leaving her and Hanna for too long, so I started dressing up at the house and coming back home at the end of the night. We chose to see it as something akin to poker night with the guys and didn't belabor the differences.

To be a good team player, I put away the picture of me as Alice I had kept on my bedroom dresser and stashed all my crossdressing gear into two large trunks and an out-of-the-way closet. That way, family and friends could come by to see our little snooky-pie and roam the house without Melissa having to worry about who was in on my secret and who wasn't. Going out and letting my hair down weekly felt great, though I certainly didn't want to miss any more time with her and Hanna.

Now that time had become more precious, I had to reevaluate my need for ongoing therapy. Although life wasn't everything I had dreamed of, I felt I had adjusted well to being a crossdresser and worked out a darn good lifestyle for myself. Like a Catholic at confession, I appreciated the weekly ritual of confiding in Caroline, but I was running out of new things to talk about—or at least, things that couldn't be just as easily discussed with Melissa, Lilly, and other people in my life. So I thanked her heartily, bade her farewell, and assured her that she would be the first person I'd call if I ran into trouble down the road.

As my frustrating experience with Posner had given way to more fulfilling experiences with Joshua and Caroline, I had found psychotherapy instrumental in meeting the challenges of crossdressing and adulthood in general. I'm sure it could help a lot of other TGs and wives too. But please be careful in choosing a therapist. Try to find someone with prior transgender experience. (www.ifge.org has a list of such people.) But more importantly, don't be afraid to ask friends for recommendations and to shop around a little if anything feels wrong.

Even though I had given up hope of a boyfriend, I still enjoyed fluttering about and flirting with anyone who looked like he had potential. Bumped from my usual Friday night by something Melissa and I had wanted to do as a couple, I came to the Queen Mary on a bustling Saturday night in March 2000 in a smooth strapless Polynesian-print dress, which I only now could pull off thanks to a clever new bra from Hagop. While dancing, I scanned the crowd and saw a man of about fifty who looked so tall, dark, and handsome you'd swear he had inspired the expression. Although he seemed to be hanging out with an older blonde "lady," I thought I caught a little eye contact, so I bopped over. "We don't usually get such handsome men in here," I began. "What's your name?"

"Frank," he said, a bit flustered by my sudden attention.

"I'm Alice," I said and swiftly turned to his companion. "What's your name?"

"Dana," she replied pleasantly.

I didn't know whether they were friends or more and didn't want to be rude. My intention was only—what it always was—to break the ice with a man, then move on. If he was interested, he could chase me down later. I turned back to Frank, who looked broad-shouldered in a striped polo shirt that hung casually over an old pair of jeans with a funny peace-sign patch over one knee, and continued, "I don't think I've ever seen you here before. Is this your first time at the Queen Mary?"

"No, I've been coming here off and on for years," he said, laughing and exchanging glances with Dana. "How about you?"

Just then, his friend excused herself and I felt bad, though she didn't seem especially miffed as she disappeared into the crowd. After Frank and I made a little small talk, he asked what kind of work I did.

"I run a string of tranny call girls," I replied, feeling frisky. Caught by surprise, he gagged on his coffee.

"Was it something I said?" I grinned coyly.

"No, no," he replied, regaining his composure. "Really?"

"Nah," I said and told him I was a psychiatrist. He seemed impressed, but not especially interested. He let me know he was a contractor who preferred residential work.

The crowd on the dance floor doubled as the room reverberated with the latest Jennifer Lopez hit. "Do you wanna go up front and see some of the show?" I shouted above the din. He nodded, and I swished ahead with confidence, feeling his eyes on my derriere, thankful for every hour of practice I'd put in.

Lucky to find an open table, and thankfully one that wasn't in the front row, we enjoyed the show and tipped the performers as they strutted by. When they paused for intermission, I touched Frank on the forearm. "Coffee?" I commented. "*That's* a funny thing to drink at a nightclub."

"I don't drink anymore. I haven't touched it for the last eight months."

"Why?" I asked reflexively.

He looked right at me for a moment. "You don't shy away from the big questions, do you?"

"Well, I *am* a shrink after all," I said, smiling. "But you don't have to go into it if you don't want to."

He explained that he had turned to alcohol as his marriage had fallen apart, all the while remaining in denial because he only drank wine, a normal thing in his Italian-American family. But when he showed up at his lawyer's office one morning sweating and shaking, he had to admit he needed help. After divorce, rehab, and a few months in AA, he claimed, he no longer felt the need to drink.

"Do you have any kids?" I asked.

"No, thank god," he said, shaking his head. "I'm so glad I don't have to have anything to do with her anymore. I had to give up so much just to keep the house." After a long sigh, he asked, "How 'bout you? What's your deal?"

"I'm married with a baby at home." I proclaimed, pulling a picture from my purse that Melissa had taken of me, as Alice, giving a bottle to our infant daughter.

"Married?" he remarked with eyebrows raised. "How does that work?"

"I was more or less this way when Melissa and I met. And we've arranged for me to have one night a week as a woman, usually on Fridays."

"Where do you live?"

"Santa Monica. How 'bout you?"

"Coldwater Canyon."

"Mind taking me for a tour?" The words jumped from my mouth, as I realized how nearby that was. Although Frank hadn't really romanced me, I guess I was feeling pretty good about him, especially how genuine he seemed. He perked up, perhaps a little too much.

"I don't mean to promise you the world," I hastened to add, "but I like looking at houses these days, and it might be a good place to talk some more and get to know each other better."

We both got into our SUVs, and I followed him to Coldwater Canyon Blvd. While stopped at a red light, I sensuously, though needlessly, fixed my lipstick in my rearview mirror just in case he might be watching me in his. We continued on through winding roads up into the hills and finally pulled into the driveway of a lovely Spanish-style house. "You don't live *in* Coldwater Canyon," I laughed, as he helped me from my car. "You live *above* Coldwater Canyon."

Once inside, he was immediately licked up and down by a black Labrador retriever he called Miko. He then showed me around the first floor, for some reason whispering as he went. He was especially proud of his home, having built it himself with the help of his crew some fifteen years ago. The rooms were filled with decorative knickknacks that seemed to show a woman's touch, even though he had said his ex-wife had moved out nearly a year ago.

My favorite thing was how his den and kitchen opened up onto a beautifully landscaped backyard and pool looking out onto the San Fernando Valley.

He grabbed two Perriers from the refrigerator and beckoned me upstairs for the rest of the tour. Most of the second floor was being used for storage or being prepared for renovation, but he had a big sky-blue bedroom with a small adjoining balcony overlooking the backyard. He gestured for me to sit down on the bed next to him.

A bit concerned, I asked, "Why can't we hang out in the den, in front of the fireplace?"

"Because Magdalena has a little apartment next to it."

"Magdalena?"

"My housekeeper."

"Oh, I didn't realize that," I said, putting it all together, while trying to settle myself onto his bed as daintily as I could.

After we talked a while longer, he lit a candle on the night table and turned off the light. I snuggled close, wanting to make it easier for him, and right on cue, he put his arm around me and kissed me. His warm hand felt luxurious on my bare shoulder, and as I melted into him, his hands began to roam the length of my body.

Despite loving every minute, I had to struggle to keep my dress on—and my wig in place—before finally tearing myself away. "We really shouldn't go any further," I said, as I collected my purse and headed for the bathroom. There I fussed over my smeared makeup until I felt certain that I'd leave my well built builder with an image of me at my best. Already having given him my number, I tried to be low-key as he walked me to my car. "I hope I see you again sometime," I said.

"Me too," he replied, as he kissed me goodbye.

Of course, it's not too hard to have a passionate night with a man; the real trick is getting him interested enough to follow it up. I wasn't too worried when he didn't call the very next day, and I remained eager and optimistic as I checked my voicemail after work: Monday, Tuesday, and Wednesday— still not a word. Finally, Wednesday night the phone rang; it was Frank. He wanted to see if I'd like to have dinner with him at the Venture Inn before going over to the Queen Mary Friday. I worked hard to hide how nervous and thrilled I was.

At the restaurant and club, we were surprisingly comfortable with each other. Although I was careful not to go all the way with him later on that night, I was moved by the fact he was sharing his home and his bed with me. It felt so different from my motel experiences. Though he didn't talk much about his feelings, his actions seemed to speak clearly enough. He called to ask me out week after week, and each time, he'd meet me at the club and greet me with a kiss on the lips. At the end of the night, he'd walk me out to my car and bid me farewell the same way. Although he could be gruff, he was steady, and when he made a plan, he stuck by it. Although he wasn't the kind of person I would ordinarily like, I grew increasingly fond of him and came to appreciate his quiet strength and inner intensity. At the same time, he seemed increasingly at ease with me.

I could hardly believe it. It looked like I was going to have a boyfriend, and he was more than I could've hoped for. He had a chiseled face, wide body, and stood 6'4". In bed, he was all man and expected me to be all woman. All the same, I couldn't relax and enjoy the moment as he prepared to make love to me for the first time, because I worried whether he'd be hard enough to satisfy me. With heaven at last in view, it would be hellish to be turned away at the gate. I lay back and held my breath as he pressed himself up against me . . . and penetrated me. I was relieved to see how efficiently he could perform—perhaps even a little too efficiently.

Shortly after we started having sex, we agreed to be monogamous. I wouldn't fool around with any man but him, and he wouldn't fool around with any transgendered woman but me. Because I would still be having sex with Melissa, he'd still be free to have sex with genetic women. Though I also insisted on no sex with gay men, he assured me he wasn't interested. Even though our agreement greatly reduced the chance of sexually transmitted diseases, I insisted on condoms nonetheless.

After three decades, my worst nightmare became my greatest delight and a regular—and legitimate—part of my life. Before Frank, going to bed with a man felt like play-acting. I tolerated it because it turned me on. But after a few months with him, it felt natural. I wasn't *tolerating* anything. I loved it when he kissed me and even when he looked deep into my eyes. I looked forward to watching TV in bed and dozing off on his furry chest. And I noticed something else strange. Or should I say the absence of something? I no longer ran fantasies in my head during sex. There was no longer any need to imagine I was anyone but myself, doing anything but what I was doing. As an erotic experience, it was pure. Or was it just what the rest of the world feels like most of the time?

Although I always liked dressing up, it was especially gratifying to look my best for my new beau. Self-conscious about my height, I had generally stuck to low-heeled shoes. But now with a tall admirer who would settle for nothing less, I discovered the joy of high heels. He also wanted to see me in skirts and dresses rather than pants, and preferably something new each weekend, or at least something he hadn't seen for a while.

Because he had a beautiful pool, I just *had* to go out and get a bathing suit. In fact, I got two: a very sleek maroon one-piece and a sexy little blue-print bikini. I could wear a waist cincher under my one-piece, but my bikini hid nothing and forced me to stay in shape. I bought a comfortable nightgown in case we ever had a sleepover, and I had a little electrolysis done so that my face would feel softer next to his. He bought me a garter belt and stockings and insisted I wear them to bed with him. Oh, the things I did for king and country.

Maybe it was more in my head than anywhere else, but I savored the happy, giddy feeling of being a girl with a boyfriend. For me, it was one of those quintessential female experiences, like nursing a baby at your breast. I liked the idea of belonging to Frank, and asked for something I could wear to symbolize my commitment to him. He gave me a heart pendant, which I wore whenever I was out as a woman. We usually spoke once a week, when he would call to confirm our plans for the upcoming weekend. Though I would have preferred a little more contact, I didn't want to be a bother, so I always let him make the first call. Most of the time, we'd meet up Friday at the QM, go for dinner on Ventura or Santa Monica Boulevard, and then get back to the club just as things were heating up.

There the role of girlfriend provided new challenges. Perhaps because he still wasn't used to socializing sober, my guy shied away from people he didn't know very well and spoke mostly to me. For the most part, he liked to talk about his week at work and his views on current events. Not much of a political person myself, I did my best to let him voice his opinions, while gently steering him more toward his professional endeavors. Thankfully the triumphs and tribulations of a carpenter-turned-contractor was a topic I never tired of.

Nevertheless, these conversations could only last so long in the middle of a swinging transgender nightclub, and most of the time, it was up to me to provide the entertainment. I kept things lively by introducing Frank around and including him in the latest gossip. "When are we going to get that fine body of yours out on the dance floor?" I would tease, while offering him conversational tidbits to bite on and filling silences with cheerful chatter.

Typically we'd hang out at the Queen Mary until about midnight, then mosey over to his place, where I'd excuse myself to change into "something more comfortable." By the time I tip-toed in, in a negligee or silk robe and compulsory high heels, he would have the bedroom ready for me with the same sensitivity and respect he would show a real woman—candlelight, soft jazz, and a reverent silence that was mine to punctuate with a little pillow talk if I so desired. Lying down next to him, I'd soon feel his long muscular arm reach behind my head and around my shoulders. Then he'd pull my slender smooth shape up against his broad hairy body before completing my encirclement with his other arm. Gradually I learned to loosen up and enjoy the feeling of being trapped and gracefully accept the kisses and cuddles coming my way.

Soon he'd be feeling me up, each caress delivering a delicious prickle from the nipple clamps I now wore under my breast forms. As he dallied back and forth between my boobs, I would know it was my duty to let my hand drift down to the bulge beneath his boxers. He always had such a hard-on for me, and it made me feel ever so sexy. Often, he'd then push my breast forms aside to lovingly bite on one nipple, then the next—the pain so exquisite, I could think of nothing else.

By now, he would be dying to get up my skirt, but I liked to fight him off for a while. Besides it being the right and girlish thing to do, it seemed like a simple matter of physics. How could I feel the force of his desire if I didn't put up at least a little resistance? Of course, I would ultimately let him win, and then he could do what he liked with my "manhood," though I preferred when he made it go away by grabbing it all with his hand and slowly starting to crush and release, crush and release. The pulsating ache of it would make me delirious, while my mind would fill with the notion: *He's making you into a woman. Relax and accept it. You know you want it. You want him inside you.*

To build the tension, I'd soon push him off me, drop to the floor by the side of the bed, and harden him up even more with my lips and my tongue. Every once in a while, as if to remind me of the loaded gun in my mouth, he would lose control right then and there. But most of the time, I'd eventually clamber back into bed and settle onto my back. Spreading my legs, I'd sweetly offer myself to him and rejoice in the feeling of him, at last, pushing himself inside me. As he'd pump in and out faster and harder, I'd gaze up adoringly at him and occasionally clamor for a kiss. By now, I'd be putty in his hands and would comply with whatever position he wanted me in.

Often he liked to pull out and roll me onto my tummy, before entering my bottom with a confident thrust. As he pounded away at me with ever more fury, I'd resign myself to the gathering thunder of his climax. Then with an intense grunt, he would deliver one last jolt and collapse on top of me, all two hundred-plus pounds pressing me down into the mattress. As long as I could breathe, I was content to lie there for a while, tender and proud at having pleased him, extremely aware of his presence still inside me. Eventually shrugging him off, I'd sweep my tousled hair off my face and curl up in his arms, before dissolving into a light sleep.

Occasionally I would play with my "clit" during or just after making love, but it just didn't feel feminine and whether I came or not didn't really matter much to either of us. Looking back on my teenage fantasies, it's rather ironic to realize that life has taken me from *I need to be a girl in order to have an orgasm* to *As long as I'm a girl, I don't even need one.* Clearly my crossdressing has become—and perhaps always was—more about the pleasure of womanhood than the quest for orgasm.

Somehow, I couldn't help wondering if sex would feel different if I had a vagina. Was I making do with an unreasonable facsimile? Who knew? Surprisingly few women I knew had tried anal intercourse. But I was pleased to hear the most experienced one among them report, "It's better. It's more stimulating than regular sex, but too much to handle on a daily basis."

Nurturing the relationship was also part of my role with Frank, and I kept it healthy and strong with amiable inquiries like "Are you okay with that?" and "How does next weekend look?" Fortunately he had an enduring interest in me and the TG scene, and our partnership prospered.

In the meantime, believe it or not, it was business as usual outside the black box. If anything, with Alice so well tucked in, I was finally able to relax, stop striving, stop searching, and finally relax. I grew ever more playful and effusive around the house with Melissa and Hanna, and soon she and I learned we were going to have a son. I kidded Frank that it was because he had gotten me pregnant, and when Jacob was born in the winter of 2001, he surprised me with a funny card congratulating me on being a mommy. Though I let him in on the major things in my life, I was careful not to share too much of my male side. I always dressed as a woman whenever I saw him and stayed strictly *en femme* over the phone.

He shared the vitals of his life with me too. Over the years, he had been involved with both genetic and transgendered women. Recently married to Tori for five years, he had found refuge in the bottle as their arguments over money and the possibility of children had grown increasingly heated. Now emerging from the ashes, he seemed stable and sober, but utterly burnt out on real women—at least for the time being.

Dreamy as our dalliance was, I had to face certain facts and learn to live without everything I might've wanted. Because Frank wouldn't introduce me to anybody in his life, not even his housekeeper, I found myself in a role that was much more mistress than girlfriend. But I knew where he was coming from and was careful not to push him. Besides, it wasn't like I could introduce him to my non-TG friends without violating my commitment to keep quiet about anything going on outside my marriage.

I noticed how he turned to his old friend Ginger for family things, like Christmas dinner or a ride home after a medical procedure. I worried that he might fall in love with her—or Magdalena.

"If that happens," I said one night, anxiously in his arms, "I hope we'll still be able to keep our thing going."

"Don't worry," he replied, almost laughing at me. "Ginger's well into her sixties; I've known her for years." He seemed sincere and sealed my mouth with a kiss before I could say anything more.

Over the next few months, I gathered that he wasn't interested in finding a serious girlfriend. He really seemed satisfied with the emotional support he found in Ginger, the day-to-day companionship he found in Magdalena, and the physical fulfillment he found in me. That way, he got all his needs met without surrendering the independence and tranquility he had prized so highly since his divorce. Although I played a limited role, I felt increasingly sure of my value to him, as I understood more about him.

Besides, once Melissa and I had two kids at home, my life became busier, and I was glad he didn't expect too much of me. That made it easier for me to stay focused on her and the kids and stay true to the priority portion of my agreement with her. Perhaps he felt more secure about his hold on me too, because he took me to dinner less and less, for fear of running into people he might know. To make up for it, he encouraged me to get out on the town with Lilly and others, even men like Marv when he was in town, but of course just as friends. All in all, he and I settled into a relationship that—while not perfect—seemed to work well for both of us on an ongoing basis.

Once, a little after midnight, in August 2001, as we were walking out to our cars in the Queen Mary parking lot, my cell phone went off. Scrambling to pull it out of my purse, I answered, "Dr. Novic," trying to sound normal in case it was a patient, but not so manly as to mess with Frank's head.

"Rick, Hanna's wheezing." It was Melissa. Apparently our daughter's asthma had flared up. She was distraught. "I gave her a nebulizer a few hours ago, but she's wheezing again."

"Hang on a second," I covered the phone and turned to Frank, who had already seen the look of concern on my face. "One of the kids is sick. I gotta go," I said with regret.

"Go," he replied, almost as if washing his hands of a messy situation. But when he saw the stunned look on my face, he touched me softly on the shoulder and murmured, "I'll call you during the week," before backing off toward his car.

I climbed into my Explorer and got back on the phone with Melissa. Thinking *first things first*, I made sure Hanna didn't need an ambulance and an emergency dose of epinephrine and then asked my wife how she was.

"I need you to come home," she insisted, her voice trembling. "You know I don't ask this of you very much."

"Are you kidding me? I'm *already* on my way home," I replied making a beeline for the freeway. "Give Hanna another treatment, and I'll call you when I get close. But call me sooner if you need to."

Twenty minutes later, I called back. "How's she doing?"

"No better, no worse."

"Do you want me to come right in, in girl clothes, and start helping? Or do you want me to change?"

She told me to go ahead and change, and five minutes later, I entered our family room in male mode. Though breathing steadily, our sweet little girl was still wheezing and hyperventilating. Melissa started to panic after we tried another albuterol treatment and a dose of Orapred to no avail.

"She'll be all right," I said, "I'm gonna take her to the emergency room."

"Oh, my god, the emergency room!" my wife exclaimed.

"It's really not such a big deal," I replied, as I discreetly slipped an EpiPen (a small preloaded syringe of epinephrine) into my pocket just in case. "It's just what she needs right now. You stay here with Jake. You've been through enough tonight." Not allowing myself a moment of fear, I grabbed Hanna's favorite Elmo CD, loaded her gently into her car seat, and made haste for the hospital.

She and I arrived at Saint John's at about two a.m. and were ushered directly into the emergency room. There she was monitored by finger oximeter, and her wheezing was finally relieved by a facemask delivering albuterol and supplemental oxygen. She bucked a little at the mask, but I held her in my arms on the easy chair the nurses had provided for us until we both drifted peacefully to sleep.

Still sleeping things off at home the next day, I woke from a nap to find Melissa looking at me with a pained expression. "You have a boyfriend, don't you?" she asked, barely holding back the tears.

Caught off guard, I felt my heart race. "Whoa, whoa. Why are you? What are you—"

"Admit it. You've been coming home later for the last year or so. I've been doing my best to ignore it, but last night I couldn't help thinking about where you were, who you were with, and when you would be back."

I stared off at a painting on the wall and took a long deep breath. "I'll answer all your questions openly and honestly as long as you really want to know," I said, slowly gaining strength and turning to face her.

My dearest wife now looked away and concentrated as if to master a flood of emotions. After a moment, she turned back toward me with a look of steel. "It's true, isn't it?"

"Yes," I said plainly.

Her steely look dissolved into one of utter despair. "I can't believe I let things get this far," she growled at me and herself.

I reached out to hold her and was relieved she didn't shove me off. "Listen, I may be far from the ideal husband, but I know who and what's important to me."

Her jaw dropped a little in a way that told me she was digesting what I had said in the light of last night's events. "Just tell me, will I always come first?"

"Always. I'm not leaving you for anyone or anything," I replied. "Frankly, I'm more concerned about you some day getting fed up with me."

"Are you safe?"

"Meticulous."

She shut her eyes for a moment and said, "Well then, let's reseal the compartment. I don't want to hear any more."

"Before we do that, I just have to let you know how much I appreciate the allowances you've made for me. They've let me move forward in life without feeling like a part of me was left behind like a forgotten child." I choked up. As Lissa started to say something, I burst out, "No, let me finish. To move forward and have two children I love more than anyone in the world—anyone except their mom." With that, I collapsed into an embrace with her that seemed to last forever and express feelings that could come out in no other way.

That was over seven years ago, seven years of baby steps and first words, birthdays and ballet lessons, album releases and unlikely literary ambitions. Nowadays, Melissa and I celebrate our seventeenth year together and Frank and I—having outlived the Queen Mary *and* his two arthritic hips—taste our tenth. It's an unconventional way to live and love, but it's worked for each of us, mostly because she knows that she and the kids are paramount and he's been content with strictly once-a-week contact. Because of the unusual complexities involved, I try to stay especially attuned to Melissa. We talk about us all the time and constantly share our delights and concerns about Hanna, Jake, and each other.

Ironically my experience with Frank has given me a new understanding of Melissa's experience as the wife of a crossdresser. I suspect that somewhere deep down he too is one. If so, that's okay, but I would want him to handle most of it on his own and with me continue to be the rugged man I fell for. Sounds familiar, doesn't it?

Since it became easier to put myself in Lissa's shoes, I realized a fundamental omission in the way I justified my right to express myself. Of course, I should be free to express my femininity any way I saw fit—on my own. But if I wanted to be her partner, she had to have some say in the matter so I didn't drift too far from being the kind of person she'd want to spend her life with. Throughout our years together, I've been very grateful for her tolerance given the norms of our culture but still sometimes chafed at how she restricted my self-expression. Now, I realize that as an individual she was only negotiating for what she needed in order to be happy over the long run—and thank god she did.

◆   ◆   ◆

Over the years, my crossdressing has gone from a terrifying thrill to an irrepressible hunger to an enduring enthusiasm woven into the fabric of my life. I no longer approach each night out with prom-like anticipation, but I sure do look forward to each and every weekend. Looking back on my journey, I see four major themes worth further comment.

First, we live in a culture that allows only two gender options. You can live as a man, or you can live as a woman. Being openly androgynous or in between is not well tolerated, not if you want to avoid snickers and have a fighting chance of being attractive to either women or men. Imagine if you were a man with limp wrists and partially developed breasts. You might have a difficult time finding a woman to settle down and have a family with. Finding a man would be just as difficult and then, of course, much trickier if you and he were hoping to have children.

For a transgendered person like myself, the choice boils down to living as a crossdressing man or a transsexual woman. Although on the inside I'm in between male and female, I've chosen to live primarily as man, husband, and father. But with Melissa's understanding and love, I've been able to stretch and customize this conventional lifestyle into an alternative one, with sufficient room for my female self.

Second, I've brought energy and meaning to my life by taking my fantasies and curiosities very seriously. No matter how radical or embarrassing—if it was possible—I tried it. And you know what? Nearly everything I thought I might like, I did like. I liked being a woman so much that I made it a regular part of my life.

Of course I haven't had the pure experience of being female, because I don't always pass. So strangers, friends, and even my "boyfriend" don't fully treat me like a woman, but they definitely don't treat me like a man either. People relate to me in a manner that seems halfway between how they would relate to a woman and how they would relate to a gay man. Although I don't get the full female treatment, my time as a girl still feels relatively realistic and decidedly different from my time as a guy. The way I see it, I live a night a week as a woman, with Frank, Lilly, and April, who know me almost exclusively as Alice. And I live six and a half days a week as a man, with Lissa and the kids and others, who know me almost exclusively as Rick.

Third, I've run into realities and reached a steady state. I've been content with one night a week for several years now. Of course, the first reality factor that keeps me there, is that that's what I've agreed to with Melissa. When she and the kids are out of town, however, I often go out two nights in a row—but never a third. So even if I were single, I might like to dress up more frequently, but certainly not night after night.

Similarly, I don't think I'd be keen to crossdress around the house. It's not that the idea is unappealing. It's just that I'd run into reality factor two: It takes too long to cover my beard, let alone fuss with a wig, breast forms, and waist cincher. So it wouldn't be worth the hassle.

Nor would I be interested in dressing up as a woman around the neighborhood or at work, because of reality factor three: I don't always pass. Getting read is okay at a restaurant Friday night, but it's too stressful at the supermarket Saturday morning and could out me to all sorts of people. And although I might like working Monday morning as a female rather than male psychiatrist, I wouldn't want to be an obviously transgendered one. So, to enjoy being a woman more than a night or two a week, I would need . . . extensive electrolysis, facial feminization surgery, high-dose hormones, and a divorce. So far, I haven't been interested. I don't expect that to change.

Fourth and finally, who would I be if not constrained by reality? If I were young and single and had magical powers, how would I want to live? I would love to be able to snap my fingers and be a woman, not the attractive crossdresser I am, nor the hopefully passing transsexual I could be, but the sweet 5'7" girl I would have been, had I been born with an extra X instead of a Y chromosome. Since she would—no doubt—have a brain that was different than mine, let's say I could at least snap my fingers and inhabit her body. As long as I could freely go back and forth, then I would want to check it out right away.

As soon as I found myself occupying that softer, smaller body and speaking in that higher-pitched voice, I would love it. Whatever I might say or do at that particular moment, neither I nor anyone else would question the fact that I was female. Even if I didn't have the most feminine personality or interests, I would just seem like a gutsy no-nonsense dame—but a dame, nonetheless. That would be a situation that I would find immensely satisfying.

I know I'd like to be a woman for much of my social life and sex life. And although I'd need to polish up my people skills, I'd probably enjoy working as a woman as well. I'm not sure how I'd like relating to my family though; I would have to try it and see. I suspect there would be a bit of a mismatch between my natural likes and dislikes and the expectations people would have of me as a daughter or sister—or wife and mother, for that matter. Although

I'd want the experience of having a baby and breastfeeding her, I'm afraid I'd be a mom who'd insist on going back to work on at least a part-time basis.

Although dull in some ways, living as a man has felt right in other ways. So I've never been itching to leave it behind. I've always liked the casualness and independence of it: rolling out of bed and starting my day with no muss or fuss, wandering around alone day or night without having to worry about my safety. With a few notable exceptions, my personality and inclinations have made me a relatively easy fit for the role of son or brother, husband or father. And, of course, I know what it means to be truly and deeply loved by a woman like Melissa and wouldn't want to miss that for anything.

So even under the most ideal circumstances, I don't think I'd want to live all my days as a woman, I would prefer to snap my fingers and go back and forth. To me, that means, deep down, I'm more of an exuberant crossdresser than a frustrated transsexual. As such, I'm very happy with the remarkable opportunity I have, to experience life as a man and as a woman. It's a very full, very satisfying life. I treasure every week.

As the years go by, change will no doubt be inevitable. From a physical standpoint, I'm a forty-six-year-old with good skin, but I'll soon show signs of aging, which I plan to manage—like any other Jewish lady in L.A.—with well-timed and tasteful cosmetic procedures. But more importantly, I'll age gracefully, knowing I've spent my time well and flourished in my prime.

Perhaps the biggest changes will involve my daughter and son, who are still very young. As they grow up, I'll have to think more about how to handle my crossdressing with respect to them. The purist in me wanted to just be myself and hide nothing. In that scenario, I would occasionally show myself as a woman who loves them in addition to being a man who loves them. That way, they could learn that having a crossdressing father is okay, before society has a chance to "teach" them that it's not.

But I care dearly for my kids and don't want to burden them with a secret or have them risk ridicule on my behalf. So Melissa and I decided to play it safe and keep my womanly side secret. Yet, as Hanna and Jacob learn the basics about boys and girls, we'll make sure they know that those rules aren't set in stone. And as they can handle more, I'll let them know more about me, and I hope that they'll let us know more about who they are.

As you can tell, I've thought a lot about the challenges in my life, and as a psychiatrist, I've learned a lot about the pleasures and perils of other people's lives. So I figured that other crossdressers might enjoy my ideas on how to feel better about this unusual fate we share. Back in '96, I wrote a small heartfelt piece and submitted it to two of my favorite transgender magazines. It was rejected by one and accepted but never published by the other.

Three years later, a t-friend of mine started to write for a new magazine named *GIRL TALK* and we joked about me doing a column called "Go Ask Alice." Well, as I'd learned once before, be careful whom you kid with. A few weeks later, *GIRL TALK* editor Gina Lance approached me at the Queen Mary. "When I heard about you," she said with a wink, "I knew I didn't want any other shrink writing for us." My advice column premiered in the next issue. The warm feedback I've received from our readers ever since has stirred me to share my own story.

As a final thought to those of you within our community—or who think you might be—I would like to say, there is hope. I am Alice. I chased my white rabbit and took a long, horrifying fall. But I've landed gently in a world more wonderful than I could have imagined. If there is a secret to my success, it's finding a way to be positive and proud of the man-woman I am, and finding a woman who understands.

To those of you who live outside Genderland, I hope you have enjoyed having your consciousness raised the way mine was and been touched by this rare glimpse into the life of a crossdresser. Maybe you never before stopped and thought through what it would be like to be different from others in such a fundamental way? Maybe you have your own indelible curse, which you strive to turn into a blessing? Or maybe someone you love does? If so, I hope my story has nourished and inspired you. One by one, we can make a difference.

APPENDIX A

Intersex Conditions

By definition, intersex conditions describe people who are born with bodies that are, in one way or another, between male and female. Such conditions can be diagnosed by objective (often anatomic) findings, in contrast to transsexualism and crossdressing, which can only be diagnosed by the subjective history that a person gives of how he or she feels inside.

According to the Intersex Society of North America, these conditions occur about once in every hundred births (however, this figure may be on the high side, because the ISNA includes some conditions that are not universally considered to be intersex).[45] The most common forms are Klinefelter's syndrome (an XXY combination of chromosomes resulting in males who don't fully virilize at puberty and don't produce sperm), adrenal hyperplasia (a hormonal condition resulting in females with a penis-like large clitoris), and hypospadias (a developmental condition resulting in males in which urine exits from underneath the penis—more like it would with respect to the clitoris in females).

Appendix B

The Wide World of Women's Wear

Women have a dazzling diversity of options available to accentuate assets, camouflage flaws, and make statements. Clothes can say things like "I'm up-to-date," "I'm proud of my success," and "I know what's appropriate." Consider, for example, the range of options open to a woman when shopping for a shirt, or what she would call a top. Like a man, she may choose between long and short sleeves, but for her, there's also sleeveless, off-the-shoulder, tank top, spaghetti strap, strapless, halter, criss-cross, over-one-shoulder, scoop neck, and backless.

Then of course, every color in the rainbow is possible, rather than the whites, blues, browns, and blacks deemed suitable for a man. Next come all the fabrics from lace to chenille and finally all the fits from baggy to body sculpting. But wait, we're not done yet. A gal can decide if she wants a short top that emphasizes her small waist, or a longer one that brings out her curvy hips, or a still longer one that minimizes them. Even if she buys a simple button-down blouse, she may choose to tie it off to show her flat tummy, tuck it in to show her waist, or leave it out to hide her lack of one. Who would have thought there was such an art to going shopping and getting dressed?

I've had my own misadventures in the world of women's tops. At first, I was so worried about passing that I covered my muscular arms with long sleeves. Later, I learned I could look cute in many different styles. Even if there were some I couldn't quite pull off, I decided to try all twelve of the major ones just for the sheer fun of it. That way I didn't feel I was missing out on anything. Soon I could sit back, watch the girls on *Sex and the City*, and think, *Been there. Worn that.*

APPENDIX C

Talking the Talk

Remember, the key is *Lighten* up. *Brighten up. Be a little more tentative and a little more polite.*

To lighten up, I spoke in a lighter, softer tone, more from my throat than belly.

To brighten up, I learned to exaggerate like "How are you? I haven't seen you in a million years!" I also brightened up by learning the classic lilt—or I should say *relearning* because, way back when, I must have lilted as sweetly as my own little kids. As a thirty-two-year-old, I trained myself to lilt by stressing, stretching, and raising my pitch on key syllables of key words like "Oh, my *god*, Tracy, that's a*maaaaaz*ing!" or "That's not apple; that's *piiiiin*apple."

To be more tentative, I would raise my pitch at the end of sentences as if to say, *Are you with me so far?* For example, "I was working on this show in New York? (Look for your listener to nod) But then it got canceled? (Once again, look for some kind of acknowledgement). So then I had to get a day job?"

To be more polite, I was sure to say things like "Excuse me," and "please" and sometimes even "Excuse me, please." Swearing was mannish and unattractive. So "Oh, shit!" became "Oh, my goodness!"

Learning to speak *Girl* is like learning the English of England. Not only do you need to get the accent down, but you have to remember that it's trousers instead of pants and loo instead of bathroom. To truly talk the talk, I couldn't forget that fingernails were nails, stomach was tummy, breasts were boobs, guys were either boys or men, and "She's hot" was . . . "He's dreamy."

APPENDIX D

Latin-Style Drag Queens

Historically, Mediterranean culture has had a masculine-feminine rather than a both-partners-are-the-same approach to sex between men.[46] Apparently it derives from one of the more common forms of homosexuality in the Roman Empire, which were masculine-feminine, man-boy, and master-slave.[47] (Such forms are generally more prevalent in cultures that restrict access to women.) Latin-style masculine-feminine homosexuality extends from France, Spain, and Portugal and their prior colonies (in Latin America and Southeast Asia) through Italy, Greece, and Turkey and on into the Arab world and its prior spheres of influence (like Iran and Afghanistan).[48]

The essence of traditional Latin homosexuality is that men who want sex with men have to choose between an outwardly masculine and (presumably but not always) sexually penetrating role and an outwardly feminine and (presumably but not always) sexually receptive role.[49] The masculine men think of themselves as normal straight men and, as such, are expected to live with their parents and siblings until they marry and then, of course, with their wives and kids afterwards. However, they express their homosexuality by pursuing feminine men on the side as prostitutes or lovers.

The feminine men, in contrast, consider themselves gay and most were effeminate as young boys. Many have been treated so poorly by their families that they've had to run away and survive as drag-queen prostitutes.[50] Some ultimately find acceptance as showgirls, hair stylists, and retail clerks. No doubt this unfortunate cycle accounts for the large Latina presence at places like Peanuts—and clubs like it in other major cities.

I'd imagine another reason for the large number of Latin and Southeast Asian drag queens is body type; they're generally shorter and more androgynous than the American norm. So a young gay Vietnamese immigrant might be drawn into drag by the chance to be a magnificent woman rather than a mediocre man. Or a drag queen who doesn't pass in the Philippines might want to relocate here. Who wouldn't want to begin life anew as a completely believable woman in the bountiful land of the hairy giants?

The Latin preference for masculine-feminine homosexuality would also explain the high demand for transgendered sex workers in Los Angeles.

Hookers strut their stuff every night along Santa Monica Boulevard. Call girls advertise themselves as she-males at many popular websites and in all the alternative newspapers. The market is so good here that a queen will typically sell her services for about one and a half times what a real girl would make. And many queens, like my friend Juanita, actually enjoy their work.

But on the dark side, many do it as a last resort after being turned down for job after job. They lead lives of drugs and tricks by night and hazy sleep by day. Some have had breast implants but still aren't comfortable going around as women in the daylight. Some have been abused and sneered at so much that they've developed their own prickly temperament. A lot of these girls get their hormones on the street as well as silicone injections to fill out their lips, cheeks, hips, and butts. Unfortunately, though, the silicone can settle and stiffen over the years and end up looking freakish. Far too many of these women lead hard lives that end tragically because of suicide, drugs, violence, and the consequences of unsafe sex.[51]

APPENDIX E

American-Style Drag Queens

These are the Anglo-American gay men who like to crossdress, and there are relatively few. Yet they've done such a good job of catching the public eye that many people assume that all gay men are drag queens and all crossdressers are gay. The truth is most gay men have little use for a dress and most crossdressers have little use for a man.

My drag queen friends are gay in the sense that they are powerfully attracted to men and hardly at all to women. But they do like to dress up on a regular basis, as opposed to most gay men, who only do it for a hoot on Halloween. In this regard, they live much like crossdressers; they're boys during the week but quite often girls on the weekend.

Naively you would think it would be easier for a drag queen to find a boyfriend than for a crossdresser to find a girlfriend, but my friends explain that this isn't always the case. Although a gay man will typically be less judgmental about a boyfriend who likes to dress, he may—just like a straight woman—get very upset if the guy starts doing it too often.

Drag queens are famous as female impersonators. Ru Paul has become a widely popular singer, and some queens crossdress so well, they get modeling work—as women. DQs have an image of glamor and pride going back to Stonewall and beyond and haven't traditionally considered themselves crossdressers nor wanted to be associated with straight men stumbling around in their wives' clothes.

These days, however, girls of all kinds are coming together and lines are blurring. Some say drag queens are simply crossdressers who happen to be gay. I disagree. None of the queens I know were ever turned on by women's clothes, and their stories are different in other ways too. As children, most had girlish interests, like playing with dolls, and as adults, many enjoy careers in decorating/design, entertainment, and nursing. Most never cared much for women, but remember being attracted to men from very early on. And last but not least, they're often quite fabulous, while my girls can be quite frumpy.

What's their secret? For starters, they're naturals. One lovely queen I know who coos and clutches her pearls as a woman coos and clutches as a man too. She can't help it. She'd have to learn to be masculine, the way I've learned to be feminine.

Secondly, drag queens aren't born; they're chosen. From the abundance of young gay men, older queens notice a few especially pretty ones and say things like "Have you ever thought of performing?" After an impressionable teenager hears that enough times, a star is born. The final secret to DQ success is that they're simply getting out and shining while they're still young, as opposed to us crossdressers, who often start dressing up and going out in our forties.

Okay, they're good at it, you may think, *but if it doesn't turn 'em on, why do they do it?* I asked around, and here is what I heard. Most enjoy the artistic expression of painting and adorning themselves. Many keep dressing up because they find they look better as women than men. And quite a few like going out in drag because it gives them access to a whole different group of men, straight men.

Many of the started-out-gay transsexuals I've seen in my office identified as *reinas* or drag queens during their teens, only to decide in their twenties to go full time and be transsexual. In fact, psychologist Michael Bailey sees drag queens as an intermediate (and sometimes transitional) type between regular gay men and started-out-gay transsexuals, and crossdressers as an intermediate type between straight men and started-out-straight transsexuals.[52] He sees started-out-gay transsexuals as the most feminine of gay men and refers to them as homosexual transsexuals. He sees started-out-straight transsexuals as the most driven of crossdressers and refers to them as autogynephiles. Though I object to his excessively sexual focus and pathologizing tone, he has an intriguing way of weaving together many of the things I've observed.

APPENDIX F

Origins of Homophobia and Transphobia

In our society, we're typically suspicious of anything that seems unnatural. Homosexual behavior seems unnatural in that it's not tied to reproduction; in fact, exclusive homosexuality would preclude reproduction. Transgender behavior seems unnatural in that it's exactly the opposite of what one would expect from a male or a female. But it's beginning to look like sex and gender variations are more natural than anyone might have imagined. In *Biological Exuberance,* Bruce Bagemihl, Ph.D., observes, "The world is, indeed, teeming with homosexual, bisexual, and transgendered creatures of every stripe and feather."[53] In fact, homosexual behavior occurs in 15-30% of species closely studied,[54] and has been accepted (in one form or another) by the majority of human cultures.[55]

Because animals don't wear clothes or opt for sex-change surgery, Bagemihl defines *transvestism* as the process of individuals of one sex taking on physical or behavioral characteristics of the other sex and *transsexualism* as individuals of one sex actually becoming the other sex (right down to being fertile). Then he cites several examples of both, including many of the lovely tropical fish you may have seen on your last vacation.[56]

Moreover, transgender behavior has been accepted by many cultures. Many North American Indian tribes have a third gender-role. So a feminine man or masculine woman isn't locked into the life of a brave or a squaw; he or she can be a two-spirit.[57] Other examples include the crossdressed male Hijra, who bless weddings in India and Pakistan, as well as the Xanith of the Arabian Peninsula and the Mahu of Polynesia.[58]

So homosexuality and transgenderism are much more natural for animals and even for humans than one might think, growing up in our culture. Unfortunately though, Judeo-Christian culture has had a very narrow view of acceptable sexual and gender behavior. The Bible is very clear about homosexuality.

If a man lies with a man as with a woman, both of them have committed an abomination; they shall be put to death; their blood is upon them.

-Leviticus 20:13

And just as unrelenting on crossdressing.

A woman shall not wear a man's apparel, nor shall a man put on a woman's garment; for whoever does such things is abhorrent to the Lord Your God.

-Deuteronomy 22:5

Some of the eunuchs of prior eras may represent predecessors of today's transsexuals. But the Bible shows no tolerance for them either.

No one whose testicles are crushed or whose penis is cut off shall be admitted to the assembly of the Lord.

-Deuteronomy 23:1

No one mentioned these parts of the Bible back at my reformed temple in Buffalo. And though ordinarily proud of my Jewish heritage, I was dismayed to discover that my ancestors made dangerous bigotry part of our sacred tradition.

Contemporary Western sex-negative mores date back to the time Imperial Rome embraced Christianity.[59] From then on, Western law adhered closely to Judeo-Christian morality, and homosexuality and transgenderism were considered crimes for centuries. It wasn't until the nineteenth and twentieth centuries that perception of them began to shift from immorality to illness. Homosexual and transgendered people were then delivered from the legal system to the medical system, from the jailers to the doctors. Extensive treatments were tried, from long-term psychoanalysis to electro-shock aversion, but none had a lasting effect.[60]

Finally, the gay rights movement of the 1970s paved the way for the Western medical establishment to see homosexuality as a healthy alternative lifestyle. Unfortunately, we transgendered people have not had as strong a civil-rights movement and still struggle for such respect.

Acknowledgments

Many people have made important contributions to this book. To protect their privacy, I would like to honor them by first name only: Bert, Marlene, Abby, Mike, Cindy, Diane, Linda, Eric, Naomi, Philip, Darya, Brianna, and Stephanie.

I'd like to thank you, my readers, for your encouragement and support and welcome you to share any comments or questions you may have with me at richard.novic@verizon.net.

Glossary

Admirer. A man who admires transgendered women

CD. Crossdresser (a man turned on by imagining he is a woman, nearly all such men are primarily straight)

DQ. Drag queen (a gay man who likes dressing up in women's clothes)

FTM. Female-to-male transsexual

Getting read. Identified as a man in a dress

GG. Genetic girl (a "real woman")

MTF. Male-to-female transsexual

Passing. Not being identified as a man in a dress

TG. Transgendered (whether CD, TS, or DQ)

T-girl. Transgendered girl (whether CD, TS, or DQ)

Tranny. Same as above

Tranny Chaser. A sometimes derogatory way to refer to a man who admires transgendered women

Trans. Transgendered (whether CD, TS, or DQ)

Transitioning. Switching from living day to day as a man to living day to day as a woman (a.k.a. going full time)

TS. Transsexual

TV. Transvestite (basically same as crossdresser)

Endnotes

1. Robert J. Rowe, *Bert & Lori: The Autobiography of a Crossdresser* (Amherst, NY: Prometheus Books, 1997). This is the only prior published memoir by a crossdresser I discovered.

2. Nathaniel McConaghy, *Sexual Behavior: Problems and Management* (New York and London: Plenum, 1993), 162.

3. Vern L. Bullough and Bonnie Bullough, *Crossdressing, Sex, and Gender* (Philadelphia: University of Pennsylvania Press, 1993), 300.

4. D.F. Swaab and M.A. Hofman, *Trends in Neuroscience 18* (1995): 264-270.

5. J.N. Zhou, M.A. Hofman, L.J. Gooren, D.F. Swaab, "A Sex Difference in the Human Brain and Its Relation to Transsexuality," *Nature* 378 (6552, 1995): 68-70; F.P. Kruijver, J.N. Zhou, C.W. Pool, M.A. Hofman, L.J. Gooren, D.F. Swaab, "Male-to-Female Transsexuals Have Female Neuron Numbers in a Limbic Nucleus," *Journal of Clinical Endocrinology and Metabolism* 85 (5, 2000): 2034-2041.

6. Anne A. Lawrence, www.annelawrence.com (Seattle, 2007), "A Critique of the Brain Sex Theory of Transsexualism."

7. Bullough and Bullough, 327-330.

8. Ibid., 294.

9. Vivienne Cass, "Sexual Orientation Identity Formation," in *Textbook of Homosexuality and Mental Health*, ed. Robert Cabaj and Terry Stein (Washington, DC: American Psychiatric Press, Inc., 1996): 227-251.

10. Time and time again since then, I've seen she was right, although I think it would be more precise to say, *"If truth be told, everyone has their troubles."*

11. Reinhold Niebuhr, The Serenity Prayer in *Way of Light: A Manual of Praise, Prayer, and Meditation,* compiled by Howard C. Robbins (1933). Later on, as a psychiatrist myself, I found the Serenity Prayer relevant to

many of my patients and their struggles. Of all the wise words people look to in times of need, these are the most precious.

12. John Talamini, *Boys Will Be Girls: The Hidden World of the Heterosexual Male Transvestite* (Washington D.C.: University Press of America, 1982).

13. Bullough and Bullough, 293-295.

14. Rachel Urquhart, *Chic Simple Women's Wardrobe* (New York: Alfred A. Knopf, 2000), 82.

15. Donald Symons, *The Evolution of Human Sexuality* (London: Oxford University Press, 1981); Deborah Tannen, *You Just Don't Understand: Women and Men in Conversation* (New York: Ballantine Books, 1991).

16. Mike Caro, *The Body Language of Tells* (Van Nuys, CA: Gambling Times, Inc., 1984): 32-33.

17. Donald Symons, *The Evolution of Human Sexuality* (London: Oxford University Press, 1981).

18. J. Michael Bailey, *The Man Who Would Be Queen: The Science of Gender-Bending and Transsexualism* (Washington, D.C.: Joseph Henry Press, 2003): 76-77.

19. Discovery Channel, Studies reviewed in *Science of the Sexes* (Silver Springs, MD: Discovery Communications, 2003).

20. Virginia Prince and P.M. Butler, "Survey of 504 Cases of Transvestism," *Psychological Reports* 31 (1972): 903-917. Deanna was essentially paraphrasing the above study.

21. Peggy J. Rudd, *My Husband Wears My Clothes* (Katy, Texas: PM Publishers, 1990).

22. Abraham H. Maslow, *Toward a Psychology of Being* (Hoboken, New Jersey: John Wiley & Sons, 1968).

23. Mavis Jukes, *It's a Girl Thing: How to Stay Healthy, Safe, and In Charge* (New York: Alfred A. Knopf, Inc., 1996).

24. Jo Ann Roberts, *Art & Illusion: A Guide to Crossdressing*, Volumes 1 and 2 (King of Prussia, PA: Creative Design Services, 1985).

25. None of us realized at the time that the Big Bad Wolf is actually from *The Three Little Pigs* rather than *Little Red Ridinghood*.

26. Anne Vitale, "Being Gender Dysphoric: A Developmental Review", *Gender and Psychoanalysis, An Interdisciplinary Journal* Vol. 6 No. 2, Spring 2001, pp 121-141.

27. Ray Blanchard, "The Concept of Autogynephilia and the Typology of Male Gender Dysphoria," *Journal of Nervous and Mental Disease* (1989) 177(10), 616-623; R. Blanchard, I. Rachansky, B. Steiner, "Phallometric Detection of Fetishistic Arousal in Heterosexual Male Cross-Dressers," *Journal of Sex Research* (1986) 22(4), 452-462.

28. Anne A. Lawrence, www.annelawrence.com (Seattle, 1998), "An Introduction to the Concept of Autogynephilia."

29. Vito Russo and Armistead Maupin, *The Celluloid Closet,* (Los Angeles: Reflective Image Inc., 1995).

30. James Krajeski, "Homosexuality and the Mental Health Professions," in *Textbook of Homosexuality and Mental Health:* 17-31.

31. A. K. Malyon, "Biphasic Aspects of Homosexual Identity Formation," *Psychotherapy: Theory, Research and Practice* (1982b) 19:335-340.

32. Gina Lance, "Modern Day Mecca: The Legendary Queen Mary Night Club," *GIRL TALK* magazine, Vol. 2 No. 2 (2000), 6-8.

33. I later realized a flaw in my reasoning caused by the fact that the right to masquerade as a man was never a goal of women's lib—although perhaps it should have been.

34. Jacobo Schifter, *From Toads to Queens: Transvestism in a Latin American Setting* (New York: Haworth Press, 1999): 9-12.

35. Vern L. Bullough and Thomas S. Weinberg, "Women Married to Transvestites: Problems and Adjustments," *Journal of Psychology and Human Sexuality* 1 (1988): 83-104.

36. Renee Richards with John Ames, *Second Serve* (New York: Stein and Day, 1983): 191-195.

37. Bullough and Bullough, 294.

38. Bailey, 62.

39. Ibid., xi.

40. Richard C. Pillard and James D. Weinrich, "The Periodic Table of the Gender Transpositions: Part I. A Theory Based on Masculinization and

Defeminization of the Brain," *Journal of Sex Research* 23 (November 1987): 425-454.

41. Jack Morin, *Anal Pleasure & Health* (San Francisco: Down There Press, 1998); Stephen E. Goldstone, *The Ins and Outs of Gay Sex: A Medical Handbook for Men* (New York: Dell Publishing, 1999).

42. J.J. Allen, *The Man in the Red Velvet Dress: Inside the World of Crossdressing,* (New York: Birch Lane Press, 1996).

43. Gregory Herek, "Heterosexism and Homophobia," in *Textbook of Homosexuality and Mental Health:* 101-113.

44. Herpes and warts, for instance. Goldstone, 69, 73.

45. Intersex Society of North America, www.isna.org (Seattle: 2000-2002), "What Is Intersex? What Do These Diagnoses Mean?"

46. Stephen O. Murray, *Latin American Male Homosexualities* (Albuquerque: University of New Mexico Press, 1995): 11-14.

47. Craig A. Williams, *Roman Homosexuality: Ideologies of Masculinity in Classical Antiquity* (New York: Oxford University Press, 1999): 3-8.

48. Stephen O. Murray and Will Roscoe, *Islamic Homosexualities: Culture, History, and Literature* (New York: New York University Press, 1997): 3-10; Maura Reynolds, "Kandahar's Lightly Veiled Homosexual Habits," *The Los Angeles Times,* April 3, 2002.

49. Francisco Gonzalez and Oliva Espin, "Latino Men, Latino Women, and Homosexuality," in *Textbook of Homosexuality and Mental Health:* 587-592.

50. Dave Gardetta, "The Game of Vice," *Los Angeles* magazine, December 2004, 174.

51. Schifter, 39.

52. Bailey: 179-181.

53. Bruce Bagemihl, *Biological Exuberance: Animal Homosexuality and Natural Diversity* (New York: St. Martin's Press, 1999), 9.

54. Ibid., 31.

55. Gilbert Herdt, *Same Sex Different Cultures: Gays and Lesbians Across Cultures* (Boulder, CO: HarperCollins Publishers, 1997), 10.

56. Bagemihl: 36-42.

57. Sabine Lang, "There Is More Than Just Women and Men," in *Gender Reversals and Gender Cultures: Anthropological and Historical Perspectives,* ed. Sabrina Petra Ramet (New York: Routledge, 1996): 183196.

58. Bailey: 134-136.

59. John Boswell, *Christianity, Social Tolerance, and Homosexuality* (Chicago: University of Chicago Press, 1980).

60. Terry Stein, "A Critique of Approaches to Changing Sexual Orientation," in *Textbook of Homosexuality and Mental Health:* 530-531.

CPSIA information can be obtained at www.ICGtesting.com
Printed in the USA
LVOW10s1416100914

403429LV00001B/100/P